THE MALE MACHINE

THE MALE MACHINE

Marc Feigen Fasteau

A DELTA BOOK

Published by
Dell Publishing Co., Inc.
1 Dag Hammarskjold Plaza
New York, N.Y. 10017

Delta ® TM 755118, Dell Publishing Co., Inc.

ISBN: 0-385-28623-6

Printed in the United States of America

15   14   13   12   11   10   9

CW

Extracts reprinted from *Commentary*, by permission. Copyright
© 1972 by the American Jewish Committee.

Extracts reprinted from *The Best and the Brightest*, by David
Halberstam. Copyright © 1969, 1971, 1972 by David Halberstam.
Reprinted by permission of Random House, Inc.

Extracts reprinted from *Love and Will*, by Rollo May. By permission
of W. W. Norton & Company, Inc. Copyright © 1969 by W. W.
Norton & Company, Inc.

"It's All Right to Cry" reprinted by permission. Copyright © 1972 by
the Free To Be Foundation, Inc. Reprinted by permission of the Free
To Be Foundation, Inc.

Extracts reprinted from *The Two-Career Family*, by Lynda Lytle
Holmstrom. Copyright © 1972 by Lynda Lytle Holmstrom.
Reprinted by permission of Schenkman Publishing Co., Inc.

Extracts reprinted from *Nixon Agonistes*, by Garry Wills. Copyright
© 1969, 1970 by Garry Wills. Reprinted by permission of Houghton
Mifflin Company.

Extracts reprinted from "Men and Work," an unpublished
paper, University of Michigan, 1973, by permission of the
author, Judith Bardwick.

For Brenda,
who showed me what it
means to love another person

Acknowledgments

I am indebted to James Harrison, Donald Levinson, and Mary C. Howell, who read individual chapters involving their fields of expertise and helped me avoid errors of fact and perspective. I am grateful also to Franklin Thomas for suggesting the title; to Robert Fein, Joseph Pleck, and Warren Farrell, for generously making their files available to me; and to Mitchell Pines for research assistance. I wish to thank Joyce Johnson, whose careful editing and sense of literature helped make a collection of ideas into a book, Veronica Windholz, who cheerfully shepherded the manuscript through numerous revisions and retypings; and Faith Sale who copyedited the manuscript with an acute eye for substance as well as style. Finally, my debt to Brenda Feigen Fasteau is immeasurable. She has led me, over the years, to many of the ideas in this book, and her insights and suggestions have made every part of it better.

Contents

Introduction

About three years ago, I was invited to a dinner at which "the revolutionizing of institutions in America" was to be the main intellectual course.
"Nothing programmed," the host explained, "just a few people with a
shared interest in radical change in the future." A license to voice our most
idealistic thoughts was to be the order of the evening.

The company was rarefied: one college president turned iconoclast, one
very creative businessman, the dean of an experimental college, a pioneer in
encounter group techniques, and a judge with expertise on children and the
family. I was flattered to be there; all the more so because the judge and I
were the only women, and she was a distinguished authority forty years my
senior.

As promised, the talk was futuristic and innovative. A pleasant sense of
communion and adventure infected us all, as if we were musicians listening
to our own improvisations. But when the first course was finished, I noticed
that only the judge and I got up to help the host's young daughter clear the
table. The men didn't move. I wondered: Should I mention this fact? How
could I be justified in interrupting an important conversation with such a
commonplace thing? Fortified by feminism but with a lot of misgivings, I
finally pointed out that the institution of who got served and who did the
serving was a very basic one, and could use some revolutionizing.

Everyone took it well. The college president still didn't budge, but he did
pass his plate. The encounter expert smiled serenely, apparently accustomed
to being confronted with almost anything at Esalen, and complimented me
on my perception. Together with the host, he even got up to help. But a half
hour later when the main course was finished, the same thing happened
again: The men philosophized, and the women served. I repeated my sentence, still feeling as if I were breaking a basic code of civilization, and got
some smiles and abstracted help as a result.

When we were ready for dessert, we were deep into the future of the multinational corporation. Nonetheless, Mr. College President interrupted himself to observe that he took his coffee black, while Mr. Esalen asked for cream, please, confessed to a weakness for sweets, and continued his predictions about the fate of the world's resources.

The judge looked at me. I looked at the judge. And suddenly there erupted from this calm and measured person the sharpest sentence of the night. "If you got up to serve and generally became self-sufficient," she said to the distinguished males, "it might be the first and only revolutionary thing you have ever done in your lives."

Of such moments, sisterhood is born. Women in patriarchal situations can look across the boundaries of age and class, even of century and country, and recognize each other's lives. But such moments, no matter how brief or commonplace, also demonstrate the most important, strategic lesson of feminism: that the power relationships in our daily lives both reflect and create the political system at large, and therefore one cannot be changed without the other.

This lesson may seem obvious and commonsensical, but it isn't. The men at that dinner table couldn't resist the lure of abstraction—that wonderful device which allows us to concentrate on the top without changing who serves whom, or who moves into the house next door—and neither could many of the most radical male thinkers of the past. Even Marx, for instance, supposed that revolution was mainly a top-down process. He theorized that the status of women, along with everything else, would change automatically when the largest mechanisms of power were taken away from the capitalist few. Therefore the ends could logically justify the means. Marx had overcome his own patriarchal culture enough to understand that women's subordinate position was political, not natural. But this sexual caste system was never quite recognized as deeper than class: The state in control of the means of production (including women's bodies, as the producers of workers and soldiers) turned out to be largely a male one; and women did not become magically, logically free.

Perhaps the greatest force that works against learning the simple lesson that change is organic—that the end is affected and even transformed by the means—is the pure force and inertia of personal privilege, of the general power system writ small.

Marx, for instance, spent much of his time living, though meagerly, off the pawned jewelry and silverware of his beloved middle-class wife, Jenny, whose energies and encouragement he greatly depended on, and whose identity he entirely absorbed. Clearly, he understood this basic form of exploitation, yet he justified it by his belief in the world-changing importance of his work. Mightn't intimate hypocrisies like these have encouraged him to believe that the end could justify the means? If so, the punishment was simple and just: His prescription for revolution became less practical because of that false conviction. The need for self-justification clouded his otherwise remarkable vision, and a bad life produced bad theory.

When such hypocritical theory is reapplied to everyday life, its impracticality becomes clear. Marx died too soon to see one tragic example of that. His third daughter, Eleanor, was a brilliant exponent of her father's work and a gifted speaker who often shared the platform with George Bernard Shaw, the Webbs, and other activists of England's Fabian era. She was also physically beautiful, which accentuated the female-caste exploitation her father had not fully accounted for. She lived openly for many years with one of her father's disciples who used Marxist philosophy as part of the reason he would not marry her—and who eventually married someone else. Vilified by society and, even worse, with no identity or self-respect separate from father or lover, she committed suicide. Would she have lived such a disastrously parasitic, nonautonomous life if Marx had been forced to develop, for himself and others, a dialectic of personal change as well as institutional change? If he had not been blinded by personal privilege to the fact that women are a colonized group inside a patriarchy, just as surely as pre-industrial countries are colonized within a capitalist world?

Dishonest, bad life produces dishonest, bad theory, but, perhaps more dangerous, this theory sincerely applied courts human disaster.

Of course most theoretical work doesn't go as far as Marx in challenging basic assumptions; not even as far as our dinner table conversation. Even women theoreticians often see themselves as exceptions to the rule of female inferiority, and so don't try to upset or question the caste system—a real tribute to the depth of our socialization. In times of feminist rebellion, there are a few works (almost totally by women) that attack this most airtight and universal of power relationships—and then a lot more (by women as well, but mostly by men) that offer brilliant, backlash explanations as to why changing the sexual status quo would result in crime, mental disease, economic chaos, confused children, and the downfall of civilization. Even the few men who do advocate sex-role reform or revolution tend to see it as a device for attaining some greater good—a decreased birth rate, for instance, or an increased pool of workers. Not only does this advocacy melt as their view of the greater good changes, but their writing remains impractical and abstract; intellectually interesting, perhaps, but never an influence on our daily lives.

Does the author of a liberal treatise in favor of sexual equality believe that *his* wife should be as free an agent in the labor force as he is? Does she have veto power over the production of *his* children? Is he free of the need to prove *his* masculinity in confrontation (intellectual or financial, if not physical) with other men? Probably not. And the reader grows more certain with every passing sentence that the book itself has probably been bought at the price of one or several women suppressing their own talents, and spending a major part of their lives saying some version of, "Shh; Karl is working."

This book by Marc Feigen Fasteau is very, very different. There is honesty on every page, and somehow the reader senses that the change being discussed here is not just theory. It is practice that has been lived and tested by the author himself.

The most obvious proof of this is the author's choice of both viewpoint and example. Yes, this book is about the destructiveness of the sexual caste system and as such, it supports most feminist criticisms of current injustice. But there is none of the usual "let-me-help-you" liberalism that demands gratitude, and probably continued inferiority, in return. On the contrary, the author doesn't attempt to write, sympathetically or otherwise, about the cause of women at all. His viewpoint is his own: that of a male human being looking at the masculine stereotype, and assessing the ways that stereotype has formed or limited him and the men around him. His examples are taken from his own life, from numerous interviews with other men in a variety of jobs and social conditions, and from an analysis of the many institutions and decision-making processes that are crucially influenced by the masculine mystique. It is precisely this enlightened self-interest, this frank concern with problems of the male role, that makes him a more trustworthy feminist ally than any mere supporter or sympathizer could ever be.

To cite a racial parallel, the author is not like the white liberals who worked in urban ghettos or the rural South, the well-meaning do-gooders in leadership roles, demanding gratitude in return, and sometimes fading altogether when the neighborhood to be integrated turned out to be their own. Like the few whites who finally understood that their own neighborhoods were ghettos, and that their children were deprived of learning from human diversity in school as well as at home, he is in this struggle on his own behalf. That means he can develop a new perspective, a complementary but different set of issues, that not only strengthen the existing movement but expand it in a constructive and valuable way.

In one sense, he is a spy in the ranks, telling us how the white male elite operates on its own preserve. As a possessor of Establishment credentials—Harvard Law School, experience in the upper legal and political circles of New York and Washington, the works—he enlightens us about class as well as sex. This means he can assess the effect of the *machismo* factor on foreign policy, or the effect of clubhouse psychology on business, in ways that an outsider would never have the expertise or the confidence to do. But even more essential, he can bring the full range of human emotions and perceptions to bear on a very factual and intimate experience of his own —those emotions and perceptions called "feminine" as well as those called "masculine." Because his goal is to achieve and express a unity of human emotions, he can make each experience universal and available to us all.

The Male Machine may be the beginning of a whole new wave of both theory and activism. Whether out of positive choice, as in this case, or painful necessity created by women's changing roles, men are beginning to seriously question the price of being thought superior. It is not a change often recognized by the press: Hostility, the battle of the sexes and the culturally masculine concern with confrontation still make better copy. But this wave is as obvious as it is vital. The goals of the feminist revolution cannot be achieved without a humanization of *both* sex roles. In the deepest sense, revolutionary feminism is a path, the *only* path, to humanism. Perhaps books like this and their activist expressions will drown forever the notion that the Women's Movement wants role-reversal instead of the humanization of both roles, and is therefore, anti-male.

Most important, this book is practical. And it becomes so largely because the author has not only lived or tried to live these basic changes, but because his motive has been healthy self-interest, not self-sacrifice. His theories are organic to his life.

In five years as a friend and sometimes a co-worker, for instance, I have never heard Marc use phrases like, "you people . . . ," "what the Women's Movement *should* be doing . . . ," "what she *really* means is . . ." and so on—often the clearest indicators of condescension when men are talking to or about women. He has spent an inordinate amount of time working with and lending his lawyer's expertise to feminist groups—not because he expects thanks, but because he perceives their work as ultimately lifting the burden of inhuman strength and eternal rectitude from him as a person, as well as from men as a caste. And I have seen him clear many tables, and help to prepare meals.

Even his decision to write this book represents a departure from the usual competitive career track of the young lawyer, and is therefore a step toward personal freedom. Male professionals of all kinds, and especially lawyers, warned that taking a year to write an "unrelated" book might make him look "unserious." Yet some of these same professionals, locked like most men in the air-tight compartment of the "masculine" role, have reacted with relief and gratitude when they read the work itself.

This book is a complement to the feminist revolution, yet it is one no woman could write. It is the revolution's other half. True, no group of people gives up power voluntarily, and therefore women can never relax efforts to overthrow the structures of patriarchal power. But there will be male allies like this one; men who also want a world in which we can shed the crippling stereotypes of sex or race, and become the unique individuals we were born to be.

Gloria Steinem

THE MALE MACHINE

1. The Male Machine

The male machine is a special kind of being, different from women, children, and men who don't measure up. He is functional, designed mainly for work. He is programed to tackle jobs, override obstacles, attack problems, overcome difficulties, and always seize the offensive. He will take on any task that can be presented to him in a competitive framework, and his most inportant positive reinforcement is victory. He has armor plating which is virtually impregnable. His circuits are never scrambled or overrun by irrelevant personal signals. He dominates and outperforms his fellows, although without excessive flashing of lights or clashing of gears. His relationship with other male machines is one of respect but not intimacy; it is difficult for him to connect his internal circuits to those of others. In fact, his internal circuitry is something of a mystery to him and is maintained primarily by humans of the opposite sex.

These delightful creatures service him with love and devotion induced by recognition of his superior design and the importance of his functions. He wields his authority over them effortlessly and magnanimously. Attempts at insurrection are easily quashed by reminding the would-be rebels of the facts of life—a quick pulse from the warning light and a simple but awe-inspiring flex of mechanical muscle usually does the job—while he rewards the most loyal and beautiful of his servants with the fruits of his labor and sexual performances that meet standards certified by Drs. Reuben and Comfort.

Of course, the male machine is not a real person, but a stereotype, an ideal image of masculinity shared, with minor variations, by nearly every male in America. No one fully conforms to it—despite our best efforts, we remain human—but it is the most fundamental standard, the yardstick against which we measure ourselves as men. To the extent that we fail to meet its injunctions, even by deliberate choice, we are likely to see ourselves, at least at times, as inadequate.

This personal ideal is intertwined with and supported by our dominant social philosophy. Based on the ideas of Locke, Mill, and Adam Smith, this ideology makes competition the guiding principle of moral and intellectual, as well as economic, life. It tells us that the general welfare is served by the self-interested clash of ambitions and ideas, but that the synergistic and creative results take place outside the individual, somewhere in the impersonal arena of society. The internal processes of the individual actors, their feelings and relationships with others, are denied importance. There is no set of beliefs that allows men to value themselves without regard to the market place. Nothing to tell men that discovering their own passions, accepting them, rejoicing in them, meshing them as best they can with the world and living by them is a worthy end in itself, in fact *is* the game itself, distinct although not separate from the judgment of the market place.

The male stereotype makes masculinity not just a fact of biology but something that must be proved and re-proved, a continual quest for an ever-receding Holy Grail. This book is about the effect of that quest, on men's personal lives, on their ways of doing business, and on the shaping of public policy. For the most part, I have avoided direct comparisons between men and women because, while the traditional female role is a repository for values that men sorely lack, it too is polarized and incomplete.

I expect that every reader will find something in this book that does not apply to him or to men he or she knows. The masculine stereotype does differ in some particulars from subculture to subculture—differences the exploration of which lie beyond the scope of this book—and in scattered pockets sex roles are already beginning to erode. Nevertheless, I am convinced that the variations are more style than substance at this point in our history, and that if I have been able to describe the stereotype and its effects accurately, every man will find in that description an important part of himself.

Incompetence in personal relationships is the inevitable result of belief in the masculine ideal, the degree of incompetence varying directly with the degree of belief. For me, this has been the most difficult aspect of masculine conditioning to escape. To the extent that I have been able to do so, it has required not only an intellectual understanding of what is wrong with the male ideal but also an effort to apply this understanding to my personal life. The effort has become easier as the legitimacy of the masculine ideal is more widely questioned, but I doubt whether I could have moved even as far as I have without some very unusual help. The help came from the most important person in my life, Brenda Feigen Fasteau, who cared enough, and had the perception and courage not to let me get away with the standard masculine avoidances.

If something upset me, for example, I would often refuse to talk about it. I would agree—after it became obvious, anyway—that I was upset and would make to myself, and if forced to Brenda, an intellectualized and summary explanation of what was going on. For example, if I had had some dealings with a professor at law school and had felt less at ease and assertive than I thought I should, I would make an explanation about authority figures and the Oedipal complex and refuse to discuss it further. I would state belligerently that there was nothing more to say about it and would go back to whatever work was nearest at hand—still angry with myself, naturally, and giving off angry (and, if I thought she would press me further, frightened) vibrations. At the risk of being cursed, yelled at, and, once or twice, physically assaulted, Brenda would insist that I articulate fully what I was feeling. When I wouldn't, she sometimes did the job herself. We must have been a strange sight, sitting together at the long tables in the law-school library, whispering furiously to each other, Brenda insisting and me trying to shove her away and bury my head in my books. A surge of anger and relief told me unmistakably when she was on target. What I was most often upset about was not the objective outcome of the incident, which was usually satisfactory, but the fact that I had felt even the slightest bit ill at ease. There was simply no room in my ideal image of a human being for anything but confidence and control. Brenda, amazed that I was angry at myself over such (in reality) minor insecurities, persistently asked the question, "What standard are you applying to yourself, and where does it come from?" Neither of us knew the answer then.

Learning to help Brenda was only a little easier. In those days, she found it hard to ask for help. She would give off a few small distress signals and then, if they weren't picked up, she would get angry, putting the force of her unhappiness into that anger. At first, I didn't hear the distress signals, mainly because my fear of experiencing emotions I didn't like made me tune out the part of the mind that picks up small, unarticulated variations and tremors in the emotional field of someone one knows well. She had to *tell* me when she was upset, which was not in and of itself a disaster, but more than I had to do when I needed her support. Only as I became more sensitive to (and less fearful of) my own feelings was I able to become more sensitive to hers.

I was also unaccustomed to the amount of effort it took to really help Brenda resolve a personal problem or begin to change an aspect of her personality. The effort, to get inside someone else's head, to sort out the real from the apparent misperceptions and difficulties and help to translate that insight into terms that the other person could use was something entirely new to me. I had to learn to use my feelings in addition to my intellect as instruments for registering and understanding how she felt and what she needed.

When Brenda would get angry as the result of being unhappy over something, my first instinct, especially if I had nothing (or very little) to do with the problem, was to fight back. I would get knots in my stomach and shout, "What the hell are you yelling at me for? I don't have to put up with this crap," or tell her she was nuts, both of which made matters worse. Nearly always what she needed was a reply indicating some understanding of how she felt. That made it easier for her to talk directly about and deal with whatever the issue was. For a long time, I couldn't give that response. I was too preoccupied with "not being pushed around." The less touchy I became about being tough in the traditional sense, the better able I became to put aside her surface anger and respond to the plea for help underneath. I had never known anybody that well before, or felt that I could affect another person so intimately.

Eventually, several key points emerged. First, the difficulties I had experienced in these situations were in large part the result of having internalized a particular set of values—I was judging my behavior against an ideal of invulnerability that was shared in rough outline by other men but not, for some reason, by women. Second, it was the fear of emotions associated with being vulnerable, rather than the emotions themselves—which were not disproportionate or unusual—that was the major cause of the unease that I felt. Third, in the process of trying to "protect" myself against these "unmasculine" feelings, I was somehow cutting myself off from all but a narrow range of human contact. These observations were the starting point for an interest in the concept of masculinity and its effects that led in time to this book.

2. Friendships Among Men

Walter: Arthur's been my friend for longer than I've known you. Do you know how I do it?

Maude: Yes. You have a very low standard of friendship.

—*Maude*, CBS Television

There is a long-standing myth in our society that the great friendships are between men. Forged through shared experience, male friendship is portrayed as the most unselfish, if not the highest form, of human relationship. The more traditionally masculine the shared experience from which it springs, the stronger and more profound the friendship is supposed to be. Going to war, weathering crises together at school or work, playing on the same athletic team, are some of the classic experiences out of which friendships between men are believed to grow.

By and large, men do prefer the company of other men, not only in their structured time but in the time they fill with optional, nonobligatory activity. They prefer to play games, drink, and talk, as well as work and fight together. Yet something is missing. Despite the time men spend together, their contact rarely goes beyond the external, a limitation which tends to make their friendships shallow and unsatisfying.

My own childhood memories are of doing things with my friends—playing games or sports, building walkie-talkies, going camping. Other people and my relationships to them were never legitimate subjects for attention. If someone liked me, it was an opaque, mysterious occurrence that bore no analysis. When I was slighted, I felt hurt. But relationships with people just happened. I certainly had feelings about my friends, but I can't remember a single instance of trying consciously to sort them out until I was well into college.

For most men this kind of shying away from the personal continues into adult life. In conversations with each other, we hardly ever use ourselves as reference points. We talk about almost everything except how we ourselves are affected by people and events. Everything is discussed as though it were taking place out there somewhere, as though we had no more felt response to it than to the weather. Topics that can be treated in this detached, objective way become conversational mainstays. The few subjects which are fundamentally personal are shaped into discussions of abstract general questions. Even in an exchange about their reactions to liberated women—a topic of intensely personal interest—the tendency will be to talk in general, theoretical terms. Work, at least its objective aspects, is always a safe subject. Men also spend an incredible amount of time rehashing the great public issues of the day. Until early 1973, Vietnam was the work-horse topic. Then came Watergate. It doesn't seem to matter that we've all had a hundred similar conversations. We plunge in for another round, trying to come up with a new angle as much as to impress the others with what we know as to keep from being bored stiff.

Games play a central role in situations organized by men. I remember a weekend some years ago at the country house of a law-school classmate as a blur of softball, football, croquet, poker, and a dice-and-board game called Combat, with swimming thrown in on the side. As soon as one game ended, another began. Taken one at a time, these "activities" were fun, but the impression was inescapable that the host, and most of his guests, would do anything to stave off a lull in which they would be together without some impersonal focus for their attention. A snapshot of almost any men's club would show the same thing, ninety percent of the men engaged in some activity —ranging from backgammon to watching the tube—other than, or at least as an aid to, conversation.*

My composite memory of evenings spent with a friend at college and later when we shared an apartment in Washington is of conversations punctuated by silences during which we would internally pass over any personal or emotional thoughts which had arisen and come back to the permitted track. When I couldn't get my mind off personal matters, I said very little. Talks with my father have always had the same tone. Respect for privacy was the rationale for our diffidence. His questions to me about how things were going at school or at work were asked as discreetly as he would have asked a friend about someone's commitment to a hospital for the criminally insane. Our conversations, when they touched these matters at all, to say nothing of more sensitive matters, would veer quickly back to safe topics of general interest.

In our popular literature, the archetypal male hero embodying this personal muteness is the cowboy. The classic mold for the character was set in 1902 by Owen Wister's novel *The Virginian* where the author spelled out, with an explicitness that was never again necessary, the characteristics of his protagonist. Here's how it goes when two close friends the Virginian hasn't seen in some time take him out for a drink:

All of them had seen rough days together, and they felt guilty with emotion.

"It's hot weather," said Wiggin.

---

* Women may use games as a reason for getting together—bridge clubs, for example. But the show is more for the rest of the world—to indicate that they are doing *something*—and the games themselves are not the only means of communication.

"Hotter in Box Elder," said McLean. "My kid has started teething."

Words ran dry again. They shifted their positions, looked in their glasses, read the labels on the bottles. They dropped a word now and then to the proprietor about his trade, and his ornaments.[1]

One of the Virginian's duties is to assist at the hanging of an old friend as a horse thief. Afterward, for the first time in the book, he is visibly upset. The narrator puts his arm around the hero's shoulders and describes the Virginian's reaction:

I had the sense to keep silent, and presently he shook my hand, not looking at me as he did so. He was always very shy of demonstration.[2]

And, for explanation of such reticence, "As all men know, he also knew that many things should be done in this world in silence, and that talking about them is a mistake."[3]

There are exceptions, but they only prove the rule.

One is the drunken confidence: "Bob, ole boy, I gotta tell ya—being divorced isn't so hot. . . . [and see, I'm too drunk to be held responsible for blurting it out]." Here, drink becomes an excuse for exchanging confidences and a device for periodically loosening the restraint against expressing a need for sympathy and support from other men—which may explain its importance as a male ritual.[4] Marijuana fills a similar need.

Another exception is talking to a stranger—who may be either someone the speaker doesn't know or someone who isn't in the same social or business world. (Several black friends told me that they have been on the receiving end of personal confidences from white acquaintances that they were sure had not been shared with white friends.) In either case, men are willing to talk about themselves only to other men with whom they do not have to compete or whom they will not have to confront socially later.

Finally, there is the way men depend on women to facilitate certain conversations. The women in a mixed group are usually the ones who make the first personal reference, about themselves or others present. The men can then join in without having the onus for initiating a discussion of "personalities." Collectively, the men can "blame" the conversation on the women. They can also feel in these conversations that since they are talking "to" the women instead of "to" the men, they can be excused for deviating from the masculine norm. When the women leave, the tone and subject invariably shift away from the personal.

The effect of these constraints is to make it extraordinarily difficult for men to really get to know each other. A psychotherapist who has conducted a lengthy series of encounter groups for men summed it up:

> With saddening regularity [the members of these groups] described how much they wanted to have closer, more satisfying relationships with other men: "I'd settle for having one really close man friend. I supposedly have some close men friends now. We play golf or go for a drink. We complain about our jobs and our wives. I care about them and they care about me. We even have some physical contact—I mean we may even give a hug on a big occasion. But it's not enough."[5]

The sources of this stifling ban on self-disclosure, the reasons why men hide from each other, lie in the taboos and imperatives of the masculine stereotype.

To begin with, men are supposed to be functional, to spend their time working or otherwise solving or thinking about how to solve problems. Personal reaction, how one feels about something, is considered dysfunctional, at best an irrelevant distraction from the expected objectivity. Only weak men, and women, talk about—i.e., "give in," to their feelings. "I group my friends in two ways," said a business executive:

> those who have made it and don't complain and those who haven't made it. And only the latter spend time talking to their

> wives about their problems and how bad their boss is and all that.
> The ones who concentrate more on communicating . . . are those
> who have realized that they aren't going to make it and therefore
> they have changed the focus of attention.[6]

In a world which tells men they have to choose between expressiveness and manly strength, this characterization may be accurate. Most of the men who talk personally to other men *are* those whose problems have gotten the best of them, who simply can't help it. Men not driven to despair don't talk about themselves, so the idea that self-disclosure and expressiveness are associated with problems and weakness becomes a self-fulfilling prophecy.

Obsessive competitiveness also limits the range of communication in male friendships. Competition is the principal mode by which men relate to each other—at one level because they don't know how else to make contact, but more basically because it is the way to demonstrate, to themselves and others, the key masculine qualities of unwavering toughness and the ability to dominate and control. The result is that they inject competition into situations which don't call for it.

In conversations, you must show that you know more about the subject than the other man, or at least as much as he does. For example, I have often engaged in a contest that could be called My Theory Tops Yours, disguised as a serious exchange of ideas. The proof that it wasn't serious was that I was willing to participate even when I was sure that the participants, including myself, had nothing fresh to say. Convincing the other person —victory—is the main objective, with control of the floor an important tactic. Men tend to lecture at each other, insist that the discussion follow their train of thought, and are often unwilling to listen.[7] As one member of a men's rap group said,

> When I was talking I used to feel that I had to be driving to a point,
> that it had to be rational and organized, that I had to persuade at
> all times, rather than exchange thoughts and ideas.[8]

Even in casual conversation some men hold back unless they are absolutely sure of what they are saying. They don't want to have to change a position once they have taken it. It's "just like a woman" to change your mind, and, more important, it is inconsistent with the approved masculine posture of total independence.

Competition was at the heart of one of my closest friendships, now defunct. There was a good deal of mutual liking and respect. We went out of our way to spend time with each other and wanted to work together. We both had "prospects" as "bright young men" and the same "liberal but tough" point of view. We recognized this about each other, and this recognition was the basis of our respect and of our sense of equality. That we saw each other as equals was important—our friendship was confirmed by the reflection of one in the other. But our constant and all-encompassing competition made this equality precarious and fragile. One way or another, everything counted in the measuring process. We fought out our tennis matches as though our lives depended on it. At poker, the two of us would often play on for hours after the others had left. These *mano a mano* poker marathons seem in retrospect especially revealing of the competitiveness of the relationship: playing for small stakes, the essence of the game is in outwitting, psychologically beating down the other player—the other skills involved are negligible. Winning is the only pleasure, one that evaporates quickly, a truth that struck me in inchoate form every time our game broke up at four a.m. and I walked out the door with my five-dollar winnings, a headache, and a sense of time wasted. Still, I did the same thing the next time. It was what we did together, and somehow it counted. Losing at tennis could be balanced by winning at poker; at another level, his moving up in the federal government by my getting on the *Harvard Law Review*.

This competitiveness feeds the most basic obstacle to openness between men, the inability to admit to being vulnerable. Real men, we learn early, are not supposed to have doubts, hopes and ambitions which may not be realized, things they don't (or even especially do) like about themselves, fears and disappointments. Such feelings and concerns, of course, are part of everyone's inner life, but a man must keep quiet about them. If others know how you really feel you can be hurt, and that in itself is incompatible with manhood. The inhibiting effect of this imperative is not limited to disclosures of major personal problems. Often men do not share even ordinary uncertainties and half-formulated plans of daily life with their friends. And when they do, they are careful to suggest that they already know how to proceed—that they are not really asking for help or understanding but simply for particular bits of information. Either way, any doubts they have are presented as external, carefully characterized as having to do with the issue as distinct from the speaker. They are especially guarded about expressing concern or asking a question that would invite personal comment. It is almost impossible for men to simply exchange thoughts about matters involving them personally in a comfortable, non-crisis atmosphere. If a friend tells you of his concern that he and a colleague are always disagreeing, for example, he is likely to quickly supply his own explanation—something like "different professional backgrounds." The effect is to rule out observations or suggestions that do not fit within this already reconnoitered protective structure. You don't suggest, even if you believe it is true, that in fact the disagreements arise because he presents his ideas in a way which tends to provoke a hostile reaction. It would catch him off guard; it would be something he hadn't already thought of and accepted about himself and, for that reason, no matter how constructive and well-intentioned you might be, it would put you in control for the moment. He doesn't want that; he is afraid of losing your respect. So, sensing he feels that way, because you would yourself, you say something else. There is no real give-and-take.

It is hard for men to get angry at each other honestly. Anger between friends often means that one has hurt the other. Since the straightforward expression of anger in these situations involves an admission of vulnerability, it is safer to stew silently or find an "objective" excuse for retaliation. Either way, trust is not fully restored.

Men even try not to let it show when they feel good. We may report the reasons for our happiness, if they have to do with concrete accomplishments, but we try to do it with a straight face, as if to say, "Here's what happened, but it hasn't affected my grown-up unemotional equilibrium, and I am not asking for any kind of response." Happiness is a precarious, "childish" feeling, easy to shoot down. Others may find the event that triggers it trivial or incomprehensible, or even threatening to their own self-esteem—in the sense that if one man is up, another man is down. So we tend not to take the risk of expressing it.

What is particularly difficult for men is seeking or accepting help from friends. I, for one, learned early that dependence was unacceptable. When I was eight, I went to a summer camp I disliked. My parents visited me in the middle of the summer and, when it was time for them to leave, I wanted to go with them. They refused, and I yelled and screamed and was miserably unhappy for the rest of the day. That evening an older camper comforted me, sitting by my bed as I cried, patting me on the back soothingly and saying whatever it is that one says at times like that. He was in some way clumsy or funny-looking, and a few days later I joined a group of kids in cruelly making fun of him, an act which upset me, when I thought about it, for years. I can only explain it in terms of my feeling, as early as the age of eight, that by needing and accepting his help and comfort I had compromised myself, and took it out on him.

"You can't express dependence when you feel it," a corporate executive said, "because it's a kind of absolute. If you are loyal 90% of the time and disloyal 10%, would you be considered loyal? Well, the same happens with independence: you are either dependent or independent; you can't be both."⁹ "Feelings of dependence," another explained, "are identified with weakness or 'untoughness' and our culture doesn't accept those things in men."[10] The result is that we either go it alone or "act out certain games or rituals to provoke the desired reaction in the other and have our needs satisfied without having to ask for anything."[11]

Somewhat less obviously, the expression of affection also runs into emotional barriers growing out of the masculine stereotype. When I was in college, I was suddenly quite moved while attending a friend's wedding. The surge of feeling made me uncomfortable and self-conscious. There was nothing inherently difficult or, apart from the fact of being moved by a moment of tenderness, "unmasculine" about my reaction. I just did not know how to deal with or communicate what I felt. "I consider myself a sentimentalist," one man said, "and I think I am quite able to express my feelings. But the other day my wife described a friend of mine to some people as my best friend and I felt embarrassed when I heard her say it."[12]

A major source of these inhibitions is the fear of being, or being thought, homosexual. Nothing is more frightening to a heterosexual man in our society. It threatens, at one stroke, to take away every vestige of his claim to a masculine identity —something like knocking out the foundations of a building —and to expose him to the ostracism, ranging from polite tolerance to violent revulsion, of his friends and colleagues. A man can be labeled as homosexual not just because of overt sexual acts but because of almost any sign of behavior which does not fit the masculine stereotype. The touching of another man, other than shaking hands or, under emotional stress, an arm around the shoulder, is taboo. Women may kiss each other when they meet; men are uncomfortable when hugged even by close friends.[13] Onlookers might misinterpret what they saw, and, more important, what would we think of ourselves if we felt a twinge of sensual pleasure from the embrace.

Direct verbal expressions of affection or tenderness are also something that only homosexuals and women engage in. Between "real" men affection has to be disguised in gruff, "you old son-of-a-bitch" style. Paradoxically, in some instances, terms of endearment between men can be used as a ritual badge of manhood, dangerous medicine safe only for the strong. The flirting with homosexuality that characterizes the initiation rites of many fraternities and men's clubs serves this purpose. Claude Brown wrote about black life in New York City in the 1950s:

> The term ["baby"] had a hip ring to it. . . . It was like saying, "Man, look at me. I've got masculinity to spare. . . . I can say 'baby' to another cat and he can say 'baby' to me, and we can say it with strength in our voices." If you could say it, this meant that you really had to be sure of yourself, sure of your masculinity. [14]

Fear of homosexuality does more than inhibit the physical display of affection. One of the major recurring themes in the men's groups led by psychotherapist Don Clark was:

> "A large segment of my feelings about other men are unknown or distorted because I am afraid they might have something to do with homosexuality. Now I'm lonely for other men and don't know how to find what I want with them."

As Clark observes, "The spectre of homosexuality seems to be the dragon at the gateway to self-awareness, understanding, and acceptance of male-male needs. If a man tries to pretend the dragon is not there by turning a blind eye to erotic feelings for all other males, he also blinds himself to the rich variety of feelings that are related."[15]

The few situations in which men do acknowledge strong feelings of affection and dependence toward other men are exceptions which prove the rule. With "cop couples," for example, or combat soldier "buddies," intimacy and dependence are forced on the men by their work—they have to ride in the patrol car or be in the same foxhole with somebody—and the jobs themselves have such highly masculine images that the men can get away with behavior that would be suspect under any other conditions.

Furthermore, even these combat-buddy relationships, when looked at closely, turn out not to be particularly intimate or personal. Margaret Mead has written:

> During the last war English observers were confused by the apparent contradiction between American soldiers' emphasis on the buddy, so grievously exemplified in the break-downs that followed a buddy's death, and the results of detailed inquiry which showed how transitory these buddy relationships were. It was found that men actually accepted their buddies as derivatives from their outfit, and from accidents of association, rather than because of any special personality characteristics capable of ripening into friendship. [16]

One effect of the fear of appearing to be homosexual is to reinforce the practice that two men rarely get together alone without a reason. I once called a friend to suggest that we have dinner together. "O.K.," he said. "What's up?" I felt uncomfortable telling him that I just wanted to talk, that there was no other reason for the invitation.

Men get together to conduct business, to drink, to play games and sports, to re-establish contact after long absences, to participate in heterosexual social occasions—circumstances in which neither person is responsible for actually wanting to see the other. Men are particularly comfortable seeing each other in groups. The group situation defuses any possible assumptions about the intensity of feeling between particular men and provides the safety of numbers—"All the guys are here." It makes personal communication, which requires a level of trust and mutual understanding not generally shared by all members of a group, more difficult and offers an excuse for avoiding this dangerous territory. And it provides what is most sought after in men's friendships: mutual reassurance of masculinity.

Needless to say, the observations in this chapter did not spring full-blown from my head. The process started when I began to understand that, at least with Brenda, a more open, less self-protective relationship was possible. At first, I perceived my situation as completely personal. The changes I was trying to effect in myself had to do, I thought, only with Brenda and me, and could be generalized, if at all, only to other close relation-ships between men and women. But, as Brenda came to be deeply involved in the women's movement, I began to see, usually at one remove but sometimes directly, the level of in-timacy that women, especially women active in the movement, shared with each other. The contrast between this and the friendships I had with men was striking. I started listening to men's conversations, including my own, and gradually the basic outlines of the pattern described here began to emerge. I heard from women that the men they knew had very few really close male friends; since then I have heard the same thing from men themselves. It was, I realized, my own experi-ence as well. It wasn't that I didn't know a lot of men, or that I was not on friendly terms with them. Rather, I gradually be-came dissatisfied with the impersonality of these friendships.

Of course, some constraints on self-disclosure do make sense. Privacy is something you give up selectively and gradually to people you like and trust, and who are capable of under-standing—instant, indiscriminate intimacy is nearly always formularized, without real content and impact. Nor does self-disclosure as a kind of comparmentalized rest-and-recreation period work: "Well, John, let me tell you about myself. . . ."

Having said all this, it is nonetheless true that men have carried the practice of emotional restraint to the point of paralysis. For me, at least, the ritual affirmations of membership in the fraternity of men that one gets from participation in "mas-culine" activities do nothing to assuage the feeling of being essentially alone; they have become a poor substitute for being known by and knowing other people. But the positive content of what will replace the old-style friendships is only beginning to take shape. I am learning, though, that when I am able to articu-late my feelings as they arise in the context of my friendships, I often find that they are shared by others. Bringing them out into the open clears the air; avoiding them, even unconsciously, is stultifying. I have found also that I am not as fragile as I once thought. The imagined hazards of showing oneself to be human, and thus vulnerable, to one's friends tend not to materialize when actually put to the test. But being oneself is an art, an art sensitive to variations in the receptivity of others as well as to one's own inner life. It is still, for me, something to be mastered, to be tried out and practiced.

3. The Conquest of Sex

If my soul is really unconquerable, I shall never fully love; for it is the nature of love to conquer all fortresses. And if I must cling to being master of my fate, I shall never be able to let myself go in passion; for passionate love always has tragic possibilities.

—Rollo May, *Love and Will*

The sex act is the only intimate contact many adult men ever have with women; it is as close as they come to crossing the barrier between the sexes. "As close as they come" because men take all their conditioning, all their ingrained ideas about how they should act and feel, to bed with them, where they tend to stifle the freedom and spontaneity that make sex personal and give it meaning. The deadening effect of the masculine stereotype is particularly poignant here because of the potential for intimacy that is being lost:

The fact that love is personal is shown in the love act itself. Man is the only creature who makes love face to face, who copulates looking at his partner. Yes, we can turn our heads or assume other positions for variety's sake, but these are variations on a theme—the theme of making love vis-à-vis each other. This opens the whole front of the person—the breasts, the chest, the stomach, all the parts which are most tender and most vulnerable—to the kindness or cruelty of the partner. [Each] can see in the eyes of the [other] the nuances of delight or awe, the tremulousness or angst; it is the posture of the ultimate baring of one's self. . . . But . . . looking is fraught with intensity; it brings a heightened consciousness of relationship. We experience what we are doing —which may be play, or exploitation or sharing of sensuality, or fucking, or lovemaking, or any form thereof. But at least the norm given by this position is personal. We have to block something off, exert some effort, to make it *not* personal. [1]

This pressure, this potential, in an act to which we are powerfully drawn is frightening to men who have to keep their psychic distance from women and from their own feelings. It explains some of the impersonality, often hostile, of men's remarks to or about attractive women they see on the street—"I'd like to get into her pants!" "How'd you like *that* warming your pecker?" etc., etc. It is the reason why men view sex as a dangerous encounter, not in the Victorian sense of its being sinful or unhealthy but as one of the ultimate tests of their masculinity: to get this close to a woman, to the feminine in her and—because of the emotions evoked—in oneself, and still be in command. For men who are most heavily steeped in the masculine ideal, often the same men who are most fearful of not measuring up, the sex act has a nasty edge of hostility.

Dave Meggyesy, former linebacker for the pro-football St. Louis Cardinals, records a teammate as saying, "I'm really going to punish the old lady tonight" to announce he was going to make love to his wife. [2] Norman Mailer, who seems to have taken up the literary wars as his route to manhood only because, to his everlasting regret, he wasn't born with the physique of a Jack Dempsey, gives the idea of sex as punishment more elaborate expression. Kate Millett, surveying Mailer's writings, found his short story "Time of Her Time" and Sergius O'Shaughnessy, its hero, a clear example:

Acting upon the principle that a female "laid" is a female subjugated, the hero strikes with his magic weapon, a penis, that his comic-strip bravado impels him to refer to as "the avenger." The attack begins when Sergius overhears his victim venture a remark on Eliot. Such pretension to intelligence appalls his sense of propriety and he is on the instant "inflamed," the avenger urging him "to prong her then and there, right on the floor of the party," "lay waste to her little independence" and set all right.

*   *   *

Things go wrong from the start . . . [t]he girl fails to succumb to that passivity which Mailer myth ordains is the only feminine route to the promised land of orgasm. . . . Nature rebukes the upstart by withholding sexual satisfaction; Sergius underlines the lesson by striking her across the face. . . .

At their final match he suffers a momentary defeat through premature ejaculation. . . . But recovering his resiliency with commendable haste, he imposes anal intercourse upon his opponent, slowly savoring "as the avenger rode down to his hilt" the outrage of pain and humiliation he has inflicted, and grimacing at the reader "she thrashed beneath me like a trapped little animal," "caught," "forced," "wounded," and so forth.[3]

As Mary Ellmann has written,

Everything conspires to make occasions of courage, in the formal and stylized sense of such occasions in the past, hard to come by. Hemingway was reduced to fighting fish, and the only land test in constant supply is fighting females. So armed intercourse must subsume all other single tournaments.[4]

This conquest orientation makes men feel obliged to make some show of sexual interest in every attractive woman they see, some movement toward putting their stamp on her, whether or not they are in fact drawn to her. "When I meet a good-looking woman and I don't make her, I have a small but very real sense of failure, I feel diminished as a man," an acquaintance reported. Women can be sexually attractive on sight, at least if one's in the right frame of mind. But much of men's reaction to them has a ritual quality, a feeling of forcing the machinery into action. Going right for the jugular, an evil woman in one of Mickey Spillane's books—written before psychiatric terminology had filtered down to the pulps—accuses Mike Hammer, the hero, after he refuses her sudden offer of her body, of being a "sissy." That gets him. "Being only human," Mike kisses her roughly, strips off her clothes and then, his manhood restored, walks out. [5]

The obligatory show can be a remark to another man, the construction worker's obscenity, insistence on eye contact, an obligation-creating and excessive gesture of gallantry, a sexual reference under circumstances which make it a distraction, even a full-fledged seduction. Real men are supposed to be ready to come through at all times. This obligation is one of the things men retreat from when they segregate themselves from women.

The heroic standard of sexual readiness and performance, although unarticulated, also heightens men's concern about their sexual adequacy. If they turn down an opportunity, they don't want their friends to know about it. This concern is especially hard on teen-agers, who are necessarily uncertain about their sexual capabilities and style. A study of youthful suicides in Los Angeles County during the 1960s found fears of sexual inadequacy to be a "very prominent" cause of suicide in boys, and, by contrast, a negligible factor for girls. [6] The sense of important but impersonal, vague and essentially unknowable criteria for masculine performance also contributes to this anxiety. Our concern with meeting external standards shifts our attention away from the actual experience and robs it of pleasure.

The mythic male that men think women adore is always less involved with the woman than the woman is with him. In a more hypocritical era, he was pulled in other directions by duty; today his distance stems from a streak of manipulative coldness: he is the handsome unsmiling man in dark glasses in the Silva Thin ads who punishes women who help themselves to his cigarettes by coolly deserting them on highways, ocean liners, cable cars, and mountain tops; or he is James Bond, whose creator never tires of describing him as looking rather cruel. The ultimate fantasy of women being seduced simply by a display of masculinity is a recurring feature of pornographic novels. "There is hardly one that does not have the same scene in which the hero, by simply exposing his 'magnificent organ, erect and quivering,' reduces the girl to quiescent jelly."[7]

Many men tend to think of making love in terms of technique, buttons to be pushed, erogenous zones to be touched, phrases to be murmured. They look for erotic stimulation everywhere but in the attempt to share fantasies and understand and respond to the individuating elements of their own and women's personalities, everywhere but their imaginations and feelings; they look instead to the uncertainty and excitement of new conquests and to more and more elaborate physical variations in lovemaking. Although it is easy today for both men and women to fall into the trap of thinking that experimenting with technique and taking on a new lover every month or so are panaceas for boredom, men are particularly susceptible to the belief that variety is a substitute for passion. To be moved by another person is not masculine, so men are afraid of being moved and try to avoid it. An executive interviewed in a Harvard Business School survey bluntly stated the case in discussing his inhibitions about expressing his feelings toward his wife: "The word 'tenderness,' " he said, "throws me off. I associate it with mothers or with artists; it is not a manly characteristic."[8]

Men develop a very rigid and narrow idea of emotional control in personal relations. They like to think that all their motivations emerge from objective considerations or the simple promptings of instinct. The distinction made by Rollo May between sex and eros is very much to the point:

> Sex can be defined fairly adequately in physiological terms as consisting of the building up of bodily tensions and their release. Eros, in contrast, is the experiencing of the personal intentions and meaning of the act. Whereas sex is a rhythm of stimulus and response, eros is a state of being. The pleasure in sex is described by Freud and others as the reduction of tension; in eros, on the contrary we wish not to be released from the excitement but rather to hang on to it, to bask in it, and even to increase it. . . . [9]

Sex, in short, is the mode of relating characterized by tumescence of the organs (for which we seek pleasurable relief) and filled gonads (for which we seek satisfying release). But eros is the mode of relating in which we do not seek release, but rather to cultivate, procreate, and form the world. *In eros, we seek increase of stimulation.* Sex is a need, but eros is a desire. [10]

Today, most men can acknowledge and satisfy sexual need fairly freely, but the masculine stereotype puts eros beyond their reach. For a man to allow himself to feel the passion of eros, the flight of imagination which fuses sexual attraction and the impulse toward intimacy with the partner, is to make himself vulnerable. It would mean that he wants, and cannot help but show that he wants, recognition of his uniqueness, an affirmation that he is known and that in the intimate world of the other person he counts, something every man, every human being, needs and desires. But once we acknowledge this desire we run the risk of having it denied; for the moment we are very much in the power of another individual. And for a man to be dependent—in particular, dependent upon a woman—is a forbidden emotional state. It does not matter that the vulnerability, the dependence in the relationship is mutual—equality in love is not one of the values of the masculine ideal.

Some men have learned to give at least a degree of personal affirmation and caring in love, but find asking for and receiving it much harder.

Just as giving is essential to one's own full pleasure, the ability to receive is necessary in the love relationship also. If you cannot receive, your giving will be a domination of the partner. . . . We speak, thus, not of receiving as a passive phenomenon, but of *active receiving:* one knows he is receiving, feels it, absorbs it into his own experience whether he verbally acknowledges it or not, and is grateful for it. [11]

In fact it is just this device, refusing to fully and openly receive, that many more subtle and sensitive men use, consciously or not, to dominate and protect themselves in their love relationships with women. These are often men who pride themselves on their ability to relate to women and repudiate the notion of women as subordinate. Nevertheless, their attentions, however perceptive, take on a false, impersonal quality. They are interested in the personality of their partner—but as a subject for analysis, not as the basis for their own feeling response. They turn away any attempts to probe their own feelings. They feel safer in the relationship if their emotional responses are not stirred up, if attention is focused away from their fantasies; wishes, and fears. They are concerned about women's reactions in sex and are technically proficient, but their concern ultimately is entirely with themselves, however anxious they are that the women be "satisfied." They want to see ecstasy in the faces of their partners, but only to assure themselves of their manhood, not to mingle that ecstasy with their own. Ingrid Bengis has captured the aridity of these performances:

> Of course, under ideal conditions I . . . would want a wholly adequate lover— "adequate" meaning sensitive, enthusiastic, imaginative, spontaneous and affectionate as well as potent. . . . In less than ideal conditions, however, I would prefer to be in bed with a man whose overenthusiastic fantasies, pent-up sexual drive, and authentic involvement made him ejaculate prematurely, than to have sex with a man who can keep it up for an hour because he does daily exercises, testing himself out on every woman he can find. . . . As for "skills," no woman wants a technocrat in bed next to her; she wants a human being like herself. [12]

I do not mean to suggest that preoccupation with performance is easy to avoid. Everything in our upbringing conspires to create it. It used to be enough (enough for men, at least) to get it up and get it in; nice girls didn't have orgasms, anyway, and getting her to let you in was full proof of masculine force and charm. Some men still live in that world. But for those men who read sex manuals, the idea that every woman could have and enjoy orgasm brought the immediate corollary that providing it, on schedule, in the approved manner and every time, is not just something nice, but a "fail not at your peril" test of masculinity. If sex now included orgasm for women, then men, like efficient machines, should give it to them. A problem, like anything else, to be studied and broken down into piéces—the right techniques, the right moves, a little practice and any man worth his salt ought to be able to do it on command. Since orgasm is thought to be the only real point of making love, physically competent performance, delivering the goods, easily becomes the sole basis for men's sexual self-esteem.

A friend told me of the time when he and another man were playing tennis with an energetic woman friend. First she played against him, then against the other man. Finally, both were worn out and she was still going strong. "How dare you not satisfy me?" she said teasingly. The double meaning made both men uncomfortable. "What men are really afraid of in women's liberation," my friend explained, making explicit the point of his story, "is that women will make sexual demands that men can't meet. After a while, you know, you can use your hands or your mouth, but that's it, you just can't do anything more."

One result of the performance ethic is a new version of the "good woman"/"bad woman" dichotomy. Today the "good woman" is one who allows men the illusion of sexuality without risk of failure. She lets him give her orgasm, or fakes it. Or she accepts the blame for failure, attributing the problem to her refusal to "accept her feminity," to "surrender herself," to submit completely to the man, to accept—if one reads between the lines—her innate masochism.

The "bad woman" today is the one who is not sexually satisfied and who complains—of inadequate technique, of the absence of feeling, of anything that puts some of the responsibility for her unhappiness on the man. Even the woman of genuine passion whose only demand is for a response of matching intensity is a secret object of fear as well as attraction for men. Women who call men's bluffs by refusing to follow the bold-male-pursuer/shy-female-prey roles also tend to frighten men. We have in effect a new covert sexual ideal of "nameless, cooperative, uncritical women," who are sexually responsive but do not openly take the initiative. [13] Its popular expression is the Playboy Bunny, but Henry Miller, ahead of his time, carried the idea to its logical conclusion. In *Tropic of Capricorn* he spelled out his version of the "dumb blonde": an amnesiac deaf-mute, identified only as "the girl upstairs," "probably the best fuck I ever had." [14]

But the fundamental problem of performance-ethic sexuality is that it is self-defeating, even on its own terms:

> The excessive concern with technical performance in sex is actually correlated with the reduction of sexual feeling. . . .
>
> The more one must demonstrate his potency, the more he treats sexual intercourse—this most intimate and personal of all acts—as a performance to be judged by exterior requirements, the more he then views himself as a machine to be turned on, adjusted and steered, and the less feeling he has for either himself or his partner; and the less feeling, the more he loses genuine sexual appetite and ability. The upshot of this self-defeating pattern is that, in the long run, *the lover who is most efficient will also be the one who is impotent.* [15]

Although statistical evidence is not available to prove it, psychiatrists, family counselors, and other professionals in the field overwhelmingly believe that the rate of impotence has jumped substantially in recent years. [16] For example, a 1970 survey of *Psychology Today* readers revealed that slightly more than one-third of the male respondents "have difficulty achieving an erection." Impotence can be caused by syphilis, diabetes, lower spinal-cord injury, and, according to traditional psychoanalytic theory, excessive dominance of either parent or early warnings against masturbation. [17] But since it seems unlikely that any of these factors was on the rise in the last decade, we had best look elsewhere for the cause of the current increase in impotence. One psychiatrist has attributed it to the more open and more exacting demands of newly liberated women for sexual performance:

The male concern of the 1940s and 1950s was to satisfy the woman. In the late 1960s and early 1970s, it seems to be "will I have to maintain an erection to maintain a relationship?" This idea is permeated with feelings of "who calls the shots" and "who is sex for." There is a reversal of former roles: the role of put-upon Victorian woman is that of the put-upon man of the 1970s. [18]

It is probably true that some women, in response to years of self-abnegation and sexual frustration, are overreacting and hostilely demanding depersonalized machinelike performance aimed only at their own gratification. But all the feminists with whom I have discussed the matter are convinced that such women are a small minority, that most are still a long way from even healthy self-assertion in bed. The increase in reported impotence, it seems to me, is due to other factors, factors in which male stereotypes about sex play the central role:

First, given that men's basic model for relationships is dominant-submissive/superior-subordinate, some men undoubtedly interpret women's demands for satisfaction as attempts to "take over and run the show," to reverse the traditional arrangement. Naturally, this can be a turnoff.

Second, some men are unable to relate sexually to women who participate as equals in the initiation and pleasures of sex. Sexual behavior, like other behavior in human relationships, is mostly learned, and the only script many men know is the one where they initiate, direct, and judge the performance. The new scenario is disorienting and does not stimulate the previously developed erogenous zones of their psyches. Not being on top, in "missionary position," for example, is upsetting to many men.

Third, it does not take much in the way of demands from a woman for a man who views sexuality as largely a matter of mechanics to begin to believe that she, also, values him solely for machinelike efficiency.

Fourth, because men expect themselves to be always ready and able, they probably count as impotence the times when, for one reason or another, they really didn't feel like sex but tried anyway. Since they are no longer the only initiators of sex, this is happening more than in the past. Furthermore, as Masters and Johnson have pointed out,[19] a few misunderstood incidents of this kind can easily produce the genuine article.

Fifth, women are not letting men get away with totally inadequate performances as much as they used to. For many men, it used to be enough to satisfy the ego to just get it up and get it in, never mind for how long. And women didn't complain because they were afraid to be labeled as castrators. Today, both because of women's legitimate demands and the general increase of knowledge and expectations of sexual pleasure, more men go to professionals for help—i.e., become *reported* cases of impotence—than they did before. It is also possible that women's complaints, however justified and tactful, push some premature ejaculators over the edge into full-fledged flaccidity.

The essential boredom of the mechanical, performance-oriented approach to sex was made clear to me when I saw a pornographic movie not long ago. The film, of the no-holds-barred variety, had been described by reviewers as artistic for the genre, and I anticipated being sexually aroused. But once the action began in earnest, my attention and interest flagged. All the acrobatics, ménages, and variations were there. But the various men showed no feeling at all, never changed expression, and the woman's sexual frenzies were completely self-absorbed. The lovers never even looked at each other. The close-ups—shots of penises moving in and out of vaginas, the analogous shot during anal intercourse, both together; penises, vaginas, tongues, mouths and ejaculations in oral sex—were even more of a turn-off. By focusing in this way the film maker had made it impossible for the viewer to see anything but the various organs in action. Without a picture even of the full human body, which is always expressive of some feeling, some relation to others, these shots, supposedly the erotic highpoint of the film, suggested nothing so much as the working of machines, and were just as stimulating.

I have also known women who separate sex and feeling in the ways I have been attributing to men. But these women, at least in my experience, are relatively few and their inability to feel often arises indirectly out of a general powerlessness—it is commonplace, for example, that people who feel ineffectual at work are also apathetic in sex and other other aspects of their private lives.

Men, on the other hand, are directly denied the freedom to experience and express emotion in all but the most narrow channels. Their constraints are more invisible, experienced almost entirely as internal because our larger culture is shaped around the masculine values out of which they grow. It seems to me that these constraints are not only different from the constraints upon the self-realization of women but also affect men's capacity to relate personally to other people in specific ways which are more crippling. We have already seen some of their effects on men's sexuality. There are others.

Some tension and anxiety is inherent in erotic passion. To desire someone in the full sense of the word is to have wishes and hopes—for sex, for intimacy, for union and incorporation of the other's qualities and personality—which we see the possibility of satisfying, but which have not yet been fulfilled. What the masculine disdain for feeling makes it hard for men to grasp is that the state of desire, of conscious movement toward imagined possibilities, is one of the best, perhaps *the* best, part of the experience of love:

> We have been led astray . . . to think that the aim of the love act is the orgasm. The French have a saying which, referring to eros, carries more truth: "the aim of desire is not its satisfaction but its prolongation." Andre Maurois, speaking of his preference for lovemaking to which the orgasm is not the goal but an incidental conclusion, quotes another French saying, "Every beginning is lovely." [20]

We hear over and over again from the men who seem to be

happiest in their jobs that what they enjoy most is the process of building something from nothing, of taking an idea and making it work. It is the process itself that is most important to them, although society puts the emphasis on the end product; the pleasure in the doing sneaks in the back door. For men the workplace is the arena that counts. They persuade themselves that their feelings and demands grow out of the requirements of the job and the masculine business of competition and conquest, rather than feminine displays of "personality." And there they relish the imagining, the stirring up of possibilities—in this case, directed at things, ideas, clients, patients. Men don't know how to do this in their love relationships, much less think of it as desirable. The ideal relationship with a woman is seen as one of constant freedom from tension, complete relaxation, evenness, stasis. For most men, courting and seduction are nuisances. The focus is almost exclusively on reaching the goal of conquest with all possible speed. Once won, women are supposed to be rest stops for men. Mary Ellmann captures the prescribed tone for the supportive relationship:

> The remarks of sexual columnists indicate that the supportive stance is essential not only in company, where one might expect the barbs of other husbands and other wives to require the most vigilant protection of the one husband's self-esteem, but also in the privacy of the home. . . . The children's hour, the advice runs, should give way to the husbands' hour, in which their wives, over the prune whip, put their paragons together again. . . . How can you, the counselors whine, expect these men to go out and succeed tomorrow if you call them failures tonight? Rebuild them, bolster them, help them, like hamsters, to refill their little pouches of confidence. The implied inadequacy, so groping and gullible, is appalling.[21]

The quality of the interchange pictured by Ellmann is one of flaccid, emotionally passive receiving, the application of an anesthetic. In this atmosphere, or anything like it, eros doesn't stand a chance. The creation, savoring, and enjoyment of passion, once the object is no longer new, are the result of active imagination and intentionality—just those faculties men put in cold storage in their relationships with lovers and wives.

The flight from passion affects men's approach to making love, as well as their inclination to do so. Bengis contrasted her sexual experience with a woman to those she had had with men:

> For men, sex was aim-oriented. There was a beginning, a middle, and an end. For me, and for many other women, it had never been that way. Kissing Dee was just as important as sharing an orgasm. It was that way for her as well as for me. The real pleasure came from intimacy in all of its forms. Dee could afford to say, "We don't have to rush things." So could I. There was none of the frantic concern with "Doing it" that was such a crucial part of relations with men. There was just being close. Whatever happened would happen.[22]

I'm not sure whether physical differences between the sexes serve to explain some of this, but I doubt it. Men are often sexually aroused and capable of orgasm faster than women, although the exceptions to the rule are numerous enough to indicate a cultural rather than a physiological explanation. In any event, men tend to force and hurry things, almost as though they were thinking, "Now that I've got it up, I'd better get it in before it goes away." Or, more commonly, feeling that they aren't into the real thing, haven't reached the objective, unless and until coitus has begun. They tend not to enjoy the slow mutual building of desire, fueled, paced, and given meaning by awareness of a matching response in the other person. Also, it is difficult for men to *let* this interplay develop, to, in a sense, *wait* for it to happen. We still have a Victorian belief in a clear dichotomy between active and passive, with passivity firmly labeled as a feminine trait which men try their best to rid themselves of. To a mind holding these beliefs, any process which is not completely under conscious control is perceived as passive. The sexual play I have been describing, involving the interplay of conscious and unconscious (or "instinctual") responses in a state of intense awareness, is thus experienced as frightening.

Men's response even to being touched or caressed by a partner must be one of action; they cannot allow themselves to simply feel and communicate pleasure. They cut themselves off from the finer-grained, more langorous pleasures of sensuality and tend to push ahead to the sex act, where the appropriate response, at least on the surface, is much more exclusively physical and conventionally active. For example, one man found things were different after his wife became a feminist and he took a critical look at the male sex stereotypes:

> Our sexual life has undergone a tremendous change, because I was no longer prepared for her to just lie back and look at the ceiling like Mother Mary while I fucked away and humped myself to death. I deserve a little bit of looking at the ceiling too.[23]

In the sex act itself, some of the same forces which force and hurry things before coitus may still be at work, albeit even farther from consciousness. A friend told me in an interview that, several years ago, he was ejaculating prematurely during intercourse. Three minutes and it was all over, despite his best intentions and efforts. He couldn't do anything about it until he realized that he was so concerned about orgasm—hers, his, the timing—that he was paying no attention to what he was feeling. When he began to think of these emotions and sensations not merely as way stations but as experiences to be enjoyed for their own sake, two changes occurred: He became more acutely aware of what he was feeling, making it possible for him to slow the rate of stimulution temporarily and lower his level of sexual excitement whenever he felt himself approaching premature climax. But, equally important, the act of focusing positively on these feelings, their nuances and variations, and on the answering initiatives and responses, dissolved what had been an unconscious discomfort with the state of sexual excitement and a resulting haste to end it. The premature ejaculation stopped. He had discovered a basic paradox of human behavior—trying to ignore, to "conquer" feeling leads not to more self-control and freedom but to less.

4.   The Roots
of Misogyny

Jeffrey, a friend's son, is seven years old and likes a girl of the same age who lives in his apartment building. But when he learned that she was going to transfer to his school, he got an agitated look on his face. "It'll spoil everything," he said. And it nearly has. The other boys in his class tease him and beat him up if they see him playing with her. Things got so bad that one day, when his mother came to school to walk Jeffrey and his friend back to his house so they could play together, the girl, without a word, carefully walked ten yards behind so the other boys wouldn't think Jeffrey was going to play with her. When she and Jeffrey had a fight, her ultimate act of betrayal was to tell the boys that she and Jeffrey had sleep-over dates. She knew he would catch hell from them.

In a second-grade class I visited, I asked the boys whether they played with the girls. Obviously expecting approval, they told me proudly that they didn't. One was embarrassed enough to start a fight when the other boys accused him of liking a particular girl.

A subscriber to *Ms.* magazine, in a letter to the editor, described a scene in which a five-year-old boy was being teased by four other boys of about the same age. Unable to endure any more, pushed to the point of tearful rage, he turned to the leader of the group and, with a look of pure hatred, screamed the most horrible insult he could think of: "You girl!"[1]

This antipathy of little boys toward little girls is so common as to be unremarkable. A "girls—ugh!" line is a standard part of family style television comedies involving pre-pubescent boys, one which calls forth universal sympathetic recognition from grown men. The "funny story" at the end of a CBS network news broadcast one night, for example, was how a twelve-year-old had won a championship horseshoe-pitching match in which his thirteen-year-old brother had also competed. The twelve-year-old had provoked the older boy, who had responded by hitting him, and injuring his own throwing hand, thus hampering his performance the next day. How had the victor precipitated the fight, asked the newscaster? Cut to filmed interview with the kid: "I called him a girl," he said, and he grinned the grin of someone who thinks he has done something expected and amusing. Cut back to matching grin of comfortable male complicity from the newscaster as he says, " . . . and good night from CBS News."[2]

It is a wishful delusion to believe that this kind of hostility toward females is merely a passing phase that somehow disappears with time. It is not. Elaborated and layered over with other feelings, it is the key to the way adult men feel about women. Let us look at its roots.

As early as ages four and five, boys learn what is expected of them as males and restrict themselves to what they believe are suitably masculine activities.[3] What this means in large part is not being like a girl, or, what is the same thing, not being a "sissy." A few years later, they are quite capable of expanding on this point. Eight- and eleven-year-old boys in a study of sex role pressures on male children, by psychologist Ruth Hartley, described girls in these terms:

> They have to stay close to the house; they are expected to play quietly and be gentler than boys; they are often afraid; they must not be rough; they have to keep clean; they cry when they are scared or hurt; they are afraid to go to rough places like rooftops and empty lots; their activities consist of "fopperies" like playing with dolls, fussing over babies and sitting and talking about dresses; they need to know how to cook, sew, and take care of children, but spelling and arithmetic are not as important for them as for boys.[4]

This image of girls, reeking of limitation and restraint, is not just the product of parental and peer-group indoctrination. Our schools also do their share in perpetrating it. For example, California's first-grade reading text, published by Harper & Row, paints this picture of girls and their proper relationship to boys:

> [Mark and Janet are brother and sister. Janet gets new skates. She tries them and falls.]
>
> "Mark! Janet!" said Mother. "What is going on here?"
>
> "She cannot skate," said Mark. "I can help her. I want to help her. Look at her Mother. Just look at her. She is just like a girl. She gives up."
>
> [Mother forces Janet to try again.]
>
> "Now you see," said Mark. "Now you can skate. But just with me to help you."
>
> [Janet, needless to say, never makes a similar remark to Mark.][5]

This is not atypical. A survey of thirty commonly used children's textbooks[6] showed females were described more often than males as lazy and incapable of direct action as well as more likely to give up easily, collapse in tears, betray secrets, and act on petty or selfish motives. Nearly all the adult female characters (found in only four percent of stories with an adult protagonist) were shown as assistants to men. Madame Curie, for example, appears as little more than a helpmate to her husband and another male scientist. Among the descriptions of present-day professionals, there was only one working female, a scientist. The three other male scientists in the same chapter are shown working alone on projects demanding originality and exacting mental effort, while the text and picture caption for the woman scientist state that she is not working independently and that the idea she is testing was assigned to her by others. Given this picture of females, it is not surprising that the boys in the Hartley study described their own characteristics as the polar opposites:

> [Boys] have to be able to fight in case a bully comes along; they have to be athletic; they have to be able to run fast; they must be able to play rough games; they need to know how to play many games—curbball, baseball, basketball, football; they need to be smart; they need to be able to take care of themselves; they should know what girls don't know—how to climb, how to make a fire, how to carry things; they should have more ability than girls; they need to know how to stay out of trouble; they need to know arithmetic and spelling more than girls do.[7]

The "not like a girl" aspects of being a boy come out even more clearly in the answers to Hartley's question, "What is expected of boys?" which gets at behavior tacitly approved by grownups:

> They believe grown-ups expect them to be noisy; to get dirty; to mess up the house; to be naughty; to be "outside" more than girls are; not to be cry-babies; not to be "softies," not to be "behind" like girls are; and to get into trouble more than girls do. Moreover, boys are not allowed to do the kind of things that girls usually do, but girls may do the kind of things that boys do.[8]

The situation is practically perfect for inducing anxiety. The ideal toward which a boy's parents and peers pressure him is vague and elusive, defined as much by what he should *not* do and be as by what is approved, and, most important, calling for total repression of his feelings of vulnerability and dependence.

Fathers, believing in a slightly more grown-up version of the same ideal, try to conceal from their sons the few departures from the male ideal they permit themselves or cannot avoid, thereby passing on the same dehumanized image of masculinity. The result, Hartley says, is "an overstraining to be masculine, a virtual panic at being caught doing anything traditionally defined as feminine, and hostility toward anything even hinting at 'femininity,' including females themselves."[9]

The mechanism is familiar. When we fear and dislike qualities in ourselves, we "project" this hostility onto others who remind us of or have the unwanted characteristics. Jews who wish they were WASPs dislike other Jews who "act Jewish." Blacks who are insecure in their middle-class style avoid and dislike "funky" ghetto blacks who remind them of their origins. Women whose self-esteem is threatened by their own frustration with their roles as housewives feel hostility toward women who articulate these feelings. In the same way, boys want so desperately to be different from girls that anything that appears to close the gap, any similarity in behavior that they are aware of, is frightening. My neighborhood tree-house gang, for example, arranged the foot- and hand-holds leading up to our tree house so "no girls can get up there." There were no secret male rituals we wanted to indulge in; it just made us feel different and more manly to keep girls out.

Of course, boys don't see the male and female roles as merely different. To be a boy—prospectively a man—is clearly superior. Although many girls want for a period of time to be boys and do their best to act like boys (so many in fact that we have a word—*tomboy*—to describe them), very few boys want to be girls.[10] Naturally, they project these differences into the future. The boys in Hartley's study thought grown women are, among other things, fearful, indecisive, stay-at-homes, physically weak, squeamish about seeing blood, unadventurous, more easily hurt and killed than men, and afraid of getting wet or getting an electric shock. They thought that women "have a way of doing things the wrong way," that they scream instead of taking charge in emergencies, fuss over children's grades, and very easily become jealous and envy their husbands (although it is conceded that they make their children feel good). Of women's traditional activities they said,

> "They are always at those crazy household duties and don't have time for anything else." "Their work is just regular drudging." "Women do things like cooking and washing and sewing because that's all they can do." "Women haven't enough strength in the head or in the body to do most jobs." [11]

By contrast, they thought that grown men had to be strong, protect women and children in emergencies, do rough, dirty and unpleasant work, earn money, care for their children and get along with their wives, and that they get tired a lot. On the positive side, however, men are usually in charge of things, they mess up the house, "mostly do what they want to do," decide how to spend the money, and get first choice of the most comfortable chair. Although they get mad a lot, they laugh and make jokes more than women. They are more fun to be with than mothers, more exciting to have around, and they have the best ideas. [12] With this vision of the future, what boy (or girl, until the pressure of social and physical reality becomes too great) would not choose the male role with its dual load of responsibilities and enticing perquisites?

Consciousness of these perquisites begins very early. My kindergarten informant, a self-assured girl of five, reported how it was when the boys and girls played Red Light–Green Light–One–Two–Three together. For readers who have forgotten or who didn't go to kindergarten, the leader of the game stands at the front of the room, with eyes covered and says "Red Light–Green Light–One–Two–Three" as fast as possible, while the other players try to move up as close to the front of the room as they can. When the leader opens her or his eyes, any player still moving has to go back to the starting line. My informant reported that the boys would readily go back to the starting line when caught by a boy leader but that when she or another girl was the leader they would refuse to go back. In her case, one came up, pushed her aside, and, restoring the natural order of things, pronounced himself the leader.

In adult life, the expression of these attitudes may be muted because of sexual attraction, the demands of family life, and social disapproval of open hostility to women. But, underneath, they remain, reinforced through the years by our institutions and culture, shaping nearly every aspect of men's adult relationships with women, and never to be outgrown.

Most grown men no longer state openly their opinions about the nature of women, especially if those opinions mark women out as clearly inferior and destined for subordination. No one today will pronounce, as Nietzsche once did, that a man "must conceive of woman as a possession, as property that can be locked, as something predestined for service and achieving her perfection in that."[13] The growing incredulity and militance of women has imposed a degree of caution and camouflage. Open antagonism and contempt, Mary Ellmann has pointed out, has largely retreated into fiction, "the conventional sanctuary of unimpeachable utterance."[14] A more acceptable posture is that of wishful reverence for the "real woman" of yore—"women aren't women any more."[15] Nevertheless, as the literature of the women's movement and numerous psychological surveys[16] convincingly demonstrate, the image of the ideal woman as passive, illogical, able to express tender feelings, security-minded, oriented toward home and children, vain, self-effacing, unambitious, and dependent on and subordinate to men still pervades our culture. Individual men may be more enlightened as to particular elements of the feminine stereotype—the idea that women should not work or not work seriously, for example—but when these men are required to accept the ramifications of such enlightenment in their personal lives a swift regression can usually be observed. Some classic lines are: "Someone has to take care of the children and she's better at it." "Her job is important, but when I get home I want a Martini ready and waiting." "Of course I want my wife to be well informed, but I don't like her disagreeing with me when we're out with other people." "I agree that women deserve equal job opportunities, just like blacks, but I can't put Linda in charge of the whole department—I mean, I could never work for a woman." "No, I don't want my wife to throw the game when we play tennis. She should play as hard and as well as she can. Things just got uncomfortable when she started beating me regularly, so we stopped playing. She doesn't have anything else to do all week except to go to those damn tennis lessons, you know."

Changes in men's beliefs about women have so far been superficial, at the level of intellect rather than feeling. Under pressure from our egalitarian ethic and the women's movement, more socially conscious men are beginning to agree in general terms to ideas about women which they are emotionally unable to accept in their personal relationships. The realization that they may not in fact be superior to, or even very different from the women they live or work with is frightening—and fear produces hostility. This reaction, as one would expect, is strongest among men who most need the prop of male superiority. A survey of twenty thousand readers of *Psychology Today*, for example, showed:

> Men who are uncomfortable over the prospect of equal women are also more uneasy with women in general (30 percent compared to 14 percent of the whole male sample); they have deceived women more often in order to have sex (31 percent of the threatened men said "frequently" compared to 23 percent of the others); the majority of their good friends are men (61 percent compared to 53 percent); and—most strikingly—they are three times as likely as unthreatened men to have negative reactions to intercourse (18 percent to 5 percent). Indeed, the more threatened a man was, the more likely he was to attribute sexual problems to members of the women's movement.[17]

Antagonism to the aims of the women's movement has also triggered a resurgence of efforts, scholarly and otherwise, to prove that sex roles are "natural," the result of genetic and

hormonal differences between men and women rather than social learning. A mainstay of this school in recent years has been
the drawing of analogies between human beings and other
primates.[18] Among certain species of baboons, for example,
patterns of organization have been observed which appear to be
roughly analogous to those alleged to be "inherent" in human
beings: the males, especially the largest and strongest, protect
the troop from predators, direct its movements, and keep order;
the females take care of the young, stay near the center of the
troop, and extend their sexual favors most readily to the males
highest in prestige and authority; positions of authority among
males are established through a combination of prowess in
ritualized combat and the ability to form and maintain alliances
with other powerful males. If the instinctual programing for
these behaviors is built into our evolutionary cousins because of
its survival value, the argument goes, is it not logical that the
formation of analogous patterns in human communities is due to
the survival value and persistence of similar programing in us? If
so, attempts to do away with sex roles will be futile, as Lionel
Tiger suggests in *Men in Groups,*[19] or, as George Gilder asserts in
Sexual Suicide[20] with less logic but more conviction, will create
havoc by overriding biological imperatives.

But analogies between humans and primates fail in two ways.
First, the behavioral generalizations about the animal world on
which they are based often turn out to be instances of inaccurate
projections of human stereotypes onto animals. Take "mothering" for example. The extent to which the father assumes the
burden of caring for the young varies enormously among primates, ranging from infanticide to carrying and caring for the
infant at all times except when it is being nursed.[21] The adult
male rhesus monkey usually has little or no relationship with
infants, yet recent experiments have shown that when the
mother is not available to perform the parenting function a male
will perform it quite adequately.[22]

Much has also been made of the critical evolutionary role of
aggression in animal life: Since the aggressive tendencies in

males had such strong survival value in our precursor species, it is argued that they must persist as an instinctual drive in human males. In the last few years, however, more refined observations of animal aggression have destroyed the foundations of this argument. Fights which lead to serious injury or death are extremely rare among animals of the same species living in normal, nonlaboratory conditions. Much intraspecific fighting is ritualized, with no serious injury inflicted (rival stags locking horns, for example). Virtually all intraspecific aggression is subject to inhibitory mechanisms that prevent major injury or death (the weaker of two quarreling wolves, when in danger of serious injury, will expose his belly and throat to the other, who then stops the attack and walks away).[23] Presumably these inhibitions exist in animals because they have survival value for the species. However helpful to our survival they would be, there are no such rigid inhibitions on human aggression.

This points to the second, and fundamental, error in these arguments by analogy: Human beings are radically distinguished from all other animals by their freedom from instinctual determination. We have less instinctual knowledge than baboons when we are born, but our capacity for varying responses is infinitely greater. Self-consciousness, the need for self-esteem, and the ability to create and manipulate complex symbolic systems—found only in humans and made possible by a uniquely large neocortex—allow human beings to ascribe a wide range of different meanings to the same event and to act accordingly. Animals do not measure their actions against a conscious internal ideal; they may defend their young, but they will not die for an idea, a country, or to prove to themselves that they are qualified members of their sex.[24]

With human beings it is extremely difficult to separate out the influences of anatomy and conditioning on the development of sex roles and identity because different treatment of boys and girls begins literally at birth.[25] During the first two years, for example, mothers talk to and smile at girl babies more than boy babies. Boys are touched—kissed, hugged, rocked etc.—more for the first six months (perhaps because of their greater irritability), but after that they are touched less than girls. Beginning when boy babies are six months old, mothers are more likely to discourage them than girls from seeking physical contact by picking them up and facing them away or by distracting their attention with objects of some kind, probably out of a belief that it is more important for boys to develop autonomy.

Drs. John Money and Anke Ehrhardt[26] overcame the usual parallelism between upbringing and biological sex by studying a particular kind of hermaphrodite, genetic females born with female internal sex organs but masculine-looking external genitalia. If diagnosed at birth, the condition can be corrected by surgical feminization and cortisone treatment to suppress the overproduction of androgen that produced the ambiguous genitalia.* If left untreated, the girl develops all the secondary sexual characteristics—facial hair, large muscles, narrow hips, lower voice—of a boy. To isolate out the effect of conditioning, Money and Ehrhardt compared three pairs of such cases.[27]

In the first pair, one was diagnosed at birth and given the prescribed feminizing treatment; the other was misdiagnosed as a boy until age three-and-a-half, when the correct diagnosis was made but it was decided to allow the child to continue living as a boy. Appropriate surgery was done and cortisone therapy used to delay puberty until the normal age. In each case, gender identity and sex role—measured by traditional indices of

---

* In a comparison of such fetally androgenized girls diagnosed and treated at birth with a control group of normal girls, Money and Ehrhardt reported that more of the girls with adrenogenital syndrome were "tomboys" as measured by their own and their parents' assessment, preference for athletic "boys" games, lesser concern with fashionably feminine clothes and adornment, lesser although substantial interest in marriage and babies, and a greater interest in having a career other than or in addition to being a housewife. (There was no higher degree of lesbianism or aberrant sexual behavior than in the control group.) The authors speculated that the differences may have been the result of a "masculinizing" effect of androgen on the fetal brain,[28] but this conclusion seems unwarranted. As endrocrinologist Estelle Ramey has written, parental concern and ambiguity about the sexual identity of the girls with adrenogenital syndrome was conveyed to these children despite corrective procedures, and this difference in postnatal experience would account for the reported variations in behavior.[29]

"feminine" and "masculine" interests and proclivities—followed the sex of assignment.

In the second pair, one was also reared as a boy and the other as a girl. But treatment of a child raised as a girl was delayed until she was twelve, when masculine secondary sex characteristics had already begun to appear. The other child had been misdiagnosed and raised as a genetic male, but, as the result of a mistaken treatment with cortisone through age thirteen, had undergone substantial breast development. Despite their discordant hormonal sex, secondary sex characteristics, and ambiguous external genitals, both children firmly identified themselves as members of the sex of rearing, thought of their secondary sex characteristics as deformities they were eager to be rid of, were attracted sexually to members of the opposite sex, and displayed interests generally considered characteristic of their assigned sex.* For example, the child raised as a boy liked to hunt, fish, and race his motorbike. Treatment for both was in accordance with this gender identity.

In the final pair, each child had requested and, after investigation, received a sex reassignment, one from boy to girl and the other from girl to boy. In both cases, as in other requests for sex change studied by Money, it was found that parents had never really made up their minds about whether the child was a boy or a girl and had transmitted this ambiguity to the child.

Money and Ehrhardt also studied a pair of school-age identical twins. Both were born as normal males, but one lost his penis in a circumcision accident and was reassigned as a girl in infancy and given the first stage of surgical reconstruction. "Her behavior as a little girl," Money and Ehrhardt reported, "is in remarkable contrast to the little-boy behavior of her identical twin brother."

After about eighteen months, Money and Ehrhardt have con-

---

* An early study of thirty-one such females brought up as women despite prolonged exposure to excess androgens both in utero and postnatally, and despite externally male sex characteristics uncorrected through puberty, showed that all but five tested out as typical American women in virtually all aspects of behavior, life goals, and self-image.[30]

cluded, the influence of conditioning on gender identity is so strong that it is impossible to reassign effectively the sex of a child raised as a member of the other sex, regardless of the child's genetic, gonadal, and hormonal situation. It is easier and more advisable to use hormone therapy and surgery to bring the child's body into conformity with her or his learned sex role than to undo the effects of conditioning.[31]

Historically, the traditional sex roles must have grown out of practical arrangements necessary to childbearing in primitive societies. Women were either nursing infants or pregnant much of their adult lives, conditions which limited their mobility, while hunting game for food put a premium on men's physical strength and speed. A division of labor in which women stayed at home and took care of the children and men went out and hunted made sense. The greater physical strength of men may also have had something to do with their primacy within the primitive family: in the absence of restraining norms, the threat of superior force is an effective means of establishing dominance.

Today, the male/female division of labor, with all its complicated psychological, political, economic and cultural elaborations, is obsolete. It has lost whatever correspondence with objective conditions it may once have had. In America today physical strength and speed of foot are of negligible importance, especially in more highly valued and rewarded work. Women spend only a small part of their lives bearing children and even for most of that period are not incapacitated from tasks that men perform.

Because masculine and feminine behavior patterns are not biologically determined, men and women have a disorderly tendency to, exhibit traits reserved for the other sex. Keeping the stereotypes straight can be a difficult task for the traditionalist. "The base of male conceit," according to Norman Mailer, is "that men [can] live with truths too unsentimental for women."[32] But what is less sentimental than the prosaic "feed-the-children-before-you-spend-our-last-few-dollars-printing-your-manifesto" attitude of which women are accused? And what is more romantic and sentimental than the charge of the light brigade or the grand schemes of dynastic, commercial, and national empire which only men are said to have the scope to conceive? What, for example, are we to make of Ian Fleming's observation about his arch-masculine hero, James Bond: "Like all harsh, cold men, he was easily tipped over into sentiment"?[33]—an observation recently confirmed for our junior counterspies by a study conducted by William Kephart of the University of Pennsylvania. Kephart found that over a lifetime the American male becomes infatuated and falls in love more often than the female, while women see their boy friends' faults more clearly and are much less driven by romantic compulsions.

Sometimes new and subtle distinctions are called into service to restore order. For example, in nineteenth-century literature, when women displayed mental instability or various forms of spiritual disturbance they were simply demonstrating the natural weakness of the female mind. Today,

> such disturbances have become a secondary sexual characteristic of the fictional male, in whom they suggest the integrity of a constitution which cannot withstand the torment of experience. . . . Psychopathology is in: madness is energy, even if it is expended upon yanking up morning glories or walking around balcony rims.

> Women therefore are obliged to be sane, as though they were not sufficiently alert to be insane. Or if they are allowed some small share of abnormalities, these are kept on the slobbering or sluggish side. . . . Heroines now shriek or mope or pass out or go black in the face—they *lose* control. Meanwhile, the men, their sensibilities activated by experience, *go* or *run* mad. A new and strange field of competition has opened, between muscular and flabby neurosis, and mayhem makes misery look mean.[34]

For the most part, men handle the problem of keeping the stereotypes straight with a variation on the scheme of opposites. Where the general categories fail, men fall back on describing women as the opposite of what they, as individuals, think they are like, and even as the opposite of what they are like at any given moment. This device, needless to say, is used unconsciously, allowing the speaker to maintain an image of himself as consistent, an important masculine trait.

But if the twists and turns of definition as to what behavior can be considered masculine and what feminine can sometimes be obscure, the basic assumptions and imperatives which shape men's attitudes toward women come through loud and clear. First, we—men and women both—believe in the either/or theory of human personality even if we do not always conform to it: a person who is tough is always tough; a person who is tender and soft is always tender and soft; we do not expect people to be tough in one situation and tender in another according to the demands of the occasion, to have both responses in their repertoires. Second, men believe that to be masculine they have to be radically different from women. Third, men believe they are better than women and that, in order to retain their masculine self-image when they deal with women, they must dominate and outperform them in every area except child rearing, homemaking, amateur culture, and the management of social life. Fourth, the areas assigned to women are thought of as less important and difficult than those assigned to men, and men, to keep their masculine identification and status, try to stay out of them.

Let us see in more detail how these general psychological imperatives and the particular components of the masculine ideal affect men's relationships with women in the different contexts in which they deal with each other.

5. Women as Colleagues

For men to play their roles, women have to play theirs—or be kept in them. This is true in every area where men and women interact, but most of all at work. Participation in work has been the mainstay of men's sense of superiority and difference. Until recently, interesting, well-paid, and prestigious work —more than any other area of life—has been almost exclusively the province of men. Where the work is less rewarding, the aura of masculinity created by keeping women out is even more important: if holding a job as a steelworker proves nothing else, it at least proves that you are a man.

The connection between the masculine stereotype and the way men treat women at work came through in a survey by the *Harvard Business Review* of its subscribers' attitudes. Executives in defense, industrial-manufacturing, construction, and mining companies were more negative than men in "less masculine" industries about working with women.[1] There are fewer women in the "more masculine" industries and male executives in them have less of a chance to unlearn their prejudices. But it also seems likely that they attract men whose stronger-than-average need for a masculinity-certifying atmosphere makes them more hostile to having women as colleagues.

Among the professions, the most prejudice and the fewest women are found in engineering, law, and medicine—traditionally thought of as masculine callings. And inside each profession, women are most strongly resisted in the more "masculine" specialties—corporate law and surgery are examples. Instead, they are tracked into family law or estates and trusts ("women bring personal warmth to working with widows and orphans"), and pediatrics or child psychiatry.[2] At the nonprofessional level as well, women are especially resented in the occupations which have the greatest cachet of manliness. This resentment and fear is so strong that over the ages it has crystallized into superstitions, some of which still linger: a woman in a ship's crew jinxes the voyage; women in mines are such bad luck that workmen walked out of a Colorado tunnel-construction job several years ago when one woman mine inspector entered the excavation. The supernatural explanations for these beliefs have fallen away, but the hostility that created them remains.

Male-led unions often support separate men's and women's job categories, so arbitrary they can only barely be rationalized by sex stereotypes. In some locals of the Amalgamated Meat Cutters, for example, the final packaging of sliced bacon—the operation closest to the actual preparation of the product for a meal—is reserved for women, while the operation of the machines that press the bacon for slicing is reserved for men—men are mechanically minded. In textile plants, repairing looms, the best-paid and most secure job, is also a male preserve, again because it is mechanical. When women first joined men on assembly lines in auto plants, many of the men refused for a time to help them out when they fell behind, a traditional courtesy extended to every new male worker.

Hostility and discrimination are present in a subtler form even in situations where women are allowed to succeed. Almost always, the woman's activity is specialized or one which takes place in back rooms, away from the organization's public. Jobs requiring specialized knowledge and techniques, Michael Korda pointed out,

> are precisely the jobs that have a ceiling, beyond which it is impossible to rise. In business, men are well aware of the advantages of mobility, of learning something about every aspect of the process so as to run it, rather than becoming immersed in the details of one department or operation. Again and again, women rise to success, mastering the details of their jobs, only to find that they have been outflanked by men who have mastered nothing but the ability to "manage."[3]

Specialized work done by women is used and often presented as their own by men they work for. As a result women's success tends to be contained, granted personally by their bosses—"Joan is doing a great job *for* Tony." They are seldom permitted to feel that it has been earned through performance which meets generally recognized standards.

In all jobs and professions visibility means prestige, opportunity, and power. The lawyer who argues in court or participates in negotiations develops the all-important relationship with the client. The executive who reports to the board of directors is noticed as a "bright young man." Men reserve these out-front positions for themselves. Young women lawyers have a harder time getting out of the library than their male counterparts. A woman member of a professional association becomes the secretary of the group or the editor of its journal, never the president representing the profession before Congressional committees and the public. Women often play vital organizational roles in the boiler rooms of political campaigns, but when the time comes for highly visible appointments, they are suddenly capable only of dealing with "women's issues" like consumer affairs.

The form of responsibility men are most reluctant to grant women is, of course, supervisory authority over men. The idea sends sympathetic vibrations of humiliation and outrage through every man in the office: "Gail could do the job, probably better than Cal. But we can't put her over all those guys . . . would you like to work for a woman?"

One finding of the study of *Harvard Business Review* subscribers was that younger executives were more hostile to the idea of female colleagues than older businessmen. If the roots of discrimination against women at work were simply the outdated values and experience of another era, this difference would have been reversed. The best explanation of the actual results is that the men who are most concerned about proving their competitive masculine worth, younger men who haven't yet made it, are more threatened by having female colleagues and competitors than older men whose positions are assured at a level above that likely to be attained by women or who, either through success or failure, have lost some of their competitive zeal.

Even as professionals serving a client, men find it difficult to accept a woman's authority. When the employees of an art museum in a major city, nearly all women, organized themselves into a union, they hired a male labor lawyer to represent them. The executive committee of the union was entirely female except for one man, and the officers of the union were all women. But in the meetings in which negotiating positions were formulated, the lawyer paid visibly closer attention to the man. The women—his clients—had to fight for his attention. Despite the fact that the male committee member's views were out of step with the general consensus, the lawyer always looked to him for approval of his ideas for negotiating positions and always sat next to him. He referred to his female clients as "the girls" and "my harem" in their presence: "O.K., John, now let's see what the girls have to say." During the negotiations with representatives of the museum, he was afraid to let the women talk, sure that they would be unable to hold their own. On the other hand, he also refused to hold prenegotiation strategy sessions where tactics could be worked out, a common and invaluable practice.

That would have meant sharing some of his power with women, and despite his professional ethic of dedication to serving the interests of the client, he felt it more important to appear to the men on the other side to be in total control of "his harem."

Eventually, the committee fired him, but his attitudes are not unusual. In fact, it took several months of looking for the union president to find a labor lawyer who didn't share his predecessor's views.

Men devalue the work that women are allowed to do simply by labeling it "feminine"—or, more accurately, they devalue the woman doing the work. Women who are good at organization, follow-up, and detail are assumed to have *only* that ability and are described as having compulsive, tidy, and therefore limited minds; the same abilities in a man make him a prime candidate for controller of the company. On the other hand, inattention to detail, an indication of creativity in men, is only a sign of flightiness and lack of staying power in a woman. What is admiringly described as diplomacy or bureaucratic savvy in a man is denigrated as feminine cunning in a woman. A gift for blunt, articulate analyses gives a man the valuable reputation of having a mind like a steel trap; it turns a woman into a pushy broad.

The devaluation extends to financial reward as well. Women professionals are paid less on the average than men doing the same work.[4] In plants and factories, "women's jobs," regardless of the actual levels of skill involved, nearly always pay less than "men's jobs"—the result of years of agreement by male union officials and corporate managers, each for their own reasons, that women do not "need" and should not earn as much as men.

In discussing a woman's work, men nearly always feel compelled to make some reference, intended as disparaging, to her sex. Often men achieve the desired effect simply by reminding one another that the person they are discussing is a woman. It is the "lady" (or, in more progressive circles, "woman") lawyer, professor, police officer, etc., even when it is clear without the sexual reference exactly who is being discussed. Reminding a woman of her sex is also the last desperate offensive of a man in the process of losing an argument: "You lady executives [or "women" or "girls"] are all alike" "Listen here, honey. . ." It's a getting back to basics, a shorthand way of saying that, when all is said and done, the woman comes from and will always remain a member of an inferior caste, and she'd better remember it.

There is one way for women to get themselves taken seriously at work, and that is to become more like men than men themselves. A woman who is supercompetent, "older," devotes herself exclusively to her work (which usually means she is unmarried), who, although she may be attractive and pleasant, represses every vestige of genuine warmth and sexuality in favor of the approved front of impersonal efficiency, may eventually be accepted as one of the "boys." She doesn't pose the sexual challenge men generally read into their relationships with women. This makes her less complicated for men to deal with. Men also find her professional ability easier to take because they think of her as sexually deficient and therefore, on balance, still safely inferior: "She's great on the committee, but I'll bet she hasn't been propositioned in ten years." Even these women, however, face condescension from men, in fact *because* they have repressed their sexuality. They are perceived as somehow not quite real women.

On the other hand, any woman who does not conform to this machinelike standard finds it impossible to get men to take anything but her sexuality seriously. Most men cannot accept the fact that a sexy woman is also tough and competent. The male sexual ideal of "nameless, cooperative, and uncritical" women, and the standard of invulnerability which fosters the ideal, do not permit it.

A man working with an attractive woman may view every encounter, no matter how businesslike in purpose, as sexually charged. The obligation to make at least a perfunctory pass is reinforced by the predominant view of sexual attractiveness as a relatively impersonal matter of physical assets—one woman with good breasts and nice legs is more or less interchangeable with any other. Men don't actually come on seriously to every attractive woman they work with, but they do expect a show of ritual, ego-satisfying flirtation. And when they have the power, as with a subordinate, they often insist on it, implicitly viewing it as part of her job. This byplay is especially manageable with a secretary: if she doesn't play the game—or when an affair goes sour—she can be fired or transferred with no more explanation than that a "personality conflict" has developed.[5] But if the woman is an equal, someone who must be dealt with seriously, these same sexual overtones and obligations become unwanted complications. This is one of the subtler reasons why men keep women out of key decisionmaking groups. They know that in these situations it is essential to focus without distraction on the problems to be solved. At the same time, men are aware that, if an attractive woman is part of the group, they will feel compelled to play another game as well, that at the very least they will be distracted to the extent of having to make a conscious decision to ignore her "as a woman." It's simpler just to exclude her.

Some men recognize that most of the human warmth in their lives is created by women. And they are afraid that if women go to work at the same jobs as men they will lose the capacity and desire to perform this service. An investment banker commented during a symposium on the potential of women:

> Women pay great attention to, take pleasure in, and are finally creative about the specific kind of connection they have with other human beings, and perhaps particularly with men. . . . Ordinarily, men have no gift for this kind of thing. . . .
>
> . . . I suspect that we men live in a human world that has been deliberately and tactfully created for us by women. . . . I would be sorry to live in the impersonal world that men, left to their own devices, would create. I like my relationships with women and I trust they do, too, because they created them. . . .
>
> . . . To become adept in stock market management, women would have to learn to think like men. . . . I, for one, should not like that.

I like my women clients. I am sometimes taken aback by their
attitudes toward finance, but *I like their attitudes toward me*, and I
would be sorry to see it change.[6]

Buried in this passage lie two assumptions, both associated with
our sexual stereotypes: first, that women's primary purpose in
life is to make men happy; and, second, the familiar "either/or"
view of human personality, the idea that if a person has the
capacity to be tough and objective, he or she cannot also be warm
and caring. The net result is one more source of resistance to
recognizing women's abilities to handle positions of responsibility and power.

Finally, men try to keep women off boards of directors of
corporations, off the executive councils of unions, and out of the
smoke-filled rooms of politics because they take a positive pleasure from being a member of and working in all-male groups. The
basis for the impetus to exclude women, since it has nothing to
do with job-related misconceptions or fears and shows up in
purest form in social situations, will be explored in the next
chapter.

6. In the Social Arena

A young, Radcliffe-educated woman who has worked in television for several years (and travels in liberal, wealthy New York society) gave a composite description of the dinner parties she had attended over the last decade. "Young, attractive, well-educated, working women alternating with men around a table . . . all the men with their mouths open, talking at the women . . . all the women with their mouths closed, listening. What are the men saying? One way or another, what big deals they are." A bit stark perhaps, but essentially accurate.

Men expect to tell women things, not to be told things by them, or even to explore a subject together. The masculine approach to an attractive woman is almost invariably one of conquest; corner her, impress her with position and accomplishments, dominate her with superior intellect or, if all else fails, the fact of masculinity itself. To what end? Sometimes seduction, but just as often simply a reaffirmation that all's right with man and his world.

At a party I went to, a social anthropologist, male, urbane, a tenured professor at a well-known Eastern university, was holding forth on class and caste in a North African country. A female colleague was among the listeners. After a few minutes she tried to comment; "Well, I was there about a month ago and . . . " No stopping the flow. Finally, another woman, bolder than the rest, said loudly, "Jim, she's just *been* there." His eyes flickered toward her, he paused for half a beat, and began to talk louder and faster. To listen to a woman—really listen—is to admit her into the circle as an equal, something men find it difficult to do.

I was also struck, during the Senate Watergate Committee hearings, by the treatment of Leslie Stahl, a CBS reporter, by her two male colleagues. During a panel discussion following one of the days of hearings, they consistently refused to let her break into their extended monologues and responded only to each other; when she finally did get the floor to make a point, one of them consistently interrupted her to make the point himself.

The lack of seriousness with which men take women's opinions was brought home to me during a speaking engagement with Brenda. We were talking to employees, mostly men, of a large advertising agency about feminism—women's and men's liberation. Brenda spoke first and sat down to a few polite questions and applause. I said more or less the same thing, emphasizing the negative aspects of sexual stereotypes for men themselves. Some of the same men were now furious. One came up and waved his fist under my chin. Another jumped onto the lap of a friend to show me that he was in fact capable of close friendship with other men. Part of the explanation for their response may have been a feeling that they were being betrayed by one of their own kind . But it also seemed clear that the ideas they were able to dismiss coolly when presented by Brenda drew blood when presented by a man.

One of the things men hate most is losing an argument to a woman. Because it reverses the approved male-dominant female-subordinate order, it is a masculinity-threatening event that men try hard to avoid. Telling a woman in the middle of forcefully expressing a thought, "Smile. Don't be so grim," is a familiar defensive reflex in these situations. (A woman just doesn't say that to a man under similar circumstances.) When a "defeat" can't be avoided, the pressure to recoup in another area is enormous. Any area will do, but sex seems to be a favorite.

An extreme (one hopes) example of sexual retaliation developed when a friend of mine went to see the movie *The Battle of Algiers* with a man. Both intellectuals, they got into a deeply felt argument about the film, an argument that, according to my friend, she clearly and definitely won. He refused to abandon his position although he literally had no response to her. When they got back to her apartment he tried to force her to have sex with him. They didn't know each other well, there was no passion —the evening had been anything but sexually stimulating—and they knew they never wanted to see each other again. Apparently he felt driven to regain control, and this was the only way he could think of to do it (revealing, in the process, the way he feels about the meaning and quality of the sex act).

The posture that men often assume toward women, at least as they describe it to other men, tends to be one of uninvolved mastery. Expressions of this attitude range from the adolescent "Naw, I don't really care about her" to more "grown-up" depersonalizing references—"a cool bitch," a "groovy chick," a "great piece of ass"—that convey detachment, a relationship based on a standardized assessment of a woman's assets rather than one's own feelings for her as a person. In groups, unmarried men will ridicule and look down on one of their number who "goes soft" on a woman. The more supermasculine the group, the stronger the sanctions and fear of involvement. Gary Shaw, writing about his experience as a football player at the University of Texas, described his own and his teammates' attitudes toward women:

> To make certain I avoided any involvement, the maximum number of times I dated a girl was five. . . . Dating a girl any longer than this meant to lose control of the situation; to lose

control was to be weak. To be weak was not to be a man. As a result, I never really knew a girl in my four years of college.[1]

This same compulsive need to dominate led most of my team-mates to pursue girls who, at least on the surface, seemed safely unaggressive; the type that swooned over their "big man" and did what he wanted with no back talk. Their discussions about these girls were a funny mixture of disregard and fear . . . . "You can't let a good-looking piece get to you or she'll scramble your mind."[2]

In more urbane circles, men use subtler protective devices. Unwilling and, because they are human, often unable to avoid showing that they care about certain women as more than sex objects or ornaments, men have ritualized the gestures of defer-ence and involvement. We call the system, what remains of it, Chivalry. The surviving gestures—opening doors; letting women out of elevators first (a particularly stupid exercise in stepped-on toes and kicked ankles in crowded office buildings during rush hour); lighting cigarettes; paying in restaurants, theaters, taxis, etc.; shielding women from headwaiters and drunks; ostentatiously allowing oneself to be governed by the woman's whim (known after marriage as "humoring the old girl")—are so standardized that they are absolutely safe. A man may perform them without indicating that he has "lost control." But, like all such solutions, chivalry doesn't really work. Ritualiz-ing acts of courtesy depersonalizes them, destroys their ability to convey feeling for the particular person at whom they are di-rected. And because these gestures are depersonalized, men are required to extend them to every woman, further draining them of meaning. It is not surprising that genuinely helpful acts that involve real effort or sacrifice—like carrying heavy packages or giving up a seat on a crowded subway to a mother and baby—have atrophied as ritual courtesies. That some women still value the remaining impersonal gestures shows only that they get very little else in the way of demonstrations of involve-ment and respect from men.

Chivalry serves men better as a weapon. In situations with an undercurrent of hostility or bargaining, courtesies which force a woman into a position of having received consideration and personal favors put her at a disadvantage. Men can make chivalrous gestures without personal exposure, while women are expected to receive them as though they were personal and thus feel personally obligated. The woman "owes" a response, but since there are very few ritualized courtesies for her to return, the appropriate response for her can only be personal, whether it is being pleasant when she is angry or something more tangible—the feeling of obligation is itself a burden. When expectations clash, the bargaining element in chivalry can sometimes be stated openly—"I took you to the Four Seasons for dinner and to a forty-dollar Broadway show, and you're throwing me out after a cup of coffee and a peck on the cheek?"

Men have also been taught that they and they alone are supposed to take the initiative in relationships with women. Men ask women out; women, traditionally, have had to wait to be asked. They have taken covert steps to help the process along, but in the end they, not men, have sat waiting for the telephone to ring. The breakdown of this custom, like the breakdown of the practice that in bed men do it and women have it done to them, is both unnerving and to a lesser extent, a relief to men. It's a relief to know that you are not always the one who has to make the effort, take the first step to expose yourself to being turned down. But a woman who straightforwardly takes the initiative upsets the only script most men know how to play: "If I am not in control, is she? Am I, therefore, less of a man?" A more flexible middle ground, where control is a central issue for neither the man nor the woman, is hard for men to conceive. Dominance over others is such an important part of the male ideal that men find it hard to imagine that women who refuse to behave as tradition prescribes aren't seeking dominance for themselves—most of them are not. And, most important, any convergence of sex roles threatens men's sense that they are different from women, the linchpin of the masculine self-image.

Closely related to the question of control is a man's expectation that, once a relationship is established or a conquest at any level is made, a woman will orient herself almost exclusively toward him, will serve as auxiliary or ornament. She's supposed to take up his interests, his friends and abandon her own—supposed, in fact, to be defined primarily by her relationship to him. Eight years after graduating from college, my friend George went to a class reunion. A classmate he had known fairly well introduced himself and told George he was married to the former Cathy S. To identify and describe her further, he added, "You know, Jeff Clark's old girl friend." Jeff Clark was a former campus athletic star. Later in the day, Cathy introduced herself to George the same way—some women still have a long way to go.

Men's treatment of women as appendages is usually most extreme in marriage or other long-term ménages, but it begins well before then. A lawyer told me of an incident which destroyed her relationship with a male friend (also a lawyer). They live in different cities, so were glad for the chance to see each other at a legal convention which they both had professional reasons to attend. One day at the convention he said that he wanted her to meet some friends of his, and they planned to get together for dinner that night. At the last minute, the delegation from her state called a caucus for the same time. She told him that she would have to attend the caucus but would try to meet him and his friends later. He flew into a rage and walked out. "It was," she said, "as though I had to come to the convention only to be with him."

The male-centered view that finding a man should be the major enterprise of a young woman's life is so important to Norman Mailer that, turning things upside down in egomaniacal confusion, he makes it the basis for his grudging "approval" of the women's movement:

> It was finally obvious. Women must have their rights to a life which would allow them to look for a mate. And there would be no free search until they were liberated.[3]

One way men keep their psychic distance from women is, quite simply, to exclude them physically. From McSorley's Old Ale House in New York City (before it was integrated by court action), to the practice of having "the men" retire to the smoking room or den after dinner, to the all-male Knights of Columbus and Wall Street lunch clubs, men consistently create social institutions which bar women from membership. And not just hidebound conservatives, either. Liberal Senators give speeches urging a reordering of national priorities toward more humane concerns, and then ride across Washington to meet their friends at the all-male Cosmos Club. In New York, foundation executives, whose professional careers are dedicated to the fight against bigotry and ignorance, have lunched for decades at the Harvard Club where until 1972 only male graduates of the university were admitted as members. Senior partners of prestigious law firms and investment-banking houses, who have served in high positions in liberal Democratic administrations, meet to cultivate business friendships and close deals in men-only luncheon clubs in the financial district. Nor is the exclusion of women from social groups limited to upper reaches of wealth and power—the Elks, the Moose, and the others—do the same thing.

When women try to penetrate these "sanctuaries," no excuse is too irrational, no strategem too ridiculous to ward off the calamity. When I tried, in 1968, to integrate Lincoln's Inn, an eating club at Harvard Law School open to virtually all male students, the reaction was fervid and negative: "We won't be able to use foul language in the dining room. . . . We won't be able to talk about sports. . . . I want to be able to bring one girl to dinner at the Inn without ending up sitting next to another girl I've been taking out who is a member." None of the arguments made sense, particularly since members were allowed to bring women guests to every meal and frequently did so. The objection repeated most often, however, and the one most impenetrable to further explanation was: "The atmosphere will be ruined."

Two years later, when the question of whether women graduates of Harvard should be permitted to join the Harvard Club of New York on the same basis as male graduates was forced to the attention of its members, the same kinds of noises were made. One red-in-the-face member predicted, in a meeting, the decline of the club as the last bastion against the outside world—by which, presumably, he meant everyone but Harvard men. Another warned that women members would "put green tablecloths all over the place." There was great concern that men and women squash players could not be prevented from running into each other naked while going to and from the showers. And, when under pressure from an American Civil Liberties Union lawsuit, the club finally voted to make women graduates eligible for full membership, some members mounted a last-ditch effort to keep women out of the innermost sanctum—the Men's Bar. To get the full meaning and flavor of the struggle, you need a mental picture of this male oasis. Walnut-paneled walls, plush leather chairs, hunting trophies on the wall, brandy snifters glinting in the firelight? Not at all. It's a bare room, about thirty-by-sixty feet, with a plain bar, bare white tile walls, no furniture, and dreary lighting. It looks more like a clean lavatory in a railway station than anything else. But to keep women out of this room, some members threatened to resign.

A columnist writing for a local newspaper about the McSorley's controversy put into words what the Harvard men probably felt but found too ridiculous to spell out:

> The key issue here is whether the American male will be able to continue to find a retreat, even if only for a few passing moments, where he can regenerate his thinking for his future accomplishments. How else can a normal red-blooded American male put his thoughts together if not by drinking beer at a bar?

> Strategically, the attempt to join the men at the bar is a serious error on the part of women. If they succeed, it could be the end of the American hero as we know him today.

Women are running the risk of no longer having any more heroes on whom they can depend and to whom they can look for ultimate protection and strength.

The passions aroused in these instances suggest that something unarticulated but powerful is at work. What is it? Why does the ceremony of brandy and cigars lose its power when women are in the room? Why does the idea of a woman participating as an equal in a senior action group of the National Security Council so jar men's sensibilities? For the same reason, I believe, that the gang of boys I once belonged to kept girls out of their treehouse: not because there were secret male activities to hide, but because if a girl could join then membership would no longer prove anything about masculinity. This is the magic, the reassurance of virility by reflection, the "atmosphere" that men fight so hard to protect. The determination with which men fight to keep this prop suggests how fragile their sense of masculinity is and how hard to maintain.

For what it is worth, the long history of "men's houses," the predecessors of the modern male social clubs—from primitive South Pacific societies studied by anthropologists, to the Sodomite regiments of Thebes, Crete, and Sparta, to the Knights Templar of the Middle Ages, to certain groups of Nazi storm troopers—demonstrates their common spirit. They are nearly all characterized by fear and hatred of women, emphasis on violence and warmaking—both symbolically associated with sex—and homosexuality of the sadomasochistic variety, expressed in initiation ceremonies and in most cases repressed thereafter.[4]

Even today, the initiation rites of many middle-class men's clubs and college fraternities include the paddling of buttocks and nudity accompanied by mock homosexual assaults or sexual humiliations.[5]

When men do venture forth from their clubs, taverns, and workplaces run by male hierarchies, they face certain hazards.

One of these is encountering women who are both attractive and openly intelligent and worldly. From this kind of woman most men beat a hasty retreat. Imagine a businessman approaching an attractive woman at a cocktail party and telling her, as part of his opening gambit, what a tough day he has had with his board of directors, meeting all day to decide whether to merge his ten-million-dollar plastics company into a much larger four-hundred million-dollar chemical producer. Imagine that, instead of opening her eyes wide at the large numbers and murmuring something appreciative and impressed sounding, she says something like, "Yes, that kind of decision can be tough. In fact, I just closed a similar deal for a small manufacturer of electronic components. The antitrust problems with these vertical mergers are getting worse all the time." If our protagonist had been talking to a man, the odds are that he would pursue the conversation eagerly. To the woman, his first reaction would be surprise (natural enough, since few woman have this kind of power). Next would come confusion—he didn't really open the subject of his deal to talk about it substantively or to compare notes but mainly to impress. Should he switch gears and get into the substance, or continue to try to impress her? What if her company was worth fifty million dollars; suppose she knows more about this kind of deal than he does? The usual response to all this is a quick exit: "Excuse me, I'm going to get a refill." But men can be frightened away even by a show of critical intelligence on nonprofessional matters—a thorough and perceptive analysis of the character of other people at the party, for example. Only if the woman is old or unattractive or firmly attached to a close friend and thus out of the game preserve, not a challenge, is it possible for men to talk to her without concern about dominance.

There is evidence of the beginnings of change in some quarters. College students appear to be growing less fearful of independent and intelligent women. In a survey of seniors graduating in 1970 from an Ivy League college, an equal number—thirty percent—felt comfortable dating women to whom they did not feel intellectually superior as felt uncomfortable. Some

of the students who felt uncomfortable described their feelings
in interviews:

> I enjoy talking to more intelligent girls, but I have no desire for a
> deep relationship with them. I guess I still believe that the man
> should be more intelligent.
>
> I may be a little frightened of a man who is superior to me in some
> field of knowledge, but if a girl knows more than I do, I resent
> her.[6]

A few older men, becoming dissatisfied with their traditional
male friendships, are starting to look to women for more open
relationships. They feel, correctly, that their initiative in this
direction will be better received by women than by men.

But for some men of all generations, women who are independent and bright as well as attractive are simply the highest form
of sport, their conquest the true test of manhood. These men are
usually aggressive and successful in their professions. What they
are looking for most is the reassurance of conquest, and the more
worthy the opponent the better. Making it with a meek doe or a
dumb Venus just doesn't have the spice of battle for them—they
are titillated by a "show" of resistance or independent intelligence and judgment. Techniques vary but the ambiance is always the Maileresque sparring and grappling for weak spots.
Nearly all begin by acknowledging with mock surprise and respect how unusual it is to find beauty and brains together. It can
be as crude as, "I thought all lady lawyers were twenty pounds
overweight and wore oxfords" or as subtle as a slightly raised
eyebrow and a half-amused, half-appreciative smile when the
woman's answer to the question, "What do you do?" puts her on
the same general level of worldliness and power as the man. The
immediate effect, and unconscious intention, is to put down
women in general (otherwise why such shock at this one's accomplishments) and to deliver oneself a self congratulatory hug
for being astute enough to recognize this woman's uniqueness
and big and bold enough to deal with her.

Then, some men will draw the woman out about her work or schooling, maintaining a detached, amused attitude and making a running series of references to sex, as if to say, "You come on like a serious professional (lawyer, businesswoman, editor, etc.) and you've got all the credentials, but you and I know that all that is not the real you—a woman whose real concern is men and sex with men. You don't scare me and I'm not going to let you get away with your act." All very irritating to a woman who in all likelihood wants to be taken seriously as both a professional and a sexual being.

Other men have a more straightforward, rushing attack. Whatever the woman says is disputed, topped, or treated as unimportant. She offers idea X . . . he argues not-X. Or he says, "Well, yes, X, but X also implies X_1 and X_2. Have you considered those? You haven't, have you?" She says she is doing Y . . . he says, "Why are you wasting your time on Y? A woman with your talents should be doing Z." The assumption lurking behind this style is the ancient "women really like to be dominated and if I show her I'm in control, she'll fall into bed with me."

Another, superficially more benign, posture is that of paternalistic advice-giver. If she's developing an advertising campaign for a particular kind of product, he's done dozens of the same type and he'll tell her what he has learned from every one. If he doesn't work in the same field, he's ready with philosophical counsel about her life.

Declared feminists are a special challenge. The lure of taking one on is irresistible for the kind of man we have been discussing. Everything she stands for is a direct challenge to his view of women and their proper relationship to him. Until Brenda got so bored with it that she refused any longer to be engaged, I was a regular witness to these confrontations. The man starts out by looking for inconsistencies between what he imagines to be her feminist beliefs and her actual behavior, or he takes a particular, always extreme faction of the feminist movement and picks away at it.

Before she learned better, Brenda would engage at this same

level, the man losing point after point but never stopping because the discussion never gets to the mainspring of his various arguments—how *he* personally feels—and because the frustration of not being able to win, for this kind of man, only spurs him on to more and more frantic efforts. After about a year of this, Brenda learned either to insist on making the discussion personal, relating it to the man's own life and relationships, or to ignore him. Either shatters his sense of detachment and control.

Once a guest at a dinner party spent the entire evening trying to make a dent in Brenda. In mock alarm, he tried to feel her biceps. He tried to bait her into argument ("How can a liberated lady like you wear a peasant blouse and a skirt?"). He practically fell across the table trying to get a rise out of her. Getting no response, he finally began to openly attack her as an unfeminine bitch and me for not being a man and having a "little" mind. When it was suggested that he was the one who had no self-confidence as a man, that he was in fact afraid of women, he lost control completely and left. As he walked out the door, his last grotesque attempt at mastery was to try to get Brenda to smile.

A great depth of fear and hostility underlies even the more polite and civilized attempts to assert control over an independent woman or, especially, a feminist woman. Resistance only brings it out into the open; it does not create it. One indication of this fear is that men tend not to want to marry or establish close relationships with such women.

When I was at Harvard, most of the editors of the *Law Review*, men who had little to fear by society's standards from anyone in the way of intellectual and occupational comparisons, consistently sought out women a level below them in terms of aspiration and independence. They wanted women who were attractive, bright, well-educated (at least a B.A. from a good college), preferably had a minor occupational interest (teaching in a progressive primary school is a good one) but who felt no internal conflict about joining the Harvard Law Wives' Association.

Most men who feel the appeal of independent women are in a particularly unhappy position. They are bored with women trained into the more traditional, passive, dependent mold, but so committed to the conquest of the women they find more interesting that they cannot open up enough to make real contact with them. They are unwilling to commit themselves to anyone they can't control. [7]

The larger number of men look for and find women to whom they are superior—or who let them believe they are superior—on the basis of occupational status in the middle and upper-middle income range, on the basis of the fact of maleness alone in lower income groups. The contempt they can then feel for women allows them to feel safe. "I feel more comfortable talking about my troubles to women," a member of a men's consciousness-raising group said, "because I don't really care what they think of me."

7. Marriage and Other Intimate Arrangements

"Make Him Your Reason for Living"

—song title

What men expect from their wives,* in return for money, an erect penis, and a little attention, is a full-fledged life-support system geared to their needs and desires. As Mary Ellmann put it:

> While the selfish (i.e., the normal majority) of both sexes spend all their unmarried time in the pursuit of personal happiness, the wife, in the course of (wedding night) intercourse, is released from so mean a compulsion, and rises from the bed dedicated to the happiness of others. This ascension defines her.[1]

Men, however, do not redefine their lives upon marriage in any comparable way except perhaps to trade a certain (often mythical) adventurousness for convenience and tranquillity.

---

*For the sake of brevity, "wife" and "husband" are used throughout this chapter. But all except the legal points are applicable to men and women living in other forms of intimate, more or less permanent relationships.

Our common-law heritage designated the wife as her husband's chattel, "something better than his dog, a little dearer than his horse."[2] Blackstone, the eighteenth century English jurist explained:

> By marriage, the husband and wife are one person in law: that is, the very being or legal existence of the woman is suspended during the marriage, or at least is incorporated and consolidated into that of the husband; under whose wing, protection, and *cover*, she performs everything.[3]

Prior to the Civil War, the legal status of married women in the United States was comparable to that of blacks under the slave codes. Neither slaves nor married women had the legal capacity to hold property or to serve as guardians of their own children. Neither blacks nor women could hold office, serve on juries, or bring suit in their own names. White men controlled the behavior of both their slaves and their wives and had legally enforceable rights to the services of both without compensation.[4]

> In the earlier common law, women and children were placed under the jurisdiction of the paternal power. When a legal status had to be found for the imported Negro servants in the seventeenth century, the nearest and most natural analogy was the status of women and children. The ninth commandment—linking together women, servants, mules and other property—could be invoked, as well as a great number of other passages of Holy Scripture.[5]

Of course, the legal status of married women has improved since the nineteenth century. The Married Women's Property Acts, enacted in the 1850s, opened the door to a measure of economic independence[6] and in the last few years the pace of legislative and court-ordered reform has picked up.

But, even in the 1970s, a woman's place as subordinate, a satellite to her husband is reflected in a wide range of laws. The legal domicile of a married woman in most states is the same as that of her husband, even if they are living apart—and often this address is used to determine where she may vote, run for public office, serve on juries, be liable for taxes, sue for divorce, have her estate administered, be eligible for free or lowered tuition at a state college or university. Nearly all states with community property laws, which provide that all property acquired by either spouse during the marriage is jointly owned by both, automatically grant the husband the right to manage and dispose of the property during the marriage. This deprives a working wife of effective control of her own earnings during marriage.

For the most part, though, the wife's "incorporation" into the husband is induced and supported by more subtle, less directly coercive means. The idea, variously expressed, permeates our culture. In an ad for *Esquire*, a magazine designed to appeal to men, a young woman talks about her husband:

> Roger was an English major at Columbia ('61) and taught at UCLA before he became an actor. He has a way of saying things that I find very apt. I think that's one of the main reasons I became Mrs. Roger Davis. . . . He's the only man I know who can get high on 18th-century literature in the evening and spend the morning watching a boxer he sponsors work out in the gym. Or, go see how his racehorse, "Royal Bupers," [sic] does at the track with a copy of Robert Frost under his arm. He's that way about places, too. So we live in Beverly Hills and New York—and we'd like to have a home in Rome—Roger's favorite city in Europe. But wherever we are—life is interesting—because my husband is an interesting man.

On the television screen, a husband looks down at his wife's anxious upturned face and, because she's well preserved through regular use of Geritol, says, "I think I'll keep you." They both laugh, he heartily, she with relief, but the point has been made.

Getting down to basics, the wife of a successful executive, who said she had to be "a ray of sunshine" at breakfast because her husband "gets a corporate look on his face at dawn," reported that he expects her to be

useful, punctual, efficient, pleasant, alert and healthy. He has no
patience with the opposites of any of these. He wants me to be
feminine, to have a sense of humor without being witty, and not
to be emphatic.[7]

During a 1972 conference, 130 wives of executives who earn more
than twenty-five thousand dollars a year were told by a male
official of the Ford Motor Company that if they wanted outside
interests they "should take up painting, music, go to school but
under no circumstances take a job." The ideal corporate wife
should also "watch her figure and don't [sic] nag."[8]

The wife of a man who earns twelve thousand dollars a year
told a reporter inquiring about the impact of the women's
movement on her life:

> In our house, my husband expects me home every evening. That
> is, unless he decides to go bowling. Then I can go to the movies by
> myself or out to a neighbor's.[9]

It is not that men do not love and care for their wives. They do,
but only in the context of the *traditional marriage*, a relationship
structured to preserve the husband's sense of being different
from and superior to his wife, to allow him, if he is an upper-
middle-income professional, to pursue the kind of total commitment to career expected of him to pressure his wife into living her
life through and around his career and the friends he makes
through his work. Until very recently, he has not had to force his
wife into this role. Society has done a thorough enough job of
conditioning women before they get married. For example, at the
conference referred to earlier, another wife stated,

> I just feel appreciated by my husband. That's what enables me to
> function as a person. Oh, I'm taken for granted like most wives.
> But once in a while he says or does something that makes me feel
> important. I get my satisfaction from looking good in his eyes and
> not anyone else's.[10]

My guess is that she and her husband never talked about this basic assumption of their marriage, that she brought it to the marriage with her and he simply did nothing to change it.

In the traditional marriage, the wife's world shrinks with the passage of time to house and children, and with it her self-confidence and sense of being in touch with the outside world. The self-description "I'm just a housewife," whether delivered defiantly or shamefully, sums up how many women feel about that status. Even assuming the relationship began with husband and wife each respecting the other's capabilities to understand and cope with life and its problems, this balance almost inevitably erodes. There is extensive evidence that while marriage is good for men in terms of physical and emotional health, it is bad for women. A study made a generation ago, for example, showed that more married than unmarried women were

> troubled by ideas that people were watching them on the street, were fearful of falling when on high places, had their feelings easily hurt, were happy and sad by turns without apparent reason, regretted impulsive statements, cried easily, felt hurt by criticism, sometimes felt miserable, found it hard to make up their minds, sometimes felt grouchy, were burdened by a sense of remorse, worried over possible misfortune, changed interests quickly, were bothered when people watched them perform a task, would cross the street to avoid meeting people, were upset when people crowded ahead of them in line, would rather stand than take a front seat when late, were self-conscious about their appearance, and felt prevented from giving help at the scene of an accident.[11]

Recent studies tend to confirm these differences. One investigator found that

> overall, more of the wives than of the single women she found to be passive, phobic, and depressed; and although the total number who showed severe neurotic symptoms was small, these were evident in almost three times as many married as single women.[12]

As the wife's world shrinks, the husband's, if he is at all successful, expands. He develops new talents, knowledge, social contacts, and sources of self-esteem. It becomes harder for them to talk to each other, because their lives are so different, and yet she is more and more dependent on him for satisfaction of her intellectual, social, and sometimes political interests. Because she has few opportunities to use her capacity to think beyond the exclusively personal and particularized world of home and children, every serious discussion with him, if she has intense interests outside the domestic sphere, becomes a valued opportunity to express and prove herself. Her conversation may often carry more emotional freight than the subject or her involvement and knowledge of it warrant. One or another cause is seized on and pushed as though it were the answer to the world's problems. In part, this happens because the woman may never have an opportunity to explore this kind of subject beyond the level of general theory. She may have a curious and quick mind and be an avid reader, but the housewife's role does not bring her into the kind of working contact with the real-life complexity of social and political issues that makes one suspicious of easy moral certitudes. Moreover, since she is neither developing new theory nor in a position to act on what she reads and thinks about, often the only focus available for her intellectual energy is the passing of moral judgment and getting her husband, the closest representative of the outside world, to confirm that judgment. The husband's unwillingness to be engaged only increases her frustration.

Conversely, a man is likely to have little understanding or respect for what his wife does know about: the raising of their children and the organization of domestic life. Isolated from intimate involvement in these concerns, his feelings about them are shaped primarily by conventional sex stereotypes and his need to think himself superior. In other words, he sees his wife's day taken up with essential but low-status work requiring time, some energy, and some conveniently mysterious female quality but relatively little in the way of intelligence and initiative. He is also prevented from making an effort of imagination to enter his wife's world by his belief that it is a sign of masculinity *not* to understand it.

These inequalities, backed by the sex stereotypes, are enough to make men feel contempt, or at best good-natured condescension, toward their wives. Only people who basically feel themselves to be equals can fully respect each other; and in every area that men are taught to value, the traditional wife is an inferior.

There are, of course, areas which are important to men in which women are equal or superior. A wife has the negative power to make her husband's life miserable, if she is willing to run the risk that he will leave. In some households, the wife has virtually complete control over the family budget and its organized social life, although this is far more prevalent in blue-collar than higher-income families. Everyone has a pet story about a particular titan of finance and industry who is led around like a lamb at home by his wife. If the meaning of these stories is taken at face value, they are clearly the exceptions rather than the rule. It takes a woman of extraordinary personal strength to control, without social status of her own and/or independent means of financial support, a man who has a lot of both. Much is made of the few marriages where this does occur because it is a fearful fantasy come true for men, a kind of poetic, if not personally appealing, justice for women, and, for both sexes, a chance to puncture the pretensions of the rich and powerful.

But at another level, women of all social strata tend to be the principal guardians of the emotional equilibrium of their families. They play this role largely unacknowledged by their husbands. As we have seen, when men are upset, disappointed, in difficulty of any kind, they are reluctant to talk about their feelings. They often don't even admit to themselves, let alone to their wives, that they are upset. A thirty-eight-year-old director of a public-service organization in a New York City suburb explained:

I have a feeling that it's not very masculine to come home at night and to—if not complain—to kind of share your burdens with your wife. I feel that, "Why involve her? If you're a real man, you'll carry these things." The point is, you're imposing your needs on your wife. I think there are so many more important things to share. For example, family decisions of all kinds—when the hell you're going to paint the house, or where you're going on vacation, and what the kids are up to in school. There's all this to work out.[13]

None of this means that wives are not affected by their husbands' unhappiness. It is often expressed indirectly in ways ranging from disproportionate rage over unrelated matters to attempts to escape into virtually total silence. In either case, the women in their lives have to coax out their true feelings—then, ever so gently and delicately, try to help deal with them. They must be especially circumspect about giving advice. What most men want, or at least all that many are capable of accepting, is a kind of passive, appreciative sympathy ("The guy they promoted [instead of you] sounds like a dumb bastard; he probably plays golf with the president"). Active analysis and intervention is harder to take ("Well, that's a marketing job, isn't it? And that kind of thing has never really been your style. You don't really have the personality for selling and you haven't worked at it like you do other things. Maybe you should try for a different slot in the company"); it puts the woman, if only temporarily, in the dreaded position of dominance. Of course, many women somehow manage to give their men both kinds of help without permanently damaging the male ego, and, despite protestations of independence, men depend heavily on that support.

In stark contrast to comparisons between married and unmarried women, married men are significantly better off than unmarried men by almost every conceivable measure. The research evidence demonstrates clearly that married men are happier, less depressed, less passive, show fewer symptoms of psychological distress—including nervous breakdowns, nervousness, trembling hands, nightmares, and insomnia—show less impairment of mental health generally, make more money and commit suicide less.[14] Although it is hard to demonstrate with complete certainty that these statistics are not the result of better adjusted men selecting themselves or being selected by women for marriage, there are strong indications that the institution of marriage rather than the quality of its recruits makes the difference. For example, a comparison between married and widowed men, all of whom were "selected" for marriage at one time or another reveals the same kinds of differences that show up in the comparison between married and never-married men. The data bear out the common observation that widowed men fall apart:

> They show more than expected frequencies of psychological distress and their death rate is high. . . . That it is the deprivation itself which produces such a result can be seen in the fact that during the first half year after bereavement, one study found an increase of 40% in mortality. Five years after bereavement, the survival rate of married or remarried men in a sample of forty-seven men with an average age of seventy-six was higher than that of the never-married, the separated, the unremarried divorced, or the unremarried widowed.[15]

This same measure also shows that marriage does less for women than for men. In the year following the death of their spouses, the death rate for widowed men is twice as high as for widowed women.[16]

In the realm of emotional support, husbands, for the most part, do not give what they get. First, a woman is more likely to be open about her feelings, so the man doesn't have to work at prying them out. More important, he is less likely to make an effort to understand her feelings and needs. Such an effort would require a conscious expenditure of his own emotional energy, especially if she is upset or confused and her distress is in some way connected to him. This is something men have never learned to do. Staying calm and in control is also easier if one doesn't get involved. I still have a strong memory of my father telling my mother (and me telling Brenda during the period after we first met) to "calm down," regardless of whether calm was in fact appropriate. If men can offer practical advice or take some concrete action, they are often eager to help. Explaining something or using connections and influence to help a woman fits right into the masculine role. So does offering a (manly and silent) shoulder to cry on. But men slough off the requests for help which involve more emotional effort , more empathy. They try hard and often successfully not to notice; they say "It's just one of her moods," "Women are that way," or "I'll never understand women," or just leave the field, pleading work obligations and suggesting, if the money is available, a psychiatrist to help her toward a better "adjustment."

Of all the areas in which men fail women, this is the one that cuts the deepest and, ultimately, evokes the most contempt. Nothing contrasts more sharply with the masculine image of self-confidence, rationality, and control than men's sulky, obtuse, and, often virtually total, dependence on their wives to articulate and deal with their own unhappy feelings, and their own insensitivity, fear, and passivity in helping their wives to deal with theirs. This, more than anything else, disillusions women about their men. Bromides like "Men are just overgrown little boys" are both a description of the phenomenon and an attempt, by labeling it innocuously, to ease the pain of disillusionment: disillusionment at having subordinated yourself to a person who isn't, it turns out, special enough to justify the sacrifice, who is probably not much smarter than you are in most ways and in some very important ways is a lot less perceptive, more dependent and more childlike.

Even apart from situations of stress and unhappiness, men tend not to be good companions to their wives. Leslie Farber, a psychiatrist, has constructed two imaginary dialogues between an upper-middle-class husband and wife to illustrate the point:

Version A: He comes home. She is making dinner, diapering the baby, and so on. He greets her affectionately, asks casually, How's it going, or, Well, what's new—and she tells him. She talks about the children, appreciating, deploring, concern about Bobby's this, delight at Billy's that, she recounts her entertaining—or boring or outrageous—experiences at the supermarket, she does not omit mention of the malfunctioning vacuum cleaner, and, stirring away at the soup, wiping children's faces and spilled desserts, she discusses her response to an item of general public interest she saw on TV. She also recalls the few free moments in which she read an article called "Radical New Approaches to Being a Woman," and more speculation, philosophy and self-scrutiny flow freely until, the children more or less bedded down, or banished to homework and/or TV, dinner cleared away, and a quiet moment descending over the last cup of coffee, she turns to him, flushed, expectant, as one who has unstintingly contributed her full share of the sharing, and says, Well? How was your day? Does he start off with who called him first thing at the office that morning, and how that call caused him to doubt a decision he'd made the day before, and does he pursue momentarily the problematic nature of the kind of decision-making he's required to do and his capacity or incapacity for it, does he respond to her notions about the TV event, or engage her reactions to the article she read, being reminded of something *he* read on that most recently well-publicized of subjects and his response to it, does he. . . . But why pursue this? Once in a while he does. More often he does not. Perhaps he says, Oh, nothing much happened, just the usual rat-race. Perhaps he recites some dry, factual resume of his activities. Perhaps he grasps at some domestic thread she dangled and addresses himself to an issue concerning her or the children, or even the vacuum cleaner. Perhaps he shrugs and is silent. In any case, more often than she cares to think about, she asks with some bitterness why there must be this inequality, why she is open about her life, her thoughts, and he remains closed.

Version B: He comes home. Pretty soon she comes home. The housekeeper is seeing to the children and making dinner. He (or possibly she) fixes a couple of cocktails and they share a quiet interlude before a family (or possibly a solitary adult) dinner. Well, he says, how did it go today—and she tells him. She talks about her secretary, or co-editor or senior research assistant, or cameraman, she appreciates, deplores, analyzes, questions, wonders about the nature of her work, of her place and performance in it, tells of other, more private thoughts and concerns that popped in and out of her day. Eventually she pauses . . . and asks . . . and does he. . .? Well , once in a while he does. More often he does not.[17]

Farber's comment:

> There may be no deliberate concealment at all: all he may experi-
> ence may be a familiar blankness following her invitation or
> demand that he talk. He can stand on his right to have nothing to
> say, or he can willfully invent a facsimile of talk, but in either case
> he is left with an aftertaste of an old inferiority in the realm of real
> talk with a woman.

Although part of the explanation for Version A may be the
emotional overloading by a wife starved for adult companionship discussed above, Version B, in which husband and wife
both have lives outside the home, also rings true. The "familiar
blankness" often results, at least it did for me, from an imagined
fear that spontaneous talk will reveal unacceptable feelings—
almost anything that would show vulnerability or indicate
that the speaker doesn't "measure up" to the masculine
ideal.

This reaction is usually entirely automatic. It doesn't matter
whether men are actually experiencing any "unacceptable" feelings at the time; we have to clear our thoughts through the
conscious part of our minds to make sure before they come out.
The anxiety created by an explicit request to talk spontaneously,
or simply a felt obligation to reciprocate, triggers the "blank"
protective reaction. This constant monitoring explains the sudden lull when the conversation turns to men's personal reactions
to people and events—unless the matter has been rehearsed
before or the speaker is certain that it casts him in an unambig-
uously masculine light. In the process, impulses toward others
—affection, generosity, sympathy, sexual attraction—which
are desirable, even by the rigid standards of the masculine
ideal, are also likely to be repressed. As Rollo May has pointed
out, "The positive cannot come out until the negative does also.
This is why in psychoanalysis, the negative (the feeling that is
feared and repressed) is analyzed, with the hope—which
comes true often enough to justify the rule—that the positive
will then be able to come into its own."[18]

8. Family and Fatherhood

When the wife doesn't work outside the home and the husband has a professional or executive-level business career, it is hard to challenge the logic which allocates the supporting services role to the wife. If the husband has to spend ten to twelve hours a day on the job, he really can't do much else; his work is not only the economic but also the social mainstay for the family. The wife's "outside interests" clearly do not count for as much. If she starts a career late, or returns to one after raising children, she is almost certain to earn less money than he does, again making it logical for her to subordinate her interests to his. Even measured by yardsticks other than money, his work is likely to be judged more "important" than hers.

To break this traditional pattern, basic assumptions have to be challenged: that the only kind of worthwhile career is an all-consuming one; that the social side of an executive job requires the full participation and services of the spouse; that the wife is the only person qualified to assume major responsibility for the care of children; that the additional money, glory, or benefit to humanity derived from the concentration of energy and time (both his and hers) on his career is always more valuable than the money, glory, or benefits to humanity and the personal satisfactions to her (or, possibly, to both) that a reallocation of time and effort freeing her to pursue a career would bring; and, all else failing, that their prize masculine and feminine identities depend on his being the breadwinner and her being at home, on his superiority and her subordination. Only when these assumptions begin to be stripped away, do men have to face their unwillingness to tolerate, much less welcome, having an equal—in status, in competence, in earning power—as a mate.

When their wives propose to take a job outside the home, it is hard for men to object directly. Other wives do it— approximately sixty percent of married women work at least part time.[1] Blue collar families often need the money, and middle- and upper-middle-income men have come to accept, or at least give lip service to, the idea that their well-educated spouses need some activity to fight boredom. So men's resistance takes subtler forms, forms which reveal a lot about their underlying feelings.

Even when they favor it in theory, men tend to disparage their wives' work. One man, who said he was eager for his wife to get a job, remarked,

> It wouldn't have to be a full-time job—just something to do and people to talk to. If she got away everybody would be better off. Anything—even volunteer work—would do it.[2]

Implicit in this statement are the assumptions that his wife's commitment to work would be so superficial, and her capabilities so slight, that the actual content of her job would be unimportant.

Many blue-collar or clerical workers, forced by economic circumstances to accept the fact of a working wife, are unhappy about it. "It just doesn't seem like home to me when I know my wife is out working, " is reported as a typical expression of this feeling.[3] A New York taxi driver who thought it was all right for women to work in financial emergencies but not otherwise told me he wanted his wife at home because nobody else could cook as well. When I hypothesized a housekeeper with comparable cooking skills, he said that, in any event, he wanted to be able to get her on the phone at any time. When I hypothesized an office job where she would be reachable by telephone, he said it just wasn't right for her to work. This opposition, according to sociologist Mirra Komarovsky, is based on possessiveness—the men want to keep their wives away from the sexual opportunities provided by outside employment—and "anxiety over loss of power."[4] The relatively low status of blue-collar and clerical jobs makes almost any work by the woman a threat to the man's superiority, which is founded mainly on his position as sole breadwinner.

When upper-middle-income men face the prospect of their wives pursuing full-fledged, time-consuming, high-status careers, what emerges explicitly is their need to feel superior and to reaffirm the higher priority automatically accorded their work and emotional requirements . Most such men, as we saw earlier, don't marry their "equals," women whose ambitions include a full-time professional career. Their feelings were stated bluntly by one of the men interviewed by Lynda Lytle Holmstrom for her study of two-career families. He was very supportive of his wife having a part-time job, but said,

> I don't think I would be very happy or could I really tolerate it if she felt that she had to work full-time and have a career in which she were very ambitious and had to tie herself into her career in which a great deal of work was demanded of her and feel that she was advancing through the ranks. . . . I don't think I could really tolerate that. . . . It would be impossible at that point to have a semblance of what I would consider a happy home life.[5]

Others emphasized that the wife "could not have a career that would in any way upset the delicate balance of the husband's career."[6] Among the professional women Holmstrom studied who had divorced their husbands (already a select group because of their initial willingness to marry a "careerwoman"), a number reported that the husband's psychological need to "put her down" had been a major factor in the divorce. Said one,

> It was very destructive to me. He was a person who could never resist taking things apart. . . . Every single time I would think of something (for a master's thesis) I'd start to talk with him about it and in half an hour there wouldn't be anything left of it. And it wasn't just *that*. This was the way just about everything went, my opinions about anything. And you know, since we were both in the same field this was very painful. I don't think now that he was that much cleverer than I *(laughter)*, but it certainly seemed so at the time.[7]

Most of the men in Holmstrom's sample of families in which both spouses pursued full-time careers did *not* feel competitively threatened by their wives. But her explanation for this is revealing:

> The general cultural norm of male superiority is also seen in marriage. The husband is expected to do the more prestigious activity, or, if he does the same activity as his wife, he is expected to do it better. . . . From this point of view, "avoidance of competition" does not mean that the sexes do not compete; rather, it means that the husband should be more successful than the wife. . . .

> Among the professional group on any given measure of success, there were only one or two cases where the wife was ahead of her husband at some point in time or where the wife was ultimately more occupationally successful. Thus, there were not enough cases to determine if there is a positive correlation between the presence of feelings of competition and the wife being more successful. A larger sample would probably include more such cases, and it is predicted that such a positive correlation would occur.[8]

One woman spelled it out:

No. I never felt it , because he was always ahead (laughter) of the game, always ahead of me. . . . I don't think it would lead to competition even if we were [in the same field] because I'm very relaxed about the whole thing. . . . I always feel I'm in a different kind of category. There aren't any women actually in the field. And then because I go part time. . . .[9]

Interestingly enough, this particular woman's husband, who in fact was always far ahead of her, always had the higher-ranking job, published more, and earned more money—gave a different answer when asked if there had been feelings of competition between them:

Not very often. As long as I'm able to do my work and do it well I don't really feel too much threatened by her. If we were in the same field I guess it would be pretty bad. . . . One time I had a manuscript rejected and something else was going slowly and I think I must have felt, you know, a little inadequate. . . . But for the most part it's not been bad. . . . Her book was reviewed in (the newspaper). . . . I would have felt jealous frankly except for the fact that my book had been reviewed. . . . If somebody would say, "Well, she's pulling him along," that would be tough. But she's not because I think I'm keeping my own.[10]

Few men are willing to make significant concessions to a wife's career. Any commitment outside the home that threatens their position as the only major focus for their wives' energies and emotions is unacceptable. Here's television personality David Susskind describing in an interview why his wife, a television producer in her own right before they were married, eventually abandoned her career:

I didn't say, "Why don't you quit working!" when she appeared on the Mike Wallace show. . . . I said, "If you continue we'll be in trouble." You see, in show business a performance is like finishing a love affair. When you finish you're wringing wet and keyed up. The same as after great lovemaking. This is exactly what happened to Joyce, and it was murder for me. I found I was getting to hate her show.[11]

Apparently, his "love affair" with his work was another story entirely.

What little research there is on the attitudes of black men toward wives working outside the home presents a somewhat different picture. A 1970 survey found that, at all income levels, black men are substantially more accepting than white men of their wives holding jobs, perhaps because working women have always been a fact of life in black families. [12]

Even when status is not an issue, the prospect of a working wife raises questions about the division of labor at home.

First, it's O.K. for the wife to have a paying job—as long as she does everything else she has been doing as well. In other words, the husband's not going to do any housework. Here's a woman's-eye view of this minuet in a "liberal" household where the man thought he was bound by elementary notions of fairness:

> "I don't mind sharing the housework, but I don't do it very well. We should each do the things we're best at."
> *Meaning:* Unfortunately I'm no good at things like washing dishes or cooking. What I do best is a little light carpentry, changing light bulbs, moving furniture (*how often do you move furniture?*).
> *Also Meaning:* Historically the lower classes (black men and us) have had hundreds of years experience doing menial jobs. It would be a waste of manpower to train someone else to do them now.
> *Also Meaning:* I don't like the dull stupid boring jobs, so you should do them.

> "I don't mind sharing the work, but you'll have to show me how to do it."
> *Meaning:* I ask a lot of questions and you'll have to show me everything everytime I do it because I don't remember so good. Also don't try to sit down and read while I'm doing my jobs because I'm going to annoy hell out of you until it's easier to do them yourself.

> "We used to be so happy!" (Said whenever it was his turn to do something.)
> *Meaning:* I used to be so happy.
> *Meaning:* Life without housework is bliss. (*No quarrel here. Perfect agreement.*)[13]

Even if the man does do some of the housework, in most of the two-career families I know and in studies of both professional and blue-collar families in which both husband and wife work, it usually remains the woman's responsibility to organize it and, ultimately, see that it is done. He does her a favor, he "helps her" with what is *her* problem even if she holds a job as time-consuming and well-paying as his. [14]

Second, it's O.K. for the wife to work, but who's going to take care of the children? The changes rung on this issue involve heavier doses of ideology and rearrangements involving the man's career that may not be entirely within his power to effect. Since the Victorian era we have been the victims of the mother-hood myth, the idea that the mother, above the father and all other women, is particularly well-suited to care for the children. Panegyrics to mother love abound in the professional as well as popular literature. It is supposed to have unique, totally selfless, all-forgiving qualities which make it irreplaceable. This stereotype of motherhood has been pushed to its limit and has bred its own reaction.

> The more ideal the conception of a human function, the more resentment and suspicion it arouses: we are entirely accustomed, in the consideration of maternity, to this jolting between soul and damnation. We are as familiar with the accusation of consumptive attachment as with the praise of selfless care. . . . It is impossible for women either to give or to withhold attention without risking the injury of their children." [15]

But, however contradictory and confusing, the myth still has a substantial hold on women and is thus available to men as a weapon. It is the first, seemingly selfless, line of defense when mother wants to get a job. No combination of housekeepers, relatives, child-care centers (however excellent) will do. Nothing but mother's full-time physical presence will allow the children to grow into healthy adults. The uncritical zeal with which men seize on this argument suggests strongly that it masks other sources of resistance. A very real one is the apprehension that if the woman holds a job outside the home, especially if it is a full time job, he will probably come under pressure to take a greater role in caring for the children than if she were to devote herself exclusively to home and children.[16] Good household help is not always available, children get sick and child-care centers are scarce. It may be difficult for him to take the time from his work, either because his conception of a career demands that he do nothing else or because he has a job with inflexible hours. A factory worker and an advertising executive who work in the inner city and live an hour and a half away are examples of men in this last, *objective* bind. More flexible organization of work and an extensive network of high-quality child-care centers, some located near places of work, as well as changes in individual values are necessary before most families with children will be able to abandon the traditional roles without hardship.

There is another level of resistance, however, to masculine involvement with child care. Being a father, in the sense of having sired and having children, is part of the masculine image; but fathering, the actual care of children, is not. Men who spend a lot of time taking care of their children—washing, dressing, feeding, teaching, comforting, and playing with them—aren't doing quite what they should be. A truck driver who spent an hour with his four-year-old son and his classmates at nursery school, after being coaxed into it by a teacher, and enjoyed himself immensely asked with a pained look as he was leaving, "What'll I tell the guys at work about this?"[17] The image of a lawyer, businessman, or even a professor wheeling a baby carriage around in public is still jarring. Part of the feeling that care of children is inappropriate as a strong commitment for men comes from the fact that it is a diversion from men's "real" work, the building of a successful career. Any man who not only says that he wishes he could spend more time with his children, but actually does so is suspected by his associates of not being properly ambitious. One young lawyer with a large New York firm told me that he very much wanted to see more of his eighteen-month-old son but was afraid he wouldn't be made a partner unless he worked evenings and Saturdays.

Even if, despite all this, a man should want to play an active part in the rearing of his children, he is generally ill-prepared for it. Men have little opportunity to learn how to care for young children.

> Boys who have younger friends are viewed as strange in many neighborhoods ("how come he's not with kids his own age?"), whereas it is "natural" that girls are attracted to young children. Men who play with children they have not fathered (not their "own"), and who may not even be fathers at all, are viewed with suspicion by some ("what's *he* doing with that kid?"), while it is assumed and demanded that women like and be comfortable with children.[18]

At even younger ages, boys are discouraged from playing with dolls, the first, imaginative trying out of the parental role.*

Moreover, the role traditionally assigned to fathers and most compatible with the masculine ideal—the benevolent but authoritarian rule maker and naysayer—is no longer viable in our permissive culture. Still called in primarily to intervene in moments of high crisis or to punish, the father is today regarded as a genuine authority by neither himself nor his children. Only Draconian measures, which he no longer believes in, will extract compliance, and these fail, too, as children grow older. Except in the limited field of "doing things with" and being a "pal" to his children (mainly the boys) there are very few models for mutually rewarding relationships between men and their children. The counterpart to the motherhood myth in popular culture is the image of fathers as bumbling outsiders in the household, men without a significant role vis-à-vis children.

> For every newsnote published or broadcast that highlights a caring experience between a man and a child, the media still trot out

---

* One available antidote is a song called "William's Doll" included in the nonsexist children's record *Free to Be . . . You and Me.*

five situation comedies or norror stories that show men who are
tyrants, or incompetent, or plain uninterested in nurturing young
children. . . . Ads for Pampers show a man carrying a puppy
greeting two women holding infants. Women care for babies, is
the message, men take care of dogs.[19]

Child development specialists have produced a voluminous literature on the mother-child relationship—its importance and
uniqueness, how it should be handled, and, of course, tracing
virtually every conceivable psychological problem to deficiencies
in mothering. But there is almost nothing about the influence of
fathers on their children. Until very recently, professionals almost universally assumed that the extent of the father's responsibility and role was to support his family and back up the
mother in her dealings with the children.[20]

But there is every indication that children respond primarily to
the quality of care given them, irrespective of the sex of the
person giving it. Even young infants have been shown to be
emotionally attached to fathers as well as mothers, despite the
lesser amount of time most fathers spend with them.[21] I know a
young child, a girl, who automatically turns to her father rather
than her mother when in distress of any kind. Both love and are
affectionate toward the child. But the woman has a nine-to-five
job and the man is a law-school professor with irregular hours.
He spends more time at home with the child and is more patient
with her. The result is that, although responsive to both parents,
she "prefers" him in the way that young children were supposed
instinctually to prefer their mothers.

The community of child development specialists, itself largely
male, is beginning to shift away from the mystique-ridden view
which exalts the mother-child relationship to something impossible for fathers to duplicate. A similar shift is developing in
the law. Many state codes provide that when custody of children
is contested upon divorce the choice shall be made in the best
interests of the child and that neither parent shall be automatically preferred. Nevertheless, most courts have interpreted these

provisions so as to favor the mother, without regard to the individual qualifications of either parent, in cases involving young children. [22] This has been achieved through the use of the "tender years presumption." Here is an early and explicit statement of this presumption by a Wisconsin court:

> For a [child] of . . . tender years nothing can be an adequate substitute for mother love—for that constant ministration required during the period of nurture that only a mother can give because in her alone is service expressed in terms of love. She alone has the patience and sympathy required to mold and soothe the infant mind in its adjustment to its environment. The difference between fatherhood and motherhood in this respect is fundamental and the law should recognize it unless offset by undesirable traits in the mother. [23]

To obtain custody of their children, fathers have had to prove not just that they are the more suitable parent, but that their spouses are, in effect, "unfit mothers," a heavy and unfair burden. Until the last decade, challenges to this antiquated presumption were rare; the idea of raising their young children occurred to only a very few men, and even those few were discouraged by counsel. In the last few years, however, the number of such cases has grown and, remarkably, a sizable number have been won. [24]

Divorced fathers are also beginning to organize groups to lobby for legislation that would direct the courts unmistakably to abandon the presumption favoring maternal custody.* Since the best interest of the child does not require that one parent be given an automatic preference over the other—in fact is badly served by such preferences—it seems likely that the "tender years presumption" will come to be seen as an instance of sex discrimination forbidden by the equal protection clause of the Fourteenth Amendment and, upon ratification, the Equal Rights Amendment to the United States Constitution.

---

* A Boston group, for example, calls itself Fathers United for Equal Justice.

Another harbinger of change is the finding by the U.S. Equal Employment Opportunity Commission, in a case brought by a New York City schoolteacher, that for an employer to allow leaves for care of young children to mothers but not to fathers constitutes sex discrimination prohibited by the Civil Rights Act.[25] The New York City Board of Education, under pressure from an American Civil Liberties Union lawsuit to enforce the determination, has amended its regulations to provide such leaves to fathers and mothers of children under the age of four on an equal basis.[26]

For individual fathers, apart from the amount of time spent on the job or career, the most serious obstacle to developing rewarding and useful relationships with their children is an inflexibly masculine personality. Small children cannot be dealt with on the basis of reason alone. They don't have the ability to understand or the emotional control of adults. One has to confront and deal with their feelings. But to understand and accept another person's feelings one must be able to put oneself in his or her place, to experience a little of the feeling oneself. For men who are uncomfortable with and repress their own emotions, especially weak dependent, "childlike" emotions, this is difficult.

> One male nursery school teacher found himself angry at little boys who cried when they felt hurt or sad. His anger was so upsetting to him that he withdrew whenever little boys needed consolation or support. Under the careful and supportive probing of the head teacher in the school, who sensed his conflict, he exclaimed that "I never was allowed to cry when I was little and they shouldn't cry either."[27]

Men tend to camouflage their tender feelings toward children, to express them in roughhousing: a mock punch instead of a hug; telling a six-year-old boy on his way to a birthday party to "give 'em hell" when that isn't what is meant at all. The scene in old westerns of two friends expressing their pleasure at meeting after a long separation by slugging each other in the arm is not far from the truth in many father-son relationships. The more they like each other, the harder they hit. Sarcasm is another camouflage men use, especially in their relationships with boys. According to Tilla Vahanian, a psychologist with broad experience in family counseling, it is often a kind of self-protection against a more direct and affectionate way of speaking. But, she says, "children find it unbearable, because they don't understand that it is not all ill-tempered. They don't know how to respond. And the father doesn't realize what he's doing because it's so much a part of his growing up."[28] Until they reach puberty, men find it somewhat easier to be affectionate with their daughters. Then, uncomfortable with the sexual overtones of physical contact, they back off. Some decrease in the level of intimacy is certainly appropriate as children grow up, but much of this discomfort seems misplaced, the result of viewing all pleasurable physical contact as a prelude to sex and thus off limits when the child reaches sexual maturity.

Men's insensitivity to the inner lives of their children makes them feel that they must earn their love and respect in a mechanical way. Children respond best to whoever performs the mundane tasks of childrearing—feeding them, helping them clean up their messes, taking them to buy shoes, putting them to bed —with love and respect for their thoughts and concerns. But men tend to believe that their children's love must be coerced by more unusual and necessarily sporadic acts—buying presents, doing things with kids that they are supposed to like. And when these things fail, as they must if used as a substitute for day-to-day contact and more personal exchange, they are bewildered and hurt: "I gave him (or her) everything, and I get nothing, not even gratitude, in return."

Children know when adults are angry or unhappy, although they often don't know why, and they tend to blame themselves. Sometimes they ask about it directly and sometimes they are too afraid or confused to ask. In either situation, the adults involved can relieve their children's anxiety effectively only if they are aware of the feelings they are communicating and able to acknowledge and accept them. A father who refuses to admit to himself that he is upset and angry over a flap at the office is not only likely to take it out on his kids along with everybody else, but to be unable to explain to them that they are not the cause of his anger.

The rewards of caring for a child are real, but essentially personal, hard to measure or hang on to. This is not the kind of experience men are taught to value. It does not lead to power, wealth, or high status. As we have seen, the male stereotype pushes men into seeking their sense of self-esteem almost exclusively in achievement measured by objective, usually competitive standards. Fathers apply these criteria to their children, taking pride in their being advanced in school or good at sports "for their age;" in fact, teaching these skills is the parental task that most holds their interest. But this is only a part, and when children are young a small part, of being a parent. And all too often the father's emphasis in the teaching will shift, without his being aware of it, from the child to the task or skill itself. Instead of focusing on the child's learning, pleasure, and feelings, with the shared effort as the vehicle, he concentrates, as men are taught to do, exclusively on getting the job done. Sometimes this means impatiently taking a tool away from a child who is working slowly but with concentration and contentment on a project and finishing it himself. Sometimes, particularly in sports, it means pushing a child, especially a boy, beyond his interest or ability, creating anxiety by making him feel that his father's love and esteem depend on his reaching an arbitrary level of competence.

The masculine mania for competition also comes between fathers and their children, again especially boys. According to Vahanian, fathers often convey contradictory and tension-creating messages about competition to their children. First, the way to earn my love and approval is by being a good competitor; but, second, you'd better not beat me:

> Father gets down on his knees and he asks the kid to punch him.
> He says, in effect, "Come on, hit me, and the harder you hit me,

the better I like it. But don't hit me too hard, because then I'll hit you back." . . . They do the same thing with games, and mothers often get terribly concerned. "Why is my husband competing with a six-year-old in checkers?" The father is not just playing easy, to teach the child; he gets involved, and he has to win, and the poor kid doesn't stand a chance.[29]

The impulse runs very deep, Vahanian observes:

I know a man, for example, who really loved having children. He talks about the years when his children were small as the greatest years of his life. He especially enjoyed playing with them. But when you listen to the kids, all you hear about is the competitive games that they always played, how even at the dinner table, one was pitted against the other to see who could win out. And this father is one of the kindest men I can imagine.[30]

Many fathers have to win every time, not only in games but in their other dealings with their children. There is no doubt that the traditional manifestations of patriarchy, harsh discipline and absolute, unquestioned authority, have eroded over the last several decades, but the sense of hierarchy and the need to control on which it was based is still very much alive. Under its influence, regardless of their intellectual beliefs about child rearing, fathers often require a stultifying deference from their children. The most common complaint Dr. Vahanian hears from children about their fathers is that they can't talk to him:

What they mean is, "He's always up there, and I'm always down here." The fathers find it impossible to drop that air of authority, of talking to the kid from a distance, and telling him what to do. It doesn't have to do necessarily with the authoritarian spirit in the sense of being a Puritan or being rigidly arbitrary. It's just that the consciousness of status is so strong that there is rarely any give on the father's side, no respect for the integrity of the child's personality. The father doesn't reveal the human side of himself, he can never admit he's wrong, for example. You can't suddenly go up to a kid and say "Let's have a heart-to-heart talk." There's got to be a kind of back and forth that goes on every day. The child has to feel free to say what's on his mind without feeling he's going to be put down for it.

When fathers are challenged by their kids, they tend to lose all perspective. For example, if a boy told his parents to shut up, they would both be justifiably angry. But there would be a difference. The father would probably blow sky-high: "How dare you talk to me like that you little bastard." The mother is less likely to feel personally threatened because her self-image doesn't depend so much on her status. She can see the incident better from the kid's point of view, of his getting to the point where he feels he has no other way out. She's more likely to say: "Don't talk to me that way, I don't like it. Come back later when you can talk to me politely." And then it's over.[31]

Nevertheless, most fathers want very much to be close to their children, even if their conception of what this means is vague and inchoate, and the estrangement which their actual behavior creates is a painful disappointment.

9. Sports:
The Training Ground

Except for war, there is nothing in American life—nothing —which trains a boy better for life than football.

—Robert Kennedy as Attorney General[1]

At a tennis club I once belonged to, you could tell which man had won and which had lost just by watching the players as they came off the court and sat around the clubhouse. The winner was always more ebullient, easier and more expansive than usual; the loser didn't talk much. Even if he played well, he seemed somehow diminished and embarrassed. He might make jokes about it, but his general sense of self-esteem had been affected. Until a few years ago, I used to feel it myself, for some reason particularly when playing squash. When I won I always felt a little more secure in relation to my opponent, more able to take risks. My sense of being on top, of having proven myself to him, extended beyond the confines of the court, even though it faded quickly. When I lost, even if I had played well, it would make me feel on the defensive, even in areas having nothing to do with athletics, as though I had to scramble around to get things back into equilibrium. It took some of the fun out of the game.

Men's preoccupation with winning is reflected in the way they talk about sports—another arena in which to win and move one step up in the masculinity rankings or to lose and move down one step. "Who won?" is almost always the first question; it comes to mind even if unspoken, consciously resisted. Some writers have suggested that black men are less caught up in this syndrome than whites. Clayton Riley, referring to the astonishing agility and body control of football back O. J. Simpson, quotes a black friend:

> White boys only want to know what the final score was; they're only interested in the results. Brothers want to know what happened *in* the game, like "Did O.J. *dance*?"[2]

When learning a sport, men are nearly always impatient with themselves, feeling that they have to reach a certain level of skill right away, instead of enjoying the process of learning. In tennis, for example, men are impatient to play matches, frequently shortchanging themselves on the practice rallies needed to develop consistency and form. In skiing, male beginners and intermediates are often found on slopes much too hard for them, helplessly and sometimes dangerously out of control; learning nothing at all, and, except for the thrill of being afraid, not really enjoying themselves; proving that they can handle the tough slopes takes precedence over everything else.

The intimate association between masculinity and athletics becomes glaringly clear when women try to join the game. If women can play, then, by definition, participation does not prove anything about masculinity. Beating a woman proves nothing; losing to a woman is a major humiliation. As we have seen, this dynamic is at work in many all-male activities, but the resentment stirred up by women's attempts to break the sports barrier is more passionate than in most other areas.

One summer, for example, Brenda and I were on a beach in East Hampton and walked over to watch a volleyball game. When the game ended and some of the players—all male—left;

those remaining called for replacements so a new game could begin. Brenda and I both volunteered. For a moment it looked as though she would be allowed to play, and several women who had been sitting around, apparently content with the traditional spectator role, also got up to join the game. But the man who had brought the net and ball, backed by the other men, said no. "Why?" "You don't play well enough." "How do you know? You've never seen me play. Anyway, you don't know how well he plays either, but that doesn't seem to bother you." "You'll get hurt." "Let me worry about that, just the way you do." And so on. When we refused to get off the "court," he took down the net, picked up his ball, and went home. The incident was so threatening, at least to the man with the equipment, that although the game had been held at the same location for several years, he moved it to another beach for the rest of the summer.

Jean-Claude Killy, the champion skier, has warned that "when a woman is too aggressive in sports, she passes beyond femininity. I admire courage, but the competition skier [i.e; a woman who skis the way he does] is not my kind of woman."[3] In 1970, when a woman first played in a minor-league pro-football game, as a place-kick holder, members of the opposing team commented that she was "prancing around making folly with a man's game," and that her playing "degraded football."[4] In the last few years there have been a spate of lawsuits brought on behalf of girls who want to play Little League baseball.[5] The usual justification for barring them, false at Little League eligibility ages, is that girls are more easily hurt. Most of the objections seem to come from the Little League fathers. In New Jersey, League fathers and managers threatened to scratch the entire 1974 season rather than comply with an order of the State Civil Rights Division to let girls play.[6] How can they be out there building their sons' manhood (and vicariously boosting their own) if the—ugh—girls are out there too?

Coaches are often explicit about the masculinity-destroying prospects of female competition, because, presumably, they aren't discussing their own egos. A *Sports Illustrated* article on women in sport cited two examples as typical: Charles Maas, secretary of the Indiana State Coaches Association, commented on a decision by his state's highest court permitting girls to compete with boys in noncontact sports:

> There is the possibility that a boy would be beaten by a girl and as a result be ashamed to face his family and friends. I wonder if anybody has stopped to think what that could do to a young boy.

Ellen Cornish, a distance runner who was a member of the 1971 U.S. Olympic team, has never been able to compete for her high school—there is no girls' track program and she was not allowed to run on the boys' team. In 1972, arrangements were made for her to enter a two-mile event in a high-school meet on an exhibition basis: any points she won would not count in the meet score. "As it turns out," *Sports Illustrated* reported, "she was handicapped in an even more obvious and effective way. At the end of the seventh lap of the race, with Cornish fighting for the lead, she was pulled off the track, according to a previous agreement between the coaches. This was done to protect the male runners from the morale-shattering possibility of being beaten by a girl, a possibility that was probable."[7]

The feeling that success in athletics is a *sine qua non* of manhood is learned early. In a study of the attitudes of middle-income fathers toward their children, only one out of twenty fathers did not want his boys to be good athletes.[8] The father who pushes his son into sports with missionary zeal is so common as to be a part of our folklore. One man in his twenties, who described himself as having struck out more than any other nine-year-old on his Little Leauge team, told me that his father literally carried him screaming and yelling to the games, where his relatives from a neighboring state across the river would sit in the stands to watch him play. And when he did poorly, his father wouldn't talk to him for several hours after the game. The fact that these extreme instances are funny, as well as sad, does not mean that the more usual climate is benign.

Pressure from parents, nearly always fathers, peers, and other male adults, results in a skewing of values which tend to make sports a compulsion for many boys, the mandated center of their lives. Some boys can live with this. Stuart, a twelve-year-old "three-letter man" described his life to a reporter:

> I've been in Little League since I was 8. But I've been throwing the ball since I was 4 or 5. I like soccer, basketball and baseball best. It's all I do, play sports.[9]

Stuart may be another Rafer Johnson in the making, but what if he isn't? There probably ought to be more in his life than sports. Looking back on my junior high school days, I am sure that some of my afternoons could have been better spent on something other than playing whatever sport was in season.

Boys who can't conform easily to the athletic ideal are made to feel inadequate. They either quit completely, developing a compensatory disdain for sports as a result and giving up its genuine pleasures for the rest of their lives; or they keep trying, setting standards for themselves that have nothing to do with their own talents or desires. Images of Richard Nixon and Robert Kennedy come to mind, the first uncoordinated and the other too small, both doggedly, probably desperately, hanging on as second-string college football players. Gary Shaw asked a former football teammate at the University of Texas, who had to quit because of injuries, how he felt about it, and characterized the attitudes revealed by his answer as typical of members of the team:

> "How did you feel about quitting?"
>
> "Crushed . . . humiliated. My whole world came tumbling down. . . . I felt like I let you guys down. I'd broken the 'code.'"
>
> "What code?"
>
> "The code we had, to agree never to quit, never give in, never give up. I didn't feel like I could face any of you. I thought you would look down on me. Still to this day, Gary, I feel you and the others who stuck it out have something inside of you because of that reason. I guess I'll really never get over it.

"It took me at least three years to accept the fact that I had quit, and could still do other worthwhile things. And still, when I go back to see old players on the team or old coaches, I feel embarassed, ashamed."[10]

I felt similar pressures, though not as extreme as this. In high school, I joined the wrestling team—I wanted to "build myself up." I was at best an average wrestler, and although I didn't hate it, I didn't like it that well either. The next year when I injured my arm and had to stop, I discovered that I was glad. Without the excuse of an injury, I had not felt free to quit.

The conventional wisdom about sports is that it is valuable beyond the experience itself, that it builds character, *masculine* character. The fathers in the study mentioned earlier were not concerned with athletics because they wanted their sons to grow up to be professional athletes but because "failure along these lines seems to symbolize for the father inability to be properly aggressive and competitive, now and in the future."[11] Men I interviewed thought sports were important for their sons because participation taught them how to compete in a rough world and how to get along with other people. But does sport actually build character? And, if it does, what kind of character?

Two psychologists who have studied the effects of athletic competition on personality for eight years and tested approximately fifteen thousand athletes from the high-school gym to the professional level, have tried to answer that question:

We found no empirical support for the tradition that sport builds character. Indeed, there is evidence that athletic competition limits growth in some areas. It seems that the personality of the ideal athlete is not the result of any molding process, but comes out of the ruthless selection process that occurs at all levels of sport. Athletic competition has no more beneficial effects than intense endeavor in any other field. Horatio Alger success—in sport or elswhere—comes only to those who already are mentally fit, resilient and strong.[12]

Men who survive the attrition of our culture's highly competitive, star-oriented sports system for the most part have personalities that conform to the traditional male stereotype: high in achievement need, respectful of authority, dominant among peers, self-controlled, and low in sensitivity to other people.[13] Interestingly enough, the psychologists also noted,

> We have also seen some indications that there may be an *upper* limit on the character development needed for success in sports. Sometimes we find players who have good physical skills with immense character strengths who don't make it in sports. They seem to be so well put together emotionally that there is no neurotic tie to sport. The rewards of sport aren't enough for them any more, and they turn away voluntarily to other, more challenging fields.[14]

Could it be that such men are "so well put together" that, among other things, they simply don't need athletic success to feel adequate as men?

On the character-building front, there is also evidence that those who don't make it to the top suffer a great deal. The University of Texas football player quoted earlier is not an isolated example. With the "winning is everything" approach, money, personnel, equipment, and emotional energy are spent on a few teams of the very best athletes,* while other men either are discouraged from participating or take a psychological beating if they do. Substitutes on high-school, college, and professional teams—second-stringers who don't play much but are kept around for the good of the team—are often depressed and suffer substantial loss of self-esteem.[15] To some extent, of course, that's life, on or off the playing field. But people learn it soon enough. Why structure amateur sport—which, at least in theory, has as its purpose the pleasure and development of its participants—so that many of the participants and would-be participants lose rather than gain from the experience? People learn and gain confidence from facing challenges that, with

---

* Women's athletics, of course, are short-changed even more drastically.

effort, they can meet, not from struggling in a system geared to the interests and abilities of the very few. Amateur sport, if designed more for the broad range of ability and commitment of potential participants and made an opportunity rather than a compulsion, could build a lot more character than it does today. But that would require the coaches, and their various publics, to care more about this than about sending their football team to the Cotton Bowl. Contemplating the unlikelihood of that set of priorities, we are led directly to the question of why men watch sports and what they get out of it.

The great chunks of their lives that men spend as spectators of sports can be partly explained, of course, by intrinsic interest. Professional athletes are often incredibly skilled and graceful, and even college football has moments of drama. But game after game, sport after sport, season after season, it can't be that interesting. The same moves are made, passes thrown and caught, championships won and lost; among the pros, all the players are so good that excellence becomes routine. Visual, aesthetic interest alone is not enough to explain the emotional commitment of male sports fans. I like to watch fifteen minutes of a football or basketball game occasionally and, because tennis is the sport I play most myself, I watch tennis on television more often and I go to watch about one tournament a year. Even there, after a match and a half, I've had enough. The drama isn't personally involving enough to absorb me any longer.

But many men are caught up in emotionally meaningful ways. In most spectator sports, especially football, qualities thought to be particularly masculine are at a premium: strength, speed, coolness under pressure, teamwork, the risk of violence, and the drive to win: then there is the satisfaction of a clear-cut decision—one team is a winner, the other a loser. Men understand and identify with these values and codes even if they are not athletes themselves. By devoted spectating and rooting, they vicariously affirm their membership in the club of certified males. Nixon phones plays into the Washington Redskins locker room at half-time. Dave Meggyesy has described a particular brand of avid football fan known to the players as "jock-sniffers": "They were wealthy [men] who would contribute to the under-the-table fund [for the college team] for the privilege of rubbing shoulders with big-name football players."[16] The too-fat or too-skinny boys who take on the thankless job of team manager in high school or college are paying differently for the same associations. Ordered about ruthlessly, sometimes labled as "pussies" by playing members of the team, they hope that somehow , the aura of masculinity surrounding the players will rub off on them. Men watching sports are often doing the same thing at one remove.

Of course, it works better if you watch the game with somebody else. Women are O.K. to watch with because your manly knowledge of the game contrasts nicely with their feminine ignorance. On the other hand, they tend to lose interest. For the long viewing haul, men are much better. The main psychic payoff from watching the Super Bowl is in talking about it with other men, either at the time or later. "Did you see Unitas throw that forty-five yarder toward the left sideline?" "Yeah, I thought that two-hundred-pound motherfucker of a tackle was gonna get him, but he put it right in Berry's hand. That guy has guts." The exchange provides a mutual confirmation of manliness. Maybe this function of sports talk explains why some very intelligent and sophisticated men, accomplished in fields other than athletics, absorb incredible amounts of information about sports, and regurgitate it at the slightest excuse. They pass it off as an eccentricity, but they wouldn't have invested the time and effort in learning it unless some fairly substantial reward were involved.

Besides the weather, sport is virtually the only topic of casual conversation that crosses class barriers for men. A businessman, doctor , lawyer, writer, or banker to his doorman (or chauffeur, security guard, barber, locker-room attendant, etc.): "Quite a game last night, eh, Walter? Did you watch it?" "Yes, sir. In fact, I had five on the Knicks." "That's great, Walter . . . See you later."

Despite social and economic differences, says the interchange, we are both *men*.

Sports is also one of the few things men feel they are allowed to become emotional about. Sitting in a bar, grunting, groaning, elbowing each other in the ribs and exclaiming over the ebb and flow of a football game on the owner's TV is the closest a lot of men come to sharing strong feelings with another man. One man I know, an intelligent, progressive, and urbane government professor, is transformed at hockey games. He bounds out of his seat with every shot, yelling for his team, encouraging the players by name, shouting directions to the manager, and generally spends the evening in a high state of excitement. He discusses the games with other *aficionados* at lengths which seem incongruous for someone with so many other things on his mind. It's very clear that his interest in hockey, as well as being tied to a romantic revisitation of his own unspectacular but fondly remembered hockey-playing days, has a lot to do with the fact that he feels free in this setting to get excited and enthused and demonstrative and to communicate those feelings to other men.

Touchdowns and other moments of victory in sports provide some of the rare circumstances in which men—members of the team, mainly, but fans too if they look like they're in enough of a frenzy—are permitted to grab and hug each other. In wrestling and football, physical contact is permitted which would otherwise be labeled as homosexual. In fact, Norman Mailer, with the zeal of an inquisitioner researching mortal sin, has traced the players' habitual gesture of bottom-slapping to its origin in homosexual flirtation. [17]

For men sports provide a kind of state religion, something they can care about and share in a way which reaffirms the most basic component of their identity; Philip Roth, writing about his love affair with baseball, spelled it out:

> To sing the National Anthem in school auditorium every week, even during the worst of the war years, generally left me cold; the enthusiastic *lady* teacher waved her arms in the air and we obliged

with the words: "See! Light! Proof! Night! There!" Nothing stirred within, strident as we might be—in the end just another school exercise. But on Sundays out at Ruppert Stadium (a green wedge of pasture miraculously walled in among the factories, warehouses and truck depots of Newark's industrial "Ironbound" section), waiting for the Newark Bears to take on the enemy from across the marshes, the hated Jersey City Giants (within our church the schisms are profound), it would have seemed to me an emotional thrill forsaken, if we had not to rise first to our feet (my father, my brother, and me—together with our inimical country-men, Newark's Irishmen, Germans, Italians, Poles, and out in the Africa of the bleachers, Newark's Negroes) to celebrate the America that had given to this disparate collection of *men and boys* a game so grand and beautiful. [18]

This aspect of the male preoccupation with sport, although pathetic, is more or less benign. But it has a darker side: the use of athletic competition as a model for behavior and problem-solving in other areas of life. Competition *is* the central dynamic of organized athletics. Its other benefits (and costs), unlike those of activities which produce a tangible product rather than abstract "victories," are personal to the athlete and sometimes hard to measure. So it has been easy to make athletic competition into a superficially rational paradigm of total, unqualified pursuit of victory. And because the subtler, personal rewards and pleasures of sports are played down, in fact often destroyed by this approach, the pursuit becomes a never ending one; one's sense of achievement depends entirely on winning. Absolute team loyalty, unquestioning obedience to authority, respectful fear and hatred of the opposition, disregard of individual injury and suffering—all justified in the name of victory—these are the axioms of the sports system. As a consequence, it attracts, as its permanent managers, men with these values. [19] For example, the mother of Don Shula, coach of the Miami Dolphins, pro-football Super Bowl winners, described the history of her son's "will to win":

He hates to lose. When he was eight years old, he would play cards with his grandmother. If he lost, he would tear up the cards and run and hide under the porch. You couldn't pry him out for supper.[20]

It is just this all-out competitiveness that makes fathers view athletics as an important training ground for their sons. For example, Joseph Kennedy, the patriarch of the Kennedy family whose dedication to the precepts "win at all costs" and "second place is losing" is well-documented, made heavy use of athletic competition to inculcate these values into his children. During summers at Hyannisport, he organized arduous sailing, swimming, and tennis competitions for them. To make sure they got the point,

> he trail[ed] his children's sailboats in his power launch to note their mistakes. Those who erred and lost races were sharply scolded and sometimes sent in disgrace to eat dinner in the kitchen.[21]

President Nixon's belief that the qualities needed to win in football are the same as those needed "to win" in life is familiar to all of us.[22] Football terms and slogans appear in his Administration's statements on almost every kind of issue, but especially foreign policy. At a reception for the quarterback of the Green Bay Packers, Nixon said,

> A word about your Secretary of Defense . . . [We] know that the defense is essential if you are going to be able to win the game . . . . The defense is important, as Mel Laird has said, not because the United States wants a war, but because with that kind of defense we can discourage anyone who might want to engage in an offense.[23]

Here's Laird himself, announcing and justifying stepped-up bombing in North Vietnam and the mining of Haiphong harbor:

> We have sort of an expansion ball club that's fighting in Vietnam at the present time. The South Vietnamese will not win every battle or encounter, but they will do a very credible job.[24]

And it was reported that

> The new bombing and mining offense had left the Pentagon with the code name Operation Iron Hand. It came out of the White House as Operation Linebacker. Nixon's code name was Quarterback.[25]

John S. D. Eisenhower, son of the former President and once ambassador to Belgium, wrote a column for *The New York Times* in 1973 that was a paradigm of this kind of thinking. Entitled "The Coach, " it offered the trials of West Point football coach Earl Blaik as a predictive parable about the problems of Richard Nixon, "our nation's Coach." Its bland analogy between a football team caught cheating and a national Administration in the throes of Watergate, between a football coach with one glorious obsession—"to win"—and the President of the United States, and its easy assumption that the only important objective for both is to rebuild the team (Administration) so it can go on to "victory" is at once incredible and disturbingly familiar in its "big game" approach to life. Here is an excerpt describing the "comeback" achieved through the Coach's personality and "fight:"

> Gradually the Coach rebuilt. He took his defeats, using scrubs for a while, but he continued to rebuild with a determination that few men could muster. Gradually he and his new team came from the depths of defeat to eventual renewed success. When it finally came time for him to set aside his responsibilities as Coach, he had once more created a team that went undefeated for the season. The Coach, exonerated, retired, and the Institution was restored.[26]

If the analogizing of national and international life to football went no farther than occasional and superficial use of sportspeak, no great harm would be done. Nixon, in all likelihood, would believe that winning is everything even if he had never heard of football. But sport—especially football—reflects society's dominant, traditional masculine ethos in a particularly clear and magnified form. For this reason, and because of its role as a key masculinity-affirming ritual, sports play an active part in the dialectic between the individual and the society which perpetuates these values. In particular, it supplies a language and rationale for men to use in nonsports situations, a language which is widely understood and which reduces the more complex real-life problems of choosing objectives and weighing human costs to the simplistic imperatives of a competitive game.

10. Work

Without work all life goes rotten. But when work is soulless, life stifles and dies.

—Albert Camus

All I knew was that you had to run, run, run, without knowing why you were running, but on you went through fields you didn't understand and into woods that made you afraid, over hills without knowing you'd been up and down, and shooting across streams that would have cut the heart out of you had you fallen into them. And the winning post was no end to it, even though the crowds might be cheering you in, because on you had to go. . . .

—Allan Sillitoe, *The Loneliness of the Long Distance Runner*

Work, understood as "activity which produces something of value for other people,"[1] is crucial to every human being's sense of identity and self-esteem. As Elliot Jaques has written:

Working for a living is one of the basic activities in a man's [sic] life. By forcing him to come to grips with his environment, with his livelihood at stake, it confronts him with actuality of his personal capacity to exercise judgment, to achieve concrete and specific results. It gives him a continuous account of his correspondence between outside reality and the inner perception of that reality, as well as an account of the accuracy of his appraisal of himself. . . . In short, a man's work does not satisfy his material needs alone. In a very deep sense, it gives him a measure of his sanity.[2]

The masculine ethos recognizes the importance of work. In fact, work is the area of life into which "masculine" traits are thought to fit best and the principal adult arena for proving one's masculinity. Our dominant social philosophy, influenced by and influencing the masculine stereotype, makes work an essential determinant of moral worth. But this system of belief, while accepting and incorporating what is unquestionably one of the basic principles of human existence—the key role of work in self-actualization—narrows and distorts the meaning of work and, at the same time, makes of it what it is not: the *only* activity worth a full measure of a man's time and energy.

Apart from economic reward, men are taught to value work primarily as an opportunity for successful competition. The undebated first principal of our social philosophy, articulated by Smith and Locke and elaborated by John Stuart Mill and the Social Darwinists, is that competition in a free marketplace is good, that it results in the most efficient production of the best goods, that it pushes to the fore the best ideas, and most important, in the process selects out the best men. There have been points of disagreement, but, as Garry Wills has written, they are largely matters of emphasis:

> The Left has stressed *equality* of opportunity. The Right has stressed opportunity to *achieve*. Yet each side allows for considerable adjustment. The Left . . . stresses that welfare is meant to "put a man on his feet," so he can be a productive competitor. . . . And the Right does not deny the need to help some men get started; it just argues points of fact (i.e., does this or that welfare scheme destroy initiative instead of creating it?).[3]

The individual man proves his worth in this race not by a single victory or achievement—for there is no end, no agreed-upon goal—but moment by moment, his value rising and falling depending on the reception accorded his efforts by the market. The emphasis is not on having risen, but on rising. Wills notes the titles of the Horatio Alger stories (*Making His Way, Helping Himself, Bound to Rise, Struggling Upward*) and points out:

> The [Horatio Alger] hero did not aim at success but at succeeding—that is, at character formation and "self-improvement." . . . The self-made man is the true American monster. The man who wants to make something outside himself— a chair, a poem, a million dollars—produces something. It can be praised or condemned; but it is "out there," a thing wrought or won or subdued, apart from the self. The *self-maker*, self-improving, is always a construction in progress. The man's product is never finished, not severed from him to stand on its own. He must ever be tinkering, improving, adjusting; starting over, fearful his product will get out of date, or rot in the storehouse.[4]

The contemporary version of the Horatio Alger story (in the form of an animal fable since the straight dose has begun to jar the sensibilities) is the immensely popular *Jonathan Livingston Seagull*. The hero of the story, described by Philip Slater as "a sort of avian Charles Atlas or self-made entrepreneur,"[5] devotes his whole life to mastery and self-improvement. He trains endlessly for faster and faster flight; spurning and spurned by his more hedonistic fellows, properly heedless of the danger to others posed by his efforts, he achieves a new speed record—214 miles an hour. "It was a breakthrough, the greatest single moment in the history of the Flock," the author tells us happily. But Jonathan must continue to prove his superiority, this time by inventing Seagull acrobatics. Still the lonely pioneer, defying the limits of his body, he achieves "a reason to life." His exploits vindicate him with the flock and make him immortal—literally—not just famous. But even then his frantic striving after mastery and control does not stop. "Even when he reaches a kind of heaven," Slater writes, "it turns out to be simply another gym, where the Superbirds spend 'hour after hour every day practicing flight, testing advanced aeronautics.'"[6]

The masculine stereotype reflected in these myths has been the major vehicle for transmitting the obsession with proving oneself through competition from one generation to the next. It focuses men's attention on developing and demonstrating in their work those traits required for masculine self-esteem —rather than on the work itself as an unfettered expression of their individual personalities. Competitiveness is not only emphasized as a desirable trait in men but is seen as an absolute requirement for masculinity—real men are dominant and aggressive, traits which can only be demonstrated through competition. And since the point is to prove that one is the kind of man who "has what it takes" to succeed in the arena—not the completion of a particular project (or even a particular project at a particular time followed by another project)—the real job is never done. The authors of a study of big-business leaders in America found this to be a central and endemic problem:

> What is the point at which these men can stop, look back, and announce to themselves and their world that they have completed this long journey, that they will rest now? There does not seem to be such a point, for an essential part of the system is the need for constant demonstration of one's adequacy, for reiterated proof of one's independence.[7]

Certain jobs are considered more acceptably "masculine" than others. For example, middle-income fathers in a study by Aberle and Naegele tended to reject academic work as a possible career for their sons. Apart from the question of financial reward, they did "not consider the academic role to exemplify appropriate masculine behavior."[8] The one father who said such a role would be fine for his son described him as shy, irresponsible, bookish, and needing a woman to take care of him. It is not hard to imagine how these men would react to the idea of their sons being classical musicians (perhaps the role of orchestra conductor, the leader of other men, would be acceptable) or ballet dancers.

Men who don't choose characteristically masculine careers

often feel pressured to show that, although they are intellectuals, professors, managers of charitable institutions, they are nevertheless tough and manly. Some do it by taking the tough fundamentalist position on social issues. Since the fifties, liberal professors, encouraged by their OSS wartime experiences, have taken pains to present themselves as pragmatic men acquainted with the hard facts of power and to distinguish themselves from those who fear it. The typical voice, Wills points out, has been Arthur Schlesinger's:

> [I]n The Vital Center, he had found the tone . . . and he obviously enjoyed writing Bogart stuff out of the corners of his pen. After adopting Hemingway as his political guide, Professor Schlesinger said that modern liberalism's political leaders brought a new virility into public life, "a sense of the gusto of democracy," to rescue us from the "political sterility" of the older (classical) liberalism and the "frenzied flight from doubt" on the part of doctrinaire Leftists. . . .
>
> The [leftist] ideologue is "sentimental" in his approach to the political realities—"soft, not hard," because "he has rejected the pragmatic tradition of the men who, from the Jacksonians to the New Dealers, learned the facts of life through the exercise of power."[9]

We shall see in Chapter 12 what sound, objective counsel these intellectuals gave when they left the ivory tower to advise the New Frontier on foreign policy.

For myself, one of the reasons I went to law school rather than into one of the social sciences was that law school and the practice of law seemed to be tougher and more combative, and thus better training for vaguely envisioned positions of power and responsibility in government. In the actual practice of law, I have gotten what now seems to me to be an inordinate amount of satisfaction out of success in adversary negotiations, out of the fact of making my view prevail. Nearly all of my career decisions since law school have been heavily influenced by my estimate of where I could go next. I haven't had a specific plan in mind, but certain possibilities have been eliminated (I simply haven't considered them appealing) because they seemed somehow out of the main arena and unlikely to lead directly up, to positions of greater power and status. The point is not that the considerations which influenced me are necessarily illegitimate but that they have been so pervasive and deeply ingrained that they have often made it difficult for me to know, all other things being equal, what I *want* to do.

The focus on status goals as opposed to particular substantive work is an accepted aspect of corporate life. A psychologist working for one of the country's largest banks, institutions not known for their fiercely competitive atmospheres, told me that managers recruiting young executives look for men who express their career objectives in terms of reaching a particular level in the bank, rather than in terms of an interest in a particular aspect of banking—making commercial loans, for example. The recruiters, he observed, don't have much confidence in the applicant who says he is interested in the substance of the job itself; they sense that he might not play by the usual rules.

Once in a job, success demonstrably traceable to one's individual efforts and movement upward to the next job tend to become the primary, if not always openly stated, objectives. Psychologist Judith Bardwick, in a study of very successful men, quotes the following exchange:

Q. Why do you work so hard? Do you have any idea?

A. I don't know. I guess I enjoy it to a great extent. . . . I really hate to be a failure. I always wanted to be on top of whatever I was doing. It depends on the particular picture but I like to be on top, either chairman of the committee or president of an association or whatever.[10]

A young executive at one of the major manufacturing companies spelled out some of the specifics of this attitude for me. Malcolm was thirty-one years old, married, with children; he was from a middle-income family, had a B.A. but no graduate training, was making approximately thirty thousand dollars a year, and was very highly rated by the company. He was at the point of deciding whether or not to make a major career commitment to the company. On the one hand, he was very well paid with prospects of making a great deal more money in the future and doing some work which he liked—no equally rewarding opportunities were open to him if he chose to leave the company. On the other hand, he saw with remarkable clarity the cost to himself and to his family of continuing to work for the company. Although his ambivalence and the pressure on him to reach a decision make his observations unusually vivid and unguarded, industrial psychologists have confirmed to me that they are applicable to men in many sizable corporations. Here is Malcolm's response to questions about the emphasis among his colleagues on moving up:

The word around the company is: "You never stand still. You're either moving ahead or moving downstairs. And once they catch you standing still, you're on the way down." The aggressive, motivated individual is a generalist. And he will do any job. The way a person gets to the top, very simply, is to try to take two- and three-year stints, two years here, two years there. He's capable of moving. They like his ability to continually uproot his family. Is he willing to go out to Seattle, Washington? . . . it proves that he is interested in going to the top.

Q. What if he has an upper-middle-level job, which suits his talents to a T and he isn't interested in moving up—what's the attitude of the company?

A. The attitude of the key executives is that after a certain period of time you become ineffective. The theory is that if you stay in a job too long—say three years—you get stereotyped as an expert in the job, you're not moving ahead. The person who wants to do what we call "go for the golden ring" can't do that. You have to make your decision. In my company if you're not making over fifty-five thousand dollars by the time you're forty, you're on your way down. The age is different in other industries, I think. Here, you're washed up at about thirty-eight, thirty-nine. You're washed up at about fifty-two in others.

In the Bardwick study, the men "would frequently say that they wanted increased responsibility which was not shared, where everything would be subject to their control or decision and the outcome was success or failure."[11] Personal ambition poses no problem for the company or project if the market is working as ordained by Locke, Mill, and Adam Smith—in other words, rewarding those who do the most useful work with the indicia of competitive success. But in areas where this is not the case—areas like government, where the problems are not only vitally important but difficult for one man to "solve"—the obsession with success traceable to one's individual efforts, with mastering a problem *so as* to get on to the next challenge, is costly. It drives many of the most capable men out of government (after the glamour wears off) and keeps others from even trying. Very few of the men in the Bardwick study had spent any time at all in government service. Those few who did, despite appointment to high positions, quickly left in frustration. They were discouraged by the degree to which political accommodation and the workings of bureaucracy—an inevitable part of dealing with complex problems involving varied and important interests—limited their freedom of action. Because they were overly concerned with living up to the anachronistic ideal of making an independent success, they found little satisfaction in sharing the responsibility and were unwilling to tackle what they had labeled as problems they could not "solve":

> "Once in a while if I'm faced with a problem I can't solve—a whole bunch of social problems, say—if I get four or five problems that are major problems, I think how little I can do about that at the time and I can get kind of discouraged and say, "Well, I really should think about something else. I really should look at trying to spend my time in some other area."[12]

Because work is the main proving ground of masculinity, all the "male" traits, not just "competitiveness," must be displayed there. Toughness is valued, often as an end in itself, without real consideration of whether or not it is in fact functional. Although the particulars differ, Gary Shaw's description of the atmosphere among University of Texas football players could also be applied to an ordinary day at the office:

> All our words and actions seemed directed toward presenting a tough image. A subtle playacting to this end was used from the very first day, and would continue throughout our careers.[13]

The bank psychologist told me that it is common practice for a new regional manager to fire fifteen of his sixty branch managers, without regard to competence, just to demonstrate to his superiors that he is tough enough to handle the job. When the basic measuring stick, profitability, can't be used to distinguish among executives eligible for promotion, the decision is based on who has the greatest reputation for toughness instead of criteria functionally related to the needs of the enterprise.

Another corporate informant told me of a high-level executive with an excellent performance record who had been indirectly informed that he had no future with the company and should look for another job. He had broken down and cried at a meeting when he was told that, for reasons having to do with his boss' efforts at self-aggrandizement, a project he had spent a year developing was being taken over by someone else. The display of weakness had totally discredited him with his colleagues.

At one of the nation's largest corporations, a top executive was once assigned the task of interrupting the presentations of a promising manager by walking up to the charts being used for the talk, throwing them to the ground, stamping on them, and returning to his seat without a word. The idea was to test the speaker. He passed if he kept his cool and resumed his presentation without appearing to be upset.

Malcolm described to me a practice in his company known as "verbal brutalization":

> Verbal brutalization happens a lot. It goes something like this: "What's the so-and-so for this?" your superior says to you, and you say, "I don't know."

"Well, can you get it? Do you have it? Can you pick it up this afternoon? I need it. You come up here, the job's not complete—Oh, for cryin' out loud!" This is the approved way of telling someone that he has done an inadequate job.

So he continues to rant and rave, and you try to get out of it: "I don't want to see anything else, I don't care if you've got a program that's one of the most creative ideas I ever saw. Where's this piece of information? Let's get it here by three o'clock."

By the way, sometimes the piece of information you have to get is not a simple number. It's something that's going to take about three weeks to do. And you've got to come up with it in a couple of hours. But it's the kind of thing where usually there's an audience around—you have to understand this—not only the person being beat up and the person beating up, but a few other key executives, usually lower than the person that's doing the beating up.

Q. Is toughness an independently valued quality?

A. It's highly valued in a marketing environment. Marketing people are very action-oriented, very no-nonsense-oriented. They set the tone for the company and only they make it to the top. There are certain characteristics that the company looks for in key executives. One is the time element—an executive ain't got too much time. Second is being very curt, very NET. (We have little signs that say NET, which means "No Extra Talk." Straight to the point! We have little signs that say WRITE TO THE POINT! W-R-I-T-E to the point, get it? We have little phrases that say DON'T GIVE ME PARAGRAPHS, GIVE ME BULLETS.) Three is the ability to beat up people. And do it, by the way, when you're right. I'm not saying that the beat-up is rational, it's not rational, but it may be substantively correct.

The guy that is respected is a guy who has classic stories following him on up the line, of brutalizing people, stepping on toes. Let me tell you a story that circulated about one executive: "He walked into this building, he didn't like the wallpaper and the carpet, and he changed it around in six hours! He had a crew in there, and he changed the whole place around. What a great guy."

I once heard a man in an executive meeting make a presentation, three hours, and a director said at the end, "I heard you. You said nothing. I don't like your program. You're doing nothing." And the guy said, "But don't you—" "I saw the charts, I'm not a dummy, you're doing nothing." "But I have—" "No." Later, he said privately to this other executive, "I don't want to see this guy in the building again." Two weeks later, he was not in the building. It was simple, a very simple operation.

I had my first conscious encounter with the toughness ethic when I was in college, during the glory days of the New Frontier. I remember being impressed by the magazine profiles of leading members of the Administration. Each one was tougher than the last. McGeorge Bundy had a "steel-trap" mind, wasted no words, was always in perfect control of the meetings he chaired; all intellect, the only emotion he permitted himself was irritation over the stupidity of lesser minds. Except at dinner parties, where he was wit personified. Same for Robert McNamara. Above all, they were "pragmatic." Give them a problem, they give you an answer. No mushy talk about values or whether this particular challenge *should* be met. Orville Freeman had been a Marine. Roger Hilsman had fought behind the lines in Burma during World War II. They all worked sixteen-hour days. The Kennedys, of course, were the toughest of all. Football. PT-109. Robert Kennedy's finger in a local pol's gut, telling him, "Do it!" Jack's nerveless poise.

At the time I wanted to serve under such a President. I remember consciously measuring myself against the style the Kennedys set and wondering whether I would be tough enough. I tried to maintain a flat, even tone in conversation. I discussed only issues, the larger the better. I worried about every instance of doubt, of self-consciousness, of emotion, of not being in control of groups I was in. The men I admired seemed to feel none of these things. Since I did, how could I play the game?

I did not see then, or until years later, that, as Nancy Gager Clinch wrote, we needed:

> A national leader capable of a revolutionary approach, a person who felt the terrible need for enormous change in his heart and bones and was not content with forming the words with his lips. Kennedy was emotionally incapable of such a response, for his best emotions seemed to be locked tightly within himself. He had insulated himself too successfully from his own feelings. Thus his

undoubted natural and cultivated intelligence could only function
at half-power, for intelligence is largely motivated and broadened
by feelings. Kennedy could not see clearly because he could not
feel clearly. Although verbally articulate, he was psychologically
separated from the agonies of the nation he wished quite
genuinely to lead and help. [14]

I did not see that, like men preoccupied with rising to the top of
the companies they work for, the Kennedy Administration was
preoccupied with victory, with its own tough, cool image, with
protecting its political resources and power. And this preoccupation robbed it of the ability to focus on the actual work of meeting
the nation's needs. The men of the Kennedy Administration
knew that they wanted to accomplish, but they were blocked
from knowing what, really, they wanted to do. For all the rhetoric
about civil rights [15] and the alleviation of poverty, the consistent,
continuous effort that grows out of substantive conviction was
lacking.

The cult of toughness can also be seen in the initiation rites of
the professions and some businesses. Pledgees are typically put
through the ordeal of working incredibly long hours, a proof of
the ability to "take it." Hospital interns are worked around the
clock. Architecture students, Caroline Bird points out, are given
design problems that can't be completed by the time they are due
unless the team works through the night. [16] Law firms, especially
the big ones which can afford it, are legendary for giving young
associates impossible, and often phony, deadlines and for making them draft long complicated documents from scratch "for the
experience" instead of using others as models. Malcolm reports
that all first presentations or reports by new managers are ripped
to shreds regardless of their actual quality.

These initiation rites also reinforce other elements of the "masculine" work style. One of these is excessive belief in and re-
liance on hierarchy. The strenuous rites of passage establish that
the young will do the bidding of the old, without rhyme or
reason; and they create, through the "I-had-to-suffer-so-you

will-too" dynamic, the desire to perpetuate the hierarchy. Being somebody's boss, having power to tell him what to do—especially things he wouldn't do otherwise—has enormous psychological rewards in a system where competition is the name of the game. I have heard experienced associates in law firms refer reverentially to the partner they work with as "the senior." A minor, casual question from this presence, though not worth the effort in practical terms, sends them into the library for days. Large corporate law firms often send three representatives to negotiations. They file in like penguins, partner first, senior associate next, and then the young associate, each one's chin inclined a well-calibrated few degrees lower than the last, each progressively more subdued. At the meeting, the senior associate, who is perfectly capable of doing the work (and in fact will do it and represent the client at most working meetings), sits meekly by. He may be thirty-three or thirty-four, on the doorstep of a junior partnership, but his demeanor in the presence of the senior is that of an adolescent.

Nonetheless, my impression is that there is less actual verbal abuse of subordinates in the professions than in business. The deference seems built in, congenial to both the grandees and the juniors, but softened to some extent by a shared professionalism. Moreover, lawyers and doctors deal with lay people over whom, in their area of expertise, they have great authority. And there are usually only three to five layers in professional hierarchies, even in large law firms.

In industry, however, most employees, even executives in a large corporation, deal primarily with each other. Corporations have many more levels of authority and status and, as the report of the Special Task Force on Work in America says,

> typically organize work in such a way as to minimize the independence of workers and maximize control . . . for the organization. Characterologically, the hierarchical organization requires workers to follow orders, which calls for submissive traits, while the selection of managers calls for authoritarian traits.[17]

Later we will see to what extent this structure is actually necessary at the blue-collar level. Here is Malcolm's response to the
question of whether hierarchical deference in the executive ranks
exceeds functional limits:

> Yes, it does. There's the "It's for Joe" syndrome. This affects both
> executives and plebeians. "Got to do a project, stay tonight until
> eleven." "Why?" "*Joe said!*" There's no reason given.
>
> I'll never forget the time that I was dealing directly with a high
> executive in the company and my immediate boss was out. The
> high executive said to me, "I would like to see what you're propos-
> ing, and I would like to see it on flip charts." And I said, "Those
> charts are going to take me a year and a day. I'll just make some
> slides." When my boss came back and he asked me, "Are you
> going to see the high executive today?" I said, "Yes." He said,
> "Do you have the charts for him?" I said, "I have slides." He said,
> "*Slides?* But he wanted flip charts." I said, "Look, he agreed to
> slides. They're easier to make." "I don't care what he agreed to,"
> he yelled, "*what did he want?*"
>
> Then there's the inability of executives, in a high-level meeting, to
> say, "I don't know," to a superior. The chairman may be a vice-
> president or the president. As we're sitting around discussing
> something we're going to make a decision on, someone says,
> "What's the ratio of dollars to men out in the South?" Nobody can
> say, "I don't know, I'll do my best to find out. It will take a few
> days." Somebody has to come up with a figure. Eight-point-one
> to one. They just throw out one that's kind of in the ball park
> because they're afraid to admit to the president that they don't
> know. And the decision is made on that figure!

Another executive told me it is common practice in his company
for managers to react to questioning from subordinates as a
challenge, an opportunity to test their powers in debate—a debate, however, that the subordinate is expected, indeed required, to lose.

The deference and awe shown for higher-ups seem to exceed
the actual requirements of even the most authoritarian corporate
structures. Moreover, men *feel* this awe and need to defer, they
are not just following an externally imposed pattern of behavior.
Success on the job is virtually the entire measure of a man. Thus

men tend to see their bosses not as people—more experienced and knowledgeable, perhaps more capable in some areas, yet still fellow human beings—but instead, as beings certified as superior on the only scale that really matters. The less genuine human contact a man has with a higher-up the less chance there is for erosion of this one-dimensional view.

In addition, a man's need to control the hostility generated by the authoritarian behavior of superiors, and his unconscious fear that he might not be able to control his anger, create a defensive overreaction: he protects himself from blowing up by unconsciously generating emotions—fears, awe, an unconditional desire to please—which prevent it.

Finally, a man's exaggerated fears of dependence and of being dominated by others have the paradoxical effect of making him more servile. If a subordinate defers automatically, plays the yes-man to his boss, he never has to have a real confrontation with him, a confrontation that would sometimes end in a face-to-face assertion of authority directed at the subordinate—"Do it because I said so," or the like. The automatic servility that avoids this direct assertion of control is rationalized as unavoidable and by the fact that it is a form of behavior accepted by fellow employees. Only a few men seem really to enjoy fawning, but the imperatives of the masculine stereotype and the hierarchical structure of work often make such behavior a low-risk strategy emotionally.

When I was in Coast Guard boot camp, an extreme model of a masculine hierarchy, all three of these phenomena were taking place. I hated the discipline; I hated being ordered to do dumb things by men I didn't respect; and I hated the drill instructor since he personified all these things. But what I hated most of all was that, some of the time, I was doing more than going through the motions; I actually *felt* deferential.

Basic to all of this, of course, is an enormous emphasis on competition.

In law schools (even at Harvard where the percentage of students flunking out is minuscule and anyone who gets through is

assured of a good selection of job offers) first-year examinations
have meant hysteria for many students: studying for days without sleep; agonizing over whether a roommate or the person
across the hall is studying harder; frantic efforts to write everything down; a few nervous breakdowns—all stimulated for the
most part by concern over how well one will do *relative to others in
the class*. It was common knowledge when I was in law school
that many students who didn't make the Law Review or the other
honorary societies—in other words, who weren't in the top tenth
of the class—felt so beaten down that it took several years after
law school for them to recognize that they were, nevertheless,
highly capable lawyers. Although not as dramatic, concern about
competition continues into law practice. In an article urging law
firms to enter into a written contract with new associates, the
executive secretary of a state bar association thought it necessary
to include the following admonition in his model contract:

> In your work, however, please remember that the competition our
> firm emphasizes is competition in team work and helping other
> associates and partners do their work.[18]

For some in the race to the top, competition degenerates into acts
of sabotage. Malcolm commented:

> Executives are keyed to winning everything. There are some
> people up the line that have never lost. Loss, to them, is a personal
> crisis. They love the battle so much, because they never lose. They
> take their first loss very disparagingly. And "disparagingly"
> means: "I'll fuck the guy who got me if it takes me five years to do
> it."

If the way men conduct business is inhumane, isn't it, as the
conventional wisdom has it, at least efficient? The work of Chris
Argyris[19] of the Harvard Business School, suggests otherwise.
Argyris systematically studied the behavior of 165 top executives
in six companies of different size and function, ranging from a

research-and-development organization with 150 employees to an electronics firm with 40,000 workers. In all, 265 decisionmaking meetings were studied, by direct observation, analysis of tape recordings made during the meetings, and subsequent private interviews with participants.

Argyris found the same competitiveness in virtually all the meetings studied. In some it was openly displayed. In most it was covert, with an apparent openness and concern for the ideas of others masking an effort to gather information in order better to discredit them. Most executives, like those described by Malcolm, believed that unilateral direction and coercion is the most effective way of obtaining the cooperation of people in their firm. Again like the managers of the computer company, they viewed all emotional and interpersonal discussion as "irrelevant," "immature," "not work." In the event of an emotional disagreement, they would tell the members to "get back to facts" or to "keep personalities out of this."

One result of these attitudes, Argyris found, is the suppression of open discussion of ideas or problems that would provoke strong emotion among the participants or require analysis of "personal" aspects of their behavior or relationships. Interpersonal problems with serious consequences for the organization—antagonistic rivalries between department heads, for example—are ignored or brought up disguised as technical, intellectual problems and dealt with ineffectually. Even when it was clear that emotions and interpersonal conflicts would prevent a group of peers from functioning effectively, the executives in Argyris' study uniformly felt that they should not deal with them. No time and effort were spent trying to improve the working relationships in any of the groups observed by Argyris. Communication to peers and superiors of information that would tell executives how they felt about each other even in terms of professional competence, which would have been vital to an atmosphere of trust, was nonexistent. Executive committee members would typically tell Argyris that the relationship among committee members was "close," "friendly," "based on years of working together," but, later in the interview, admit that they had no idea how the other members felt about them.

Men's need "to have everything rationalized," to ignore "personalities," according to a New York attorney who conducts monthly seminars on negotiation for executives of major corporations, is also a substantial disadvantage in negotiation. Women, he says, are more alert to nonverbal cues and are willing to rely on intuition—their feelings about a person or situation—and for that reason generally do better.[20]

Most important, as illustrated in the manufacturing company examples, the highly competitive tone of most meetings discourages the use of the group as a sounding board. Because members feel that others present will, however politely, try to tear down any new idea, instead of attempting to refine and develop its good points, they present to the group only ideas that they believe are fully worked out, cannot be stolen and are otherwise impregnable. The assistance that the group could and, in theory, is intended to provide tends not to be given. Since workable ideas in complex areas rarely spring full-blown from one individual's mind, the germs of such concepts are often lost. Here are some of the executives' own comments made in a meeting at which Argyris discussed with the board of directors of a company some of his observations:

> A.* I would think that each of us is in some other group that is far more creative than we are when we are together.
>
> C: I think that when we meet, there is always a tendency for our contributions to be critical. As a result, the person who is doing the creating is wary. He cuts off [his new ideas] before he has gone too far. It isn't long before he loses his confidence in pursuing a new line of attack [on a problem].
>
> C: I always feel in these meetings people aren't really trying to be open or to help. Hell, I wouldn't come to this group to explore a new idea.

* Letters represent individuals.

B: I for one would never think of coming to this group with a very important idea without having presented it elsewhere. In other words, when I come out with a brand new idea, this would not be the best place . . . we tend to ask questions which try to prove our own point of view. . . .

C: Yes, and it isn't long before you realize that people are asking questions in order to "lick" you.[21]

Finally, the premium placed on avoiding messy, "emotional" scenes with peers means that the *most important questions* —questions of fundamental objectives and strategy—are not dealt with directly and openly. For it is precisely these issues that involve the greatest personal investment by individuals and thus hold the highest potential for strong feeling. Conflicts that cannot be avoided are generally "pre-discussed" by a few key principals and an arranged solution railroaded through the formal decisionmaking meeting without open discussion, eliminating the inputs of potentially valuable contributors and reducing the commitment of members who had no part in shaping the proposed solution.

These behavior patterns are not unique to business executives—Argyris has made similar observations in studies of leaders in education, research, the ministry, trade unions, and government.

I do not mean to suggest that effective group decisionmaking can be made easy simply by abandoning the masculine stereotype for a more balanced ideal. Open discussion is not always possible, especially in government, where participants often have outside constituencies who may be stirred to unwanted action by premature disclosures. Even in a more confidential and trusting environment, full use of a group's creative potential is likely to be painful. The development of the Marshall Plan for the reconstruction of post–World War II Europe by a group headed by George Kennan has been cited as an example of sound decisionmaking. The atmosphere of openness, the absence of deference to hierarchical status, and the willingness to risk self-esteem in which the Plan was hammered out did not make for a comfortable experience:

> The members of the group, Kennan informs us, were tough-minded, and "stout in argument" throughout their three weeks of constant "sweat." They took very seriously their role as critical thinkers, not sparing each other the embarrassments and humiliation of having to listen to a pet idea being subjected to incisive criticism and sometimes hacked to pieces.[22]

> As leader of the group, Kennan seems to have made it quite clear to the members that open-minded, free-wheeling, unconstrained debating was precisely what they should be doing. Everyone was urged to express any idea that might embody a useful proposal and to help spell out all the drawbacks as well as the good consequences. One of the main group norms was to subject everyone's ideas to thorough criticism. The members applied this norm to Kennan's own seemingly brilliant proposals, some of which he had painstakingly developed during the months preceding the group's deliberations: "[They] put me personally over the bumps, to drive a whole series of clichés and oversimplifications out of my head, to spare me no complications . . . . So earnest and intense were the debates in our little body in those hairy days and nights that I can recall one occasion, in late evening, when I, to recover my composure, left the room and walked, weeping, around the entire building."[23]

Revision of the masculine ideal will not spare men the anguish of criticism. But it would prevent the personal impact of criticism from being magnified out of proportion, prevent it from being any broader or more threatening a humiliation than necessary. It can open channels of communication essential to the "delicate balance of mutual suspicion and mutual trust"[24] and remove the obstacles of obsessive concern with infallibility, dominance, and victory over others. Temporary feelings of dependence, of frustration, of "losing" in deeply felt debate are painful enough without being thought of as incompatible with manhood. The traditional male ideal prevents men from taking these feelings and confrontations in stride, as part of the job. It would have dictated, for example, that Kennan feel "less of a man" because he was emotionally affected enough to weep at one point in the debate.

It comes as no surprise that for most men, work is not one of two or three major commitments but the single major focus of their lives. As Bardwick says of the men she studied, "Work was what you did—the rest was muted."[25] It is the only area of life where accomplishment is measured and rewarded by the market.

The most obvious result of this imbalance is overwork. An in-control-but-pressed-for-time look is part of the successful executive's image. Argyris found that whenever the president of a company asked for a discussion of problems that top and middle management men thought important, certain kinds of genuinely troubling issues were ignored.

> Rather, the most frequently mentioned problem (74% of the cases) was the overload problem. The executives and managers reported that they were overloaded and that the situation was getting worse. The president's usual reply was that he appreciated their predicament, but "that is life."[26]

In effect, they were reporting that all is well.

For success to really count, it must be the result of long and uncomfortable effort. Harvard Business School, as part of preparing its students for the corporate big leagues, begins classes at seven-forty A.M.; student-organized study groups meet even earlier. A corporate executive told me that most managers in the upper middle ranks of his company, earning fifty to sixty thousand dollars a year, all have managed to get offices overlooking the company parking lot. When they see their bosses get into their cars and drive out, they leave—but not before. If their superiors decide to stay until midnight or sneak out via the company helicopter or limousine, they are trapped until at least nine or ten at night.

Human nature being what it is, long hours spent on the job do not always mean long hours of actual work. At the New York law firm where Brenda worked for a time, associates would come in between nine and nine-thirty, drink coffee and read the paper until ten, take an hour and a half for lunch, play squash for an hour during the afternoon once or twice a week, at six-thirty go out for a drink and dinner at the client's expense, come back to the office about eight and work until ten or eleven. The same amount of work could have been done in a normal working day, but that would not have demonstrated the "dedication to the firm" required for promotion.

For all too many men on their way up the corporate or professional ladder, everything not related to work is slighted in terms of time and energy. Wives are important primarily as symbols, something every man should have, and as providers of a psychological and logistical base of support. One executive commented that

> the wife is the raiser of the children, the one who is given enough financial resources to deal with every single thing. The executive acts at home the way he acts in the office. "I don't want to hear about the problems. Here's the money, hire someone to handle it." It's the same whether it's a gardener or a psychiatrist.

For men like this every work crisis, no matter how minor, automatically takes precedence over any desire to spend time with their children or with women or men they care about.

A study of successful Americans—professionals, business and government leaders, and artists—found that for most of these individuals sex was "almost nonexistent, something to be stifled," or a source of fear and avoidance. They "performed" the sex act, as a necessary "nuisance," with a "minimum of fanfare"—"like any other body function . . . it needs attention from time to time."[27] The rumored sexual conquests of some public figures do not negate this point.

> Brief sexual encounters may drain off surplus tension. . . . Some may even manage to carve out a few more extended erotic interludes from their busy lives. But by and large, a successful public career is not compatible with leisurely and gratifying lovemaking.

> There are only so many hours in a day, after all, and strong involvement in a love relationship—even a marital one—will ultimately impinge upon career activities.[28]

There is another side to the overwork syndrome. A man who works late may remain at his desk more to avoid going home to his family than because his job requires it. Either he spends his leisure time with men like himself,[29] or, as one corporate manager said of two colleagues:

> An executive from the company took a vacation for the first time in two and a half years. After the first day, he couldn't take just being with his family. So he left right away to take intensive flying lessons. In six months he had a flying license which normally takes two years. Another vice-president sneaks in a drawer of work and a tape recorder to make notes on when he goes to his summer home, and pulls it out about twelve o'clock at night when everybody's asleep.

It is usually when men are in their forties that they recognize that their ambitions are not going to be fully realized: they will not be president of the corporation, a Nobel prize–winning scientist, a partner in a major law firm, a famous politician, wealthy entrepreneur—whatever they have been striving for. The reaction of many at this point is to feel depressed and worthless. In interviews with psychologists these men devalue their actual achievements, no matter how substantial. Their accomplishments didn't get them to the top, so they don't count. Searching for meaning, they ask themselves, often for the first time, whether they have enjoyed their work. A psychologist who has counseled business executives in these crises says that the most typical response to this question is something like: "I don't know . . . I must have, I've been doing it for ten years." After a period of turmoil, the crisis is generally resolved in one of two ways: either the men plod onward in the same track, with the same ideals but more or less embittered and drained of hope; or their values and the direction of their commitments change. As one personnel executive put it:

There's a feeling after a certain number of years. You think, "That's it. The company has counted me out at forty. Those bastards, I've got a lot to offer." And you see, usually they do. Some of them change their style, from a very company-oriented point of view to a very sensitive people-oriented kind of view. They become very good people managers at that point. They say, "Look, I'm down here, and I'm not going anyplace, and I'm not going to tell these people, 'You ought to do this.' I'm going to exemplify the way I think this operation should be run. From eight-thirty to six o'clock. As for me, I'll get involved in the Indian community. I'll play handball on Saturdays; I'll play tennis on Sundays. I'll be with my kids at night." But they make this decision when they know they aren't going any further.

For other men, the mid-life crisis is triggered not by failure but by success. Usually in their forties, but sometimes later, these men achieve the occupational goals and recognition they have been driving toward. For them work has become routine. They know the ropes, much of the challenge is gone. Middle age also brings consciousness of mortality, a realization that one no longer has unlimited time in which to shape and reshape one's life, a sense that one is pretty much what one will be. The combination often creates a malaise, a feeling of incompleteness surprising to men who have done what they set out to do. There is a realization that

engulfment by work has caused a loss of spontaneity in perceiving and feeling. It is not simply that they were busy—it is that they lost capacities to feel and perceive because they maximized only those personal qualities that were intrinsic to achieving success.[30]

Essential aspects of the self previously repressed, consciously or unconsciously—"other voices in other rooms," in Dr. Daniel Levinson's phrase—now seek to be heard.[31] These voices tend to represent those needs and aspects of the self traditionally labeled as feminine.[32]

Some men manage to stave off feelings of incompleteness by creating new challenges and involvement in work which allow them to avoid, at least for a time, the recognition of aging and thus keep alive the promise of eventual self-actualization through work. [33] But, interestingly, many of these successful men move in the same directions as men who haven't succeeded. There is the same tendency to turn to extramarital affairs; greater involvement in their local communities and other activities involving caring and social contact with others. A new interest in their children; on the job, a greater interest in associates and employees as people; the hobbies and clubs that other men in their circumstances take up or join.

In some of these pursuits, notably those calling for skills like those developed on the job, men tend to make the transition successfully. It is not difficult for a corporate executive to become effective in his community. Or for an experienced movie producer to shift gears and realize his middle-aged dream of bringing to the screen on a noncommercial basis eight great stage plays performed by the best actors in the world. Politics and high-level government service are the other not-too-different pursuits, although, as we have seen, effective service in these interdependent arenas often does call for a temperament less in need of total control and quick, individual recognition.

More personal avenues of self-actualization are very much more difficult. It is next to impossible to express and realize, quickly and easily, aspects of the self that have been repressed and undeveloped for forty years, and many such efforts, made with little self-awareness, fail. Affairs with women fall easily into the old conquest mold, with satisfaction limited to proof of continued sexual potency and attractiveness. The impulses toward more open, personal human contact and a fuller expression of sexuality, unarticulated to begin with, are elusive and hard to grasp. They tend to be forgotten. It is hard for a man to begin the process of getting to know his children at the age forty-five. He doesn't really know what they're like, and, more important, he doesn't know how to talk to them. All too often, the effort degenerates into trying to become their pal by doing things and playing games with them or a businesslike attempt at "making the boy into a man," with the hoped-for but only vaguely imagined emotional contact slipping away. Of course, some men do manage to establish rewarding relationships with their children; the point is that the lives they have led and a late start make it more difficult than it has to be.

Among factory workers and clerical staff of some large institutions, rejection of the dehumanizing aspects of work supported by the male stereotype does not require the stimulus of mid-life reassessment. They work for the most part under rigidly authoritarian conditions, with little chance for meaningful social interaction with co-workers, on tasks broken down in the name of efficiency to the point of mindlessness. The possibility of making it big, which sustains executives and professionals, does not exist for them. It's not that the pay is necessarily bad, or that it will not increase, but the dream of moving up, from worker to executive, from clerical worker to manager, is no longer believable. The current generation of blue-collar and clerical workers are the children who were supposed to move up. A few have, but many, despite more education and higher expectations, have not.

Abraham Maslow suggested that the needs of human beings are hierarchical and, as each level is satisfied, the next level becomes more prominent.[34] The order he posited is

1. Physiological requirements (food, shelter, etc.)

2. Safety and security

3. Companionship and affection

4. Self-esteem and the esteem of others

5. Self-actualization (being able to realize one's potential to the full)

More than ever before, the basic—the first two—needs of workers are being met, and in those situations, the focus of workers' discontents and demands seems to be shifting to the last three.[35] What they are saying, more clearly than middle management, is that they are not machines whose sole function is to work, that they want more than decent pay and a safe, physically tolerable work environment. They are raising issues basically analogous to those which executives face only when they stop rising through the ranks or when consciousness of passing time forces a reassessment: reasonable control over the pace and organization of work, an opportunity for meaningful cooperation and relationships with co-workers, some sense of useful purpose for their work beyond financial and hierarchical reward. They rate the content of work as more important than being promoted, an apparent shift away from the competitive masculine ethic.[36]

Not surprisingly, the solutions that are beginning to be found to the blue-collar and clerical "blues" also involve departures from traditional male values. One of the major work redesign efforts, unique in scope but not in basic design or results, was recently carried out by General Foods.[37] With the advice and cooperation of workers and consultants from business schools, a whole new plant and management approach were designed and put into operation. Autonomous teams of eight to twelve workers were formed and given the responsibility for larger segments of the production process, including maintenance, quality control, custodial, industrial engineering, and personnel functions. Allocation of responsibility for particular tasks was made a team responsibility. "Team leaders," chosen by management, were charged with responsibility for facilitating team decisionmaking rather than making the decisions themselves.

An attempt was made to design every set of tasks in a way that would include functions requiring higher human abilities and responsibilities. Pay raises were given for mastering an increasing number of jobs, first within the team and then in the total plant. There were no limits on the number of workers who could qualify for higher pay, so employees were encouraged to teach each other. Teams were provided with economic information and managerial decision rules, enabling them to make production decisions ordinarily made at a higher supervisory level. No plant rules were laid down by management; instead a commitment was made to let rules evolve through collective experience. Differential status symbols—separate parking lots, entrances, eating facilities, decor—were minimized. The technology and architecture were designed to facilitate rather than discourage the congregating of team members during working hours on the assumption that these *ad hoc* meetings would be enjoyable human exchanges as well as opportunities to coordinate work and learn about each other's jobs.

Often such reorganizations are combined with profit-sharing to avoid the feeling among workers that the changes are merely refined techniques for improving productivity at their expense and to create a commonality of interests that cut across hierarchical lines.[38] But in this case the initial results were striking even without profit-sharing. Industrial engineers had estimated that 110 workers would be needed to run the new plant along conventional lines; under the new system only 70 were required. Major cost savings resulted from improved yields, minimized waste, and avoidance of shutdowns—factors closely connected to work attitudes. In addition to demonstrably greater satisfaction on the job, the redesigned work setting affected employees' activities outside the plant. Many more workers than is typical in other plants owned by the same corporation or located in the same community became active in civic affairs.

Questions remain about these work reorganization efforts: How much of their success is attributable to novelty, to the fact that, if nothing else, they demonstrate to workers that someone is concerned about them? When workers learn all the jobs in their work group and want to move up, will routes into management be open? Conversely, will workers, once moving up becomes a real possibility, show themselves to be as much victims of the emulative ethic as management and demand higher level jobs at rates which outrun the growth of their skills? As workers become highly skilled, does it still make sense to assign them custodial functions in their work areas? (If so, why not assign such functions to vice-presidents as well?)

Nevertheless, these and other innovations—such as flexible (sometimes referred to as "sliding") work hours or work weeks—which recognize that work cannot be walled off from the rest of a person's life are steps in the right direction. Taken together, they are very different from the cosmetics of the human-relations school of management, which has usually meant trying to make people function more happily and, thus, more effectively—through devices ranging from Muzak to seminars on communication—within the traditional hierarchical and authoritarian work structure. Collectively, such efforts fail because they do not come to grips with the failure of work to meet a wide range of human needs. Individually, they fail because they attempt to isolate and work on a part of the problem that cannot be disengaged from its context. When managers come back from their T-groups, the new, more open ways of relating to people they learned are undercut by the actual values and practices of the organization. Either they are used selectively to support the *status quo* or they are quickly abandoned because they are out of sync with what the system in fact rewards. Innovations like sensitivity training will only become effective when competitive, hierarchical, and authoritarian attitudes toward work are tempered by the kinds of changes instituted in the General Foods experiment and by analogous shifts in individual values in both the executive and blue-collar ranks.

11. Violence: The Primal Test

... becoming more masculine does not involve simple "imprinting." One has to dare certain activities which are dangerous and can be painful. There is nothing automatic about fighting.

—Norman Mailer, "The Prisoner of Sex."

Real violence scares the hell out of most of us. But men are brought up with the idea that there *ought* to be some part of them, under control until released by necessity, that thrives on it. This capacity, even affinity, for violence, lurking beneath the surface of every real man, is supposed to represent the primal, untamed base of masculinity. And, although its restraint is required in civilized circumstances, the myth is that this restraint, however inevitable, is costly. It cuts us off from our (masculine) roots, from one of our deepest sources of (male) energy, and dulls our basic animal vitality. (Women, ignored as usual in such matters, presumably have other sources of vitality.) Kate Millett has pointed out that Norman Mailer, Hemingway's successor as our foremost literary celebrant of this myth, even finds the genesis of cancer in the repression of violent impulses:

> "The first unmanageable cell/ of the cancer which was to/ stifle his existence" made its appearance in the subject "on a morning when by/ an extreme act of will/ he chose not to strike/ his mother." . . . "his/ renunciation of violence/ was civilized too civilized/ for his cells which proceeded to revolt."[1]

We don't have to look as far afield as Mailer's theory of disease for the notion that for real men the capacity for violence is "natural." The standard male heroes of our popular movies, television, and fiction are usually distinguished and set off from other male characters by only two things: they are on the right side; and, although they don't always win, they are brave and effective fighters in the crunch. We do have male antiheroes. But they are in the minority, a reaction against the accepted type. In *The Virginian*, the prototypical western novel referred to earlier, the hero shows himself to be a man's man throughout, but the key scene takes place near the end. On the day before the Virginian is to be married, Trampas, the villain, calls him a liar and a horse thief and tells him to get out of town before sundown. His friends offer to get Trampas out of the way, but

> It had come to that point where there was no way out, save only the ancient eternal way between man and man. It is only the great mediocrity that goes to the law in these personal matters.[2]

His bride implores him to avoid the fight. But he feels he has no choice:

> "I work hyeh. I belong hyeh. It's my life. If folks came to think I was a coward . . .
>
> "Can't yu' see how it must be about a man?"[3]

The model created in *The Virginian* has been followed in other western novels and countless movies, comic books, and television shows—including *Gunsmoke*, the longest-running television show in history—but the most influential and popular of them all is the John Wayne western. The violence in these films has a wholesome, unreal quality. Wayne openly enjoys the barroom brawls and fistfights he gets into. He is initially reluctant but when forced to it he goes in grinning. He always wins, and somehow nobody gets seriously hurt—no eyes put out, no smashed noses, etc. Fights are fun, bracing, good exercise, a great way to work up an appetite. When actual shooting takes place, people die and that's too bad, but it's never really bloody or painful and nobody stays upset about the dead for very long. Wayne himself sails through these battles with incredible serenity, protecting the women, wounded occasionally although always in the shoulder or leg, sorry when friends are killed but basically cheerful—just a real man doin' his job.

In the urban setting, the parallel male hero is the private detective or secret agent. The Mickey Spillane series was the first to make it big—it has sold more than forty-two million books—and, like *The Virginian*, spelled out its hero's values quite explicitly:

> Maybe he thought he was dealing with somebody soft. "Listen, pimple face. Just for the fun of it I ought to slap your fuzzy chin all around this room, but I got things to do. Don't you go playing man when you're only a boy. You're pretty big, but I'm three sizes bigger and a hell of a lot tougher and I'll beat the living daylights out of you if you try anything funny again. Now sit down over there."[4]

James Bond, Mike Hammer's popular successor, is more understated and urbane, but when the sophisticated accessories of fine wines, caviars, and fast cars are stripped away, his basic appeal to women characters and the reader alike is the same capacity to handle danger and violence with nerveless aplomb.

One step more refined are the spy novels of John Le Carré.

There, the hero Smiley, a distinctly nonphysical British Intelligence type, deals with violence at one remove. He recognizes and makes us believe that his business is ugly, even sordid. But still his appeal and distinguishing feature is his ability, while recognizing all this, to coolly and cleverly manipulate the instruments of violence—the techniques, devices, bureaucracies, individual operatives with their stupidities and illusions—to achieve his objectives.

Characters like these exist in exotic settings and lead lives in which violence is routine. In that sense they are fantasies, although fantasies which reflect and help shape an important element of the masculine ideal. Closer to home are movies in which ordinary men are drawn into situations where they must act violently. Here the sense of violence as a male restorative comes through. *Straw Dogs*, directed by Sam Peckinpah, is a good example. The hero, David Sumner, is an American mathematician on a sabbatical in rural England with his sexpot wife. He is a mild-mannered, repressed milquetoast running away from some unexplained stateside difficulty. The climactic moment in the film comes when Sumner explains to his wife why he is fighting off a lynch mob of locals (including two men who, unknown to him, earlier raped her) that is after the village idiot, accused of another rape. Referring to their rented farmhouse, he says, during a lull in the drunken, glass-smashing assault:

> This is me. This is where I live. I will not allow violence against this house. No way.

The mayhem that follows, described by a reviewer as an "alternately dreamy and jolting sequence in which David wastes his antagonists with a combination of pluck and Yankee ingenuity," is graphically ghastly, ending with the chief rapist's decapitation in a bear trap. Sumner is not an unbelievable, nerveless machine. He panics at a rat thrown through the window and, between battles, fusses hysterically with his glasses. And the situation is so arranged that one can hardly disapprove of his actions. More to the point, however, the brutal, atrocious mess he has created is supposed to be a kind of happy ending, releasing David's blocked masculinity and winning his wife's respect and adoration. "Jesus!" he says softly, surveying the carnage, and he says it as an oath of self-appreciating wonderment. As the reviewer commented, "the prevailing emotion among [Peckinpah's] heroes is soul-destroying depression. Violence comes to such men like an oasis to someone dying of thirst."[5]

Another example is the novel *Deliverance* by James Dickey and the film of the same name, "the latest of a series of fictional escapes into the 'territory' where women do not go, where civilization does not reach, where men hunt one another like animals and hunt animals for sport."[6] The plot is simple and "classic": four men set out on a canoe trip down a wild, uncharted river through the junglelike wilderness somewhere in the South. There they run into trouble in the form of two illiterate, savage mountain men who rape one of the four and threaten to kill another. Having "no choice" under the circumstances, Lewis, the "real man" of the foursome, kills one of the mountain men with a hunting arrow. You can feel his satisfaction:

> Lewis and I faced each other across the dead man. His eyes were vivid and alive; he was smiling easily and with great friendliness.
>
> "Well now, how about this? Just . . . how *about* this?"[7]

For the first time in the story, he is quiet, calm, in touch with himself. The only trace of ambiguity comes when the two make the mistake of killing a third mountain man who they think is one of the pair that had assaulted them. But basically *Deliverance* celebrates the idea that the kill-or-be-killed situation, away from civilization and its artificial protections, is where men are most profoundly alive and, if they pass its tests, most profoundly masculine.

Hemingway and Mailer, our most accomplished literary purveyors of the cult of toughness, became cultural phenomena, symbols in their own right, because the values they espouse

resonate so deeply in the American male psyche. Both understand men's fear of violence and its horror, but honor violence
nevertheless as the crucible of manhood. Hemingway—who
could write, "Never think that war no matter how necessary nor
how justified is not a crime. Ask the infantry and ask the
dead"—could also give us lyrical descriptions of battle:

> In all that, in the fear that dries your mouth and your throat, in the
> smashed plaster dust and the sudden panic of a wall falling,
> collapsing in the flash and roar of a shellburst, clearing the gun,
> dragging those away who had been serving it, lying face down-
> ward and covered with rubble, your head behind the shield, the
> gun searching the roadside again; you did the thing there was to
> do and knew that you were right. You learned the dry-mouthed,
> fear-purged ecstasy of battle. . . . You learned . . . how to endure
> and how to ignore suffering in the long time of cold and wetness,
> of mud and of digging and fortifying. And the feeling of the
> summer and the fall was buried deep under tiredness, sleepiness,
> and nervousness and discomfort. But it was still there and all that
> you went through only served to validate it. It was in those days,
> . . . that you had a deep and sound and selfless pride.[8]

Mailer, writing in a later, franker era and with pop Freud in his
arsenal, equates masculinity with violence and ties violence
firmly to sexuality. He understands, better than almost anyone
else, the price men pay for this equation, but in the end the
exaggerated burlesque of his prose is a device to deflect criticism
rather than a genuine attempt at satire. He endorses what he
describes. Kate Millett has analyzed his attitudes toward violence, sexuality, and manhood, particularly as they appear in
Why Are We in Vietnam?, his "study of the Wasp male
psychosis":

> [T]he beguiling youth of D. J. Jethroe is introduced to tell us of the
> Alaskan bear hunt which has introduced him to "animal murder
> . . . and murder of the soldierest sort," describing his initiation
> into the company of men in a Hip-Pop diction whose metaphor is
> sexual-military: "Now remember!" he instructs the reader before
> the killing begins, "Think of cunt and ass—so it's all clear." To
> convince us that sex and violence are inextricable in the culture
> into which he is being welcomed as an adult, D. J. offers us the

evidence of his senses: "ever notice how blood smells like cunt and ass all mix in one?" Already perfectly at ease among the "sexual peculiarities of red-blooded men," at home with the hero "who can't come unless he's squinting down a gunsight;" D. J. renders the intercourse of his parents in terms of an explosion. Using a "dynamite stick for a phallus," Big Daddy himself ("he don't come, he explodes, he's a geyser of love, hot piss, shit . . . he's Texas willpower") mother Alice is scattered over the southern states, "They found her vagina in North Carolina and part of her gashole in hometown." Just as D. J. fancies his penis a gun to "those Dallas debutantes and just plain common fucks who are lucky to get drilled by him," he first gives in to the fever of the hunt when he catches sight of a great wounded bear splattering her death's blood into the forest. . . . D. J. now yearns after slaughter in Vietnam, inspired by an "itchy-dick memory of electric red."[9]

In ordinary life, the most violent pursuits are considered the most masculine—football and making war, for example. And when acolytes in these trades don't show the proper enthusiasm, one of the harshest sanctions is to be labeled unmasculine, a woman. College football players are supposed to "like to hit"[10] or, on the more realistic professional teams, "want to love to hit."[11] Dave Meggyesy described the defensive coach's reaction after he "ducked" a tackle out of "fear of getting my head kicked in":

> He said I was "afraid to stick my nose in there," as he always put it, adding that I looked "almost feminine" in making the tackle. This sort of attack on a player's manhood is a coach's doomsday weapon. And it almost always works, for the players have wrapped up their identity in their masculinity.[12]

In Marine boot camp recruits are called "faggots" by drill instructors. Their reputation as tougher and more aggressive in combat than the other armed services leads Marines to refer to the Corps as "the crotch" and to the others as "the sister services."[13] Samuel Stouffer, in his massive study of the American soldier observed,

The fear of failure in the role [of combat soldier], as by showing cowardice in battle, could bring not only fear of social censure on this point as such, but also more central and strongly established fears related to sex-typing. To fail to measure up as a soldier in courage and endurance was to risk the charge of not being a man. ("Whatsa matter, bud—got lace on your drawers?" "Christ, he's acting like an old maid.") If one were not socially defined as a man, there was a strong likelihood of being branded a "woman," a dangerous threat to the contemporary male personality. [14]

In poor neighborhoods, the equation of fighting and manhood is literal. Claude Brown, recalling his childhood in Harlem, said "Most of the cats I swung with were more afraid of not fighting than they were of fighting," He described a confrontation between himself and his father over the issue:

Dad once saw me run away from a fight. He was looking out the window one day, and the Morris brothers were messing with me. I didn't think I could beat both of them, so I ran in the house. Dad was at the door when I got there. He said, "Where you runnin' to boy?"

I said, "Dad, these boys are out there, and they messin' with me."

He said, "Well, if you come in here, I'm gon mess with you too. You ain't got no business runnin' from nobody."

I said, "Yeah, Dad, I know that. But there's two of 'em, and they're both bigger than me. They can hit harder than I can hit."

Dad said, "You think they can hit harder than I can hit?"

I said, "No, Dad. I know they can't hit harder than you." . . .

He said, "Well, damn right. . . . And, if you come in here you got to get hit by me." . . .

. . . [Finally] Mama came in the hallway and put her arms around me and said, "Come on in the house and lay down."

I went in and I laid down. I just got sicker until I went downstairs. They really did kick my ass. But it was all right. I didn't feel sick any more. [15]

This pressure to prove onself through fighting is not unique

to Harlem; nor does it come only from parents. A young Eng-
lishman was interviewed about gang life by a BBC producer:

> I don't think I could lose face, I would rather get hurt and put in the
> hospital than refuse to fight whether the geezer, whether the
> bloke is ten times bigger than me, I mean the thing is you have lost
> such a terrible lot not to be able to fight. I mean how could you
> walk out, how could you speak to them [his mates] . . . You could
> never argue a point with them after that because they would say
> he would go to one extreme but he won't fight so we win the
> argument anyway. . . . One day a bloke refused to fight two
> people . . . and everytime he says anything now they say it is all
> right we remember the time you refused to fight . . . no one will
> talk to him; . . . if we ever go out he is never included, never
> included in anything we do or say.[16]

Even in middle-income neighborhoods, where fighting is not
necessary for survival, boys are admonished to "fight back" and
not to be a "sissy," at least when the odds aren't too bad. And,
although the initiation of violence is formally discouraged, boys
are also likely to be given inconsistent messages of furtive, in-
formal approval, rationalized generally along the lines of "he's all
boy." One such message is that boys should settle their disputes
themselves and not, like girls, rat on their fellows to a teacher or
someone else in authority. (Another version of: "It is only the
great mediocrity that goes to the law in these personal matters.")

The message that fighting is the kind of thing boys do gets
through, even if it isn't acted on. For reasons no one ever articulated, the junior-high-school tree-house gang in my neighborhood provisioned itself for a war with another gang which was
supposed to exist somewhere on the other side of town. We
assembled supplies of rocks, wooden swords, shields, maces
(pieces of garden hose with four or five nails driven through one
end in different directions) and plotted raids on the other gang. I
could never actually imagine using these instruments of death
and disfigurement on anyone else, or risking having them used
on me. Although at the time I thought I was the only one with
these reservations and kept them to myself, they must have been

silently shared by most of the others—somehow we never actually marched into battle. The closest we came was an intramural war waged with rock-filled snowballs. The battle stopped when a warrior's nose was broken by a direct hit. The mystery is not why it stopped but why it began. None of us had a history of violence. Only one of the kids was the kind of lunatic who just doesn't care. The others, I am sure, had the same feeling someplace in their heads that I did: a feeling that this is goddamn dangerous, that somebody, especially me, could really get hurt. But once the idea had been broached no one was willing to take the risk of walking away from the fight or trying to call it off.

Boys learn especially that they should fight to protect or "defend the honor" of women, including sisters, mothers, and later, girl friends. That's most of the meaning to a ten-year-old of his father's admonition, "Take care of your mother, son, until I get back." Even in Claude Brown's Harlem, where violence was routine, a slur on a woman "under the protection" of a boy was cause for unusual measures:

> If somebody messed with your brother, you could just punch him in the mouth, and this was all right. But if anybody was to mess with your sister, you really had to fuck him up—break his leg or stab him in the eye with an ice pick, something vicious.[17]

For middle-income boys, whose hearts aren't really in it, this imperative can have ludicrous consequences. Roger P., a distinctly nonbrawny and unusually self-aware man, told me of an incident that took place when he was in high school in Missouri. He was riding home from school in a convertible with his girl friend Elaine. As they stopped at a light next to a school bus, an acquaintance named Steve leaned out the window of the bus and spat on her. The next day, Roger, feeling obliged to take some action, went up to Steve and, trying to fulfill his obligations while at the same time avoiding a fight, gave him an easy out, asking him, "Did you spit on Elaine?" "No, I threw some snow on her." "Oh, O.K." Roger replied with an inward sigh of relief. Later that day, however, Roger heard that Steve was bragging that he had in fact spat on Roger's girl. Roger gathered his courage, approached Steve, and said in—he reports—his most grown-up voice, "I want to talk this matter over with you after school. I'll come over to your house at six-thirty. Where do you live?" At the appointed hour Roger arrived at the house. Steve came to the door. Both of them were scared. Steve asked if he wanted to come in. Roger said, "No, is there someplace outside we can go?" They went up to the top of a hill behind the house, and stood there looking at each other. Roger asked, "Do you want to take your glasses off?" "No, they'll take care of themselves." Then, as Roger describes it, feeling like an actor doing a first read-through, he somehow brought himself to make a fist, lift his arm, and hit Steve in the face. Steve fell down. Roger jumped on him, hoping to end the whole business by keeping him from getting up. He grabbed Steve in a choke hold. "Will you apologize to Elaine?" Steve agreed and Roger let him up. They walked back to the house. Roger told Steve he was the first guy he had fought in "I don't know how long." Steve said, "I really like your car, I'd like to go riding in it." Not knowing what else to do, with his honor formally if not passionately upheld, Roger went home.

What does all this mean for adult men, in real life, men who are not counterspies, marines, or football players? Some, like Hemingway and Mailer and their less-cultivated barroom brawling, "step outside" confreres, never outgrow the equation of violence with masculinity at all. (Not surprisingly, the fastest way to provoke a demonstration of this brand of masculinity is to suggest that it is lacking, that its pretenders are "faggots."[18]) Although most men think that physical strength is a necessary attribute of manliness,[19] they generally avoid trying to settle things with their fists. Most of them have too much to lose from getting into a brawl and are afraid—sensibly, it seems to me—of getting hurt. Furthermore, they spend most of their time with other men who, like themselves, don't want to be put to this kind of test. But the fact that they don't actually lead lives filled with physical risk and violence doesn't mean that they have escaped the feeling that they are less masculine as a result.

Men are emotionally conflicted about avoiding challenges to fight. Even though it clearly doesn't make sense to take a swing at the construction worker who has just insulted your female companion (or, through her, you), one feels somehow diminished by the decision to let it pass. Until only a few years ago, I would feel a real twinge of inadequacy after refusing to respond to the challenge to get out of my car and fight hurled by motorists who did not like my driving style. Somewhere in me a voice was still saying, even though I haven't been in a fight since high school, "If you were a real man, if you had any guts, you'd get out and knock him on his ass, instead of trading insults from the safety of the car." Sometimes this conflict leads to the "hold me back or I'll kill him" phenomenon, a ploy aimed at preserving a tough reputation without risk.

Men never get tired of talking about the few times they really did blow their stack and hit somebody. Even if they say, "I never should have done it," every time they repeat the story, they want to reassure the listener, and themselves, not just that they were courageous in a pinch but also that they are capable of a self-forgetful explosion of violence, that they have that dangerous masculine inner core. I like to tell of the time when, without thinking about it, I chased a man who snatched Brenda's purse for four blocks, finally scaring him into dropping it and getting the police to take over the chase and catch him. It was a stupid thing to do; he could easily have turned on me with a knife, and there was nothing of real value in the purse. But I felt enormously proud of myself, not simply for having done it but because my response had been so automatic, so "instinctual," so reassuringly masculine. When moments of passionate violence are not available for retelling, men make do with the closest substitute. The war story, artfully embellished and told and retold by men who were never near the front lines, is part of our folklore.

It is difficult to prove, but it seems likely to me that men compensate for the gap between the male ideal of physical toughness and courage and the reality of their lives by displaying a distorted, compensatory toughness in other, often inappropriate areas susceptible to simplistic polarization—resolving personal disagreements, with both women and men; child-rearing practices; opinions on social or political issues like "law-and-order," welfare, and defense policy. This phenomenon may explain the occasional, and by contrast startling, gentleness and flexibility of men with supermale credentials. It takes Rosey Grier, a two-hundred-pound-plus former professional football player, to be able to sing "It's All Right to Cry" on the "Free To Be . . . You and Me" record as though he means it.[20] It takes former five-star general and Commander of the Allied Forces Dwight Eisenhower, as President, to end a discussion about the "tyranny" of weak nations who can pester strong ones with a calm shrug: "We must put up with it."[21] And to decide not to send troops to Vietnam in 1954.

The fact that a capacity, almost a readiness, for violence is an accepted part of the personal image of the ideal male also makes men resort to it faster as a tool of public policy. It makes men quicker to believe that the point has been reached where all other options have been exhausted; and that force will be a "solution" to the problem. We saw this type of solution at Attica prison in 1971.

Finally, in environments where one absolutely must fight to retain a masculine identity, some give up that identity or find self-destructive ways to take themselves out of the running. In certain prisons, men who can't or won't fight become abject and abused "female" homosexuals, sodomized at will by more "masculine" prisoners and stripped of dignity and autonomy. In Harlem in the late 1950s,

> A lot of cats were using horse [heroin] to get away from bebopping [gang fights]. It gave them an out, a reason for not doing it, and a reason that was acceptable. Nobody would say that you were

scared or anything like that; they would just say that you were a junkie, and everybody knew that junkies didn't go around bebopping.[22]

There is, Rollo May has written, an "ecstasy" and fascination in violence.[23] The actual experience of doing violence takes us out of ourselves, puts us in contact with deep and powerful emotions, takes away our burdensome sense of individual responsibility and plunges us into the crowd. In the most primitive way possible, it makes us feel, and thus know, we are alive. In this sense, May says, quoting William James, "the horrors make the fascination—everything is risked, we play for stakes that clearly matter."[24] Violence is also the ultimate and most primitive way for people to assert their significance, to have impact on others. So Hemingway and Mailer are describing something that is very real.

But our conception of masculinity does more than recognize this aspect of the human condition. It makes the experience of the ecstasy of violence a mythic prerequisite of men's self-esteem, thereby provoking a lot of mechanical—one might almost say "nonecstatic"—compensatory violence and discouraging understanding and control of the genuine article. Worst of all, our prevailing idea of masculinity tells men that violence is the *only* way for them to make contact with and draw strength from a crucial part of their innermost selves.

12. Vietnam and the Cult of Toughness in Foreign Policy

The Vietnam war has been for me, as it has been for many other Americans, a central influence in the evolution of my political beliefs and personal values. One of my most sustained intellectual endeavors has been the effort in the early years to decide whether the war made sense and then the longer and more difficult attempt, once it became clear to me that it was a pointless and futile undertaking, to understand what it was that kept the United States in the war. The process began in 1963, when I graduated from college and went to work as a member of Senator Mike Mansfield's staff, where my responsibilities led me to try to articulate and examine the underlying premises and rationale of our involvement. They did not stand up under scrutiny: Vietnam was not another Munich and there was no empirical or solid theoretical support for the "domino theory." In fact, the explanations were so clearly weak, that I could never quite understand how so many obviously intelligent men could believe them. Six years later, when everyone in his or her right mind knew the war was a disaster and still we couldn't get out, this nagging question connected up with an embryonic awareness of the masculine stereotype.

The precipitating event for me in making the connection was the publication of the Pentagon Papers. Here, at last, was the inside story—a good chunk of it at least—a twenty-year long view of the policymaking process, free of political if not bureaucratic posturing. I scoured the Papers eagerly for the analysis and motivation behind our involvement. But the most striking revelation of the Papers was not what they did say but what they did not say. Even at the highest and most private levels of our government, the rationale and supporting analysis for the American objective of winning in Vietnam had been incredibly flimsy. Secretary of Defense Robert S. McNamara wrote to President Johnson in March 1964:

> Unless we can achieve [an independent non-Communist South Vietnam], almost all of Southeast Asia will probably fall under Communist domination (all of Vietnam, Laos and Cambodia), accommodate to Communism so as to remove effective U.S. and anti-Communist influence (Burma) or fall under the dominance of force not now explicitly Communist but likely to become so (Indonesia taking over Malaysia). Thailand might hold for a period with our help, but would be under grave pressure. Even the Philippines would become shaky, and the threat to India to the west, Australia and New Zealand to the south and Taiwan, Korea and Japan to the north and east would be greatly increased.[1]

This is the fullest supporting discussion of the "domino theory" in the Papers. Even in memoranda discussing the broad outlines of United States policy, only an introductory paragraph (usually the shortest) is devoted to a discussion of our national interest in Vietnam. The only lengthy and careful examinations of this question in the Papers were produced by Undersecretary of State George Ball and by the CIA in response to a question from President Johnson. The CIA concluded that

with the possible exception of Cambodia it is likely that no nation
in the area would succumb to Communism as a result of the fall of
Laos and South Vietnam. Furthermore, a continuation of the
spread of Communism in the area would not be inexorable, and
any spread which did occur would take time—time in which the
total situation might change in a number of ways unfavorable to
the Communist cause. [2]

Ball's memo examining the likely effect of U.S. withdrawal from
Vietnam on a country-by-country, area-by-area basis concluded
that only in Southeast Asia proper would there be an adverse
effect and that this would be short-lived. [3] Both analyses were
dismissed by the Administration without a response on their
merits.

Why was there so little serious analysis or rethinking of United
States objectives in South Vietnam by the men holding power?
Not because their achievement was thought to be cheap. Fairly
early in the Johnson Administration, the President and his advisers were far more pessimistic in private than in public about
the actual results of past war efforts and the forecasts about the
results of each new escalation. CIA analyses consistently predicted the failure of escalation in the air and on the ground. Each
new escalation was undertaken because the Administration did
not know what else to do—getting out was (except at one point
for Robert Kennedy) unthinkable. A partial explanation for this
attitude is that Presidents Kennedy and Johnson and their advisers misapplied the lessons of history.

In the spring of 1965 Johnson said privately to columnist James
Wechsler, as he was to say to others: "I don't want to escalate this
war, I want nothing more than to get our boys home. . . . But I
can't run and pull a Chamberlain at Munich." This analogy was
often drawn. [4] But it rested on a number of very doubtful assumptions: that Communist China created and controlled the Viet
Cong in the South and could produce similar insurgencies elsewhere; or that North Vietnam itself had imperialist ambitions
and the capacity to carry them out on a scale which would
threaten the security interests of the United States; that a Com-

munist regime would be worse for the people of South Vietnam than the government they had; that even if China did not create the insurgency in South Vietnam, the struggle there was still "a test case"—despite Vietnam's unique character as a divided country and a history which made the Communists the heirs of nationalist sentiment; that Indochina was strategically vital to U.S. security; that China would somehow be able to force national Communist regimes in Indochina into actions furthering Chinese ambitions but not their own; and, finally, that if the United States won in South Vietnam, Communist parties in other underdeveloped countries would roll over and die.

These propositions can be debated, although they do not stand up under careful review. The shocking fact, however, is that nowhere in the Papers do our policymakers even articulate any of these underlying propositions, much less examine them critically. The process by which United States defeat in South Vietnam would lead to catastrophe is described only in the conclusory terms of the McNamara memo quoted above.

I made this discovery in a more impressionistic way myself in 1965 by cornering William Bundy, then Assistant Secretary of State for East Asian and Pacific Affairs, at a cocktail party, and asking him to spell out how the loss of South Vietnam to the Communists would injure the security interests of the United States. He couldn't do it. Coldly calculating, realist to the core, rational examiner of all sides of every policy issue set before him, ostensibly a believer in the systems-analysis article of faith that if effect follows cause the steps in between can and should be articulated, he hadn't even thought about it, hadn't even stated for himself the assumptions underlying the conclusion. Among other things, that conversation ended for me the lingering faith that the insiders "knew" more than those of us outside the situation-room circuit.

This incredible lacuna suggests that the "domino theory" was primarily a rationale supporting a policy chosen for other, not fully conscious, motivations. Major decisions are not made on such a transparently thin basis unless another, unstated rationale and set of values are at work. No other reasons are spelled out in the Pentagon Papers, but the feeling that the United States must at all costs avoid "the humiliation of defeat" is the unarticulated major premise of nearly every document. For example, John McNaughton, Assistant Secretary of Defense, McNamara's right-hand man and head of International Security Affairs at the Pentagon, described United States aims in South Vietnam, March 1965, as

> 70%—to avoid a humiliating United States defeat (to our reputation as a guarantor). 20%—to keep South Vietnam (and the adjacent territory) from Chinese hands. 10%—to permit the people of South Vietnam to enjoy a better, freer way of life.[5]

The Task Force on Vietnam, created by President Kennedy the day after the collapse of the Bay of Pigs invasion of Cuba and headed by Roswell Gilpatric, Deputy Secretary of Defense, reported that allied efforts should impress friends and foes alike that "come what may, the U.S. intends to *win* this battle."[6] President Johnson said on many occasions that he would not be the first American President to lose a war. For Nixon, "peace with honor"—meaning "peace without losing"—was a goal worth any sacrifice which could be sold to the American public. And the repeated admonitions of Secretary of State Henry Kissinger that it mattered "how" the United States disengaged from Vietnam, as we shall see, amount in the end to the same thing.

Statements like those quoted, consistent discounting of reports that the adverse consequences of losing in Vietnam would not be substantial, and the absence throughout the twelve years of active United States involvement of any serious analysis of the specific effects of defeat suggest that the Kennedy, Johnson, and Nixon Administrations have been emotionally committed to winning, or at least not losing, in Vietnam, regardless of actual consequences. It does matter sometimes whether a nation wins or loses, but whether it matters depends on the particular circumstances and on the specific consequences that flow from the defeat or victory. Avoiding the "humiliation of defeat," per se, is not automatically an important national objective. But for our Presidents and policymakers, being tough, or at least looking tough, has been a primary goal in and of itself.

The connection between the war and the cult of toughness has not been prominent in the flood of writings about Vietnam, but the evidence is there, subtler in the Kennedy Administration and more blatant under Johnson and Nixon.

There was the Kennedy emphasis on personal toughness. An excessive desire to prove this quality had taken early root in John Kennedy and showed itself first through wild recklessness in sports that led to frequent injuries. [7] This need was demonstrated again in the famous PT-boat incident during his Navy career. Kennedy's bravery in rescuing a shipmate after his boat was rammed and bringing the survivors to safety is well known. But during this rescue, some of his actions appear to reveal the same straining after heroics.

> Trying to signal American PT boats which patrolled a nearby channel at night, Kennedy swam alone into the dangerous passage and was almost carried out to sea by the current. There was no need for such foolishness, which endangered not only Jack but the rescue of his crew. He had eight uninjured men with him, plus a plank, lifejackets, and the island growth from which to make some sort of float or raft (as recommended by Navy survival doctrine in the South Pacific at that time) on which Kennedy and another man could have put to sea. [8]

Later, sharing his brother's values but being more outspoken, one of the first things Robert Kennedy would want to know about someone being considered as a Kennedy adviser or appointee was whether he was tough. [9] If he was—on to other questions; if not, he lost all credibility.

This attitude was reflected in the counterinsurgency fad that so captivated the Kennedy Administration. Americans, excellent specimens both physically and mentally, would be trained to be the Renaissance men of the twentieth century. They would be able to slit throats in Asian jungles, teach the natives in their own language how to use democracy and modern technology to improve their lives, and would quote Thucydides in their reports. President Kennedy once had the entire White House press corps flown to Fort Bragg, South Carolina, to watch an all-day demonstration of ambushes, counterambushes, and snake-meat eating. [10] The Special Forces epitomized, much more clearly than any civilian engaged in the messier business of politics, the ideals of the Kennedys. They were knowledgeable, they were progressive, up-to-date, they would do good, but above all they were tough, ready to use power and unaffected by sentiment.

Closely allied to the concern about toughness was the Kennedy drive to win at all costs. We have seen the efforts made by Joe, Sr. to drill this precept into the Kennedy sons. By all accounts he succeeded. Eunice Kennedy Shriver said of her brother:

> Jack hates to lose. He learned how to play golf, and he hates to lose at that. He hates to lose at anything. *That's the only thing Jack really gets emotional about*—when he loses. Sometimes, he even gets cross. [11]

Throughout his adult life, Kennedy's affable and deceptively casual manner concealed, as a friendly biographer commented, a "keyed-up, almost compulsive, competitiveness." [12]

Kennedy's actions in Vietnam can be understood only against the background of these values, which he brought with him into the Presidency and which strongly colored the interpretation he placed on certain events that occurred early in his Administration: the Bay of Pigs fiasco, his Vienna meeting with Khrushchev, and, closely tied to the summit meeting, the confrontation with the Soviet Union over Berlin.

He came into office looking for challenge in his chosen field of interest: foreign relations. In his inaugural address (which never once mentioned the domestic scene) he declared America ready to defend "freedom in its hour of maximum danger," willing to "pay any price, bear any burden, meet any hardship, support any friend, oppose any foe to assure the survival and success of liberty." David Halberstam has written,

> Almost at the same moment that the Kennedy Administration was coming into office, Khrushchev had given a major speech giving legitimacy to wars of national liberation. The Kennedy Administration immediately interpreted this as a challenge (years later very high Soviet officials would tell their counterparts in the Kennedy Administration that it was all a mistake, the speech had been aimed not at the Americans, but at the Chinese), and suddenly the stopping of guerrilla war became a great fad. [13]

Questions about the Soviet Union's or China's actual *capacity* to produce or control insurgencies around the globe, and about whether the success of a few nationally oriented Communist insurgencies would in fact affect the security of the United States were not asked. For Kennedy and his men, it was enough that they had been challenged. They believed that relaxation of tensions could come only after they had proved their toughness. [14]

The first Kennedy response—to a challenge his own Administration had created—was the Bay of Pigs invasion, an unqualified fiasco which added, as we saw in the Gilpatric Task Force Report, more fuel to the feeling that the United States had to win the next one, no matter what. [15]

The next challenge, as Kennedy saw it, was over Berlin. The division of Berlin was the remaining unresolved issue of World War II, primarily because the Allies, pressured by West Germany, refused to give up occupation rights and sign a peace treaty recognizing East Germany. Until the U-2 affair ended plans for a summit meeting with Khrushchev, Eisenhower had been moving slowly toward negotiations on the subject. In 1961, the Soviet Union was under strong pressure to close off West Berlin as an escape route for East Germans and was pressing for negotiations on a treaty which would allow them to do this.

Kennedy's staff divided on the issue. Dean Acheson, the hard-liner appointed by Kennedy to study the problem, wanted to respond to any Russian demands with an immediate show of force. As Arthur Schlesinger observed, "For Acheson the test of will seemed almost an end in itself rather than a means to a political end."[16] Kennedy's experienced experts on Russia, including Ambassador Llewellyn Thompson and Averell Harriman, disagreed. They believed that Russian aims were defensive, an attempt to consolidate and prevent the erosion of their position in Europe rather than a preliminary to an aggressive takeover of Europe. Kennedy was much closer to Acheson's position than to that of his more realistic advisers. Nancy Gager Clinch, quoting Louise FitzSimons' careful, but critical study of Kennedy foreign policy, wrote:

> President Kennedy had assumed in preparing for the summit that to fail to adhere firmly to the Western powers' occupation rights in Berlin would be to show weakness. Crisis planning in Washington was already under way and a series of military steps were under consideration to demonstrate the American will to risk war over Berlin. . . . Any Russian requests at this time seemed to be viewed as encroachment [on the Free World] by Kennedy and his most influential advisers.[17]

Harriman, the American with the longest experience and demonstrably the best judgment in dealing with the Russians, an early dove on Vietnam, and a man long past concern with proving his own toughness, advised Kennedy not to view the meetings with Khrushchev as a personal confrontation. He told him,

> Don't be too serious, have some fun, get to know him a little, don't let him rattle you, he'll try to rattle you and frighten you, but don't pay any attention to that. Turn him aside, gently. And don't try for too much. Remember that he's just as scared as you are. . . . Laugh about it, don't get into a fight. Rise above it. Have some fun.[18]

When Khrushchev, true to form, blustered and threatened in pursuit of his objectives, Kennedy disregarded Harriman's advice and retaliated in kind. After their last meeting, Kennedy met privately with James Reston of *The New York Times*. As reported by Halberstam, he told Reston of Khrushchev's attacks:

> "I think he did it because of the Bay of Pigs, I think he thought that anyone who was so young and inexperienced as to get into that mess could be taken, and anyone who got into it, and didn't see it through, had no guts. . . . So I've got a terrible problem. If he thinks I'm inexperienced and have no guts, until we remove those ideas we won't get anywhere with him. So we have to act." Then he told Reston that he would increase the military budget and send another division to Germany. He turned to Reston and said that the only place in the world where there was a real challenge was in Vietnam, and "now we have a problem in trying to make our power credible and Vietnam looks like the place."[19]

Shortly after his return to the United States, he requested 3.25 billion dollars more in defense funds, large increases in the armed forces, a doubling then tripling of the draft, authority to call up 150,000 reservists, and a vastly enlarged bomb-shelter program. Certainly a large measure of this apocalyptic response was based on a personal reaction to an unpleasant confrontation.

Khrushchev was not so stupid as to risk all-out nuclear war over Berlin. He had threatened several times before to sign a separate peace treaty with East Germany, but had never done so.[20] If he did, it was uncertain whether the East Germans would have tried to cut the access routes to West Berlin. And if they took such actions, there were, as in 1947, many gradations of diplomatic and economic pressure that could be applied before an overt military response was threatened. Nevertheless, Kennedy leaped to describe the problem in cataclysmic terms. "West Berlin," he told the American public in July 1961, ". . . above all, has now become—as never before—the great testing place of Western courage and will, a focal point where our solemn commitments stretching back over the years to 1945, and Soviet ambitions now meet in basic confrontation. . . . "[21]

In October 1961, when it became clear that the Viet Cong were winning, Kennedy felt he had no choice. Vietnam was the place to prove his Administration's toughness. He sent two of his key advisers, Walt Rostow and General Maxwell Taylor, to Vietnam. Although the mission was said to be designed to give the President a first-hand, objective view of the facts, its composition reveals otherwise. Rostow and Taylor, as Kennedy well knew, were both hard-liners and leaders of the counterinsurgency movement. In particular, Rostow's eagerness to demonstrate the accuracy of his theories of guerrilla warfare was well known.[22] The mission included no one with countervailing views. The President had stacked the deck. No one would—and no one did, in the White House on their return—consider the option of doing nothing, or of removing the economic-aid mission then in place in South Vietnam. Although rejecting direct involvement of American troops (he had been burned once at the Bay of Pigs), Kennedy did accept the Rostow-Taylor recommendation to send combat support units, air-combat and helicopter teams, military advisers and instructors and Green Beret teams, an American involvement which had grown to more than 15,000 men by the end of 1963. The fact that a special national intelligence estimate prepared by U.S. agencies reported that "80–90 percent of the estimated 17,000 Viet Cong guerrillas had been locally recruited, and that there was little evidence that they relied on external supplies,"[23] thereby belying the "Communist monolith" theory of the war, was ignored by Kennedy (as Johnson would ignore, at great cost, other intelligence reports that pointed away from involvement). To "win the next one" Kennedy had taken the key step of committing American soldiers to the war, thereby giving the military a foot in the door and drawing press and national attention to the conflict and his Administration's commitment.

By the fall of 1963, when reports in the press that Viet Cong were doing very well against the South Vietnamese army and their American advisers could no longer be denied, Kennedy himself was unhappy with the commitment and—with Attorney General Robert Kennedy, his closest adviser—may have been looking for an opening to move away from it. By then the President was able to allow his natural skepticism somewhat freer rein. His handling of the Cuban missile crisis was considered at the time to be a great success* and he had gone a long way toward demonstrating not only to the public but to himself that he was tough and in command. It did for him—at the risk of Armageddon—what a career as a general in the army had done for Dwight Eisenhower: put his toughness and manhood beyond doubt.

There is also some indication that by 1963 Robert Kennedy too was changing. According to Halberstam, he began to shed his simplistic, hard-line view of the world, and to develop "a capacity . . . to see world events not so much in terms of a great global chess game, but in human terms." He *felt* things, despite a conflicting attempt to maintain his cool. Virtually alone among the President's advisers, "his questions at meetings always centered around the people of Vietnam: What is all this doing to the people? Do you think those people really want us there? Maybe we're trying to do the wrong thing?"[25] And that fall, he was the first high official of the Administration to suggest that it was time to consider withdrawing from Vietnam.

Against these factors one must weigh President Kennedy's fear of domestic political reaction to a "pullout"—he foresaw a resurgence of the "soft on communism" charges hurled at the Democrats by Senator Joseph McCarthy during the fifties—and its effect on the impending Presidential election of 1964. Taken together with his personal emotional commitment to counterinsurgency and victory, and the growth of the American effort under his aegis up to November 1963, it seems unlikely that Kennedy would have quickly ended United States involvement.[26]

But if there was at least a chance that the Kennedys were growing away from the view that they had to win in Vietnam, President Johnson and the advisers he inherited from Kennedy were not. McGeorge Bundy and Walt Rostow, academicians who

---

*Recently, however, historians taking a second look have considered Kennedy's handling of the Cuban missile crisis to be a case of reckless, unnecessary heroics.[24]

became, under Johnson, the key White House advisers on Vietnam, were believers in the ultrarealism school of government. "Its proponents believed that they were tough, that they knew what the world was really like, and that force must be accepted as a basic element of diplomacy. . . . Bundy would tell antiwar gadfly John Kenneth Galbraith with a certain element of disappointment, 'Ken, you always advise against the use of force—do you realize that?'"[27] Bundy also had an impulse toward action. Enormously confident, both in himself and in the power of the United States, he gloried in the challenge of taking a problem apart and mastering it. His instinct was always to try something. And, of course, power accrued to the "can-do" men, men whose mastery took the form of visible action, not those who expressed doubts and attacked the proposals of others. To answer, "Nothing," to the question, "What can be done about disagreeable development X?" was passive, the mark of a loser and a weakling.[28]

The tough, no-nonsense posture, common among professors of government and history in the late 1950s and 1960s, was also a kind of protection. University intellectuals have always been suspected in America of being a little soft; exclusive devotion to intellectual matters has been thought of as not quite manly. It's legitimate to attend the university to gather knowledge and technique and even to improve oneself, but after that the real man goes out into the harsh world of action and conflict and gets things done. A tough line in foreign affairs made one sound like a man of action—even if the action was all on paper.

Johnson's single most influential adviser on Vietnam, Secretary of Defense Robert McNamara, had shown that he could get things done before he got to Washington by serving as president of the Ford Motor Company. But there was a split in his personality. His neighbors in Ann Arbor, where he had lived while at Ford, and his social friends in Washington knew him as a warm man of deep and humane feeling. But during the working day he was a different person, cold and machinelike, all emotion ruled out as antithetical to the task to be accomplished. His chief passion was rationality, a quintessentially masculine and, finally, narrow rationality based on the premise that anything worth knowing can and ought to be reduced to numbers and statistics.

> One was always aware of his time; speak quickly and be gone, make your point, in and out, keep the schedule, lunch from 1:50 to, say, expansively 2 P.M., and above all, do not engage in any philosophical discussions, *Well, Bob,* my view of *history is . . .* No one was going to abuse his time. Do not, he told his aides, let people brief me orally. If they are going to make a presentation, find out in advance and make them put it on paper. "Why?" an aide asked. A cold look. "Because I can read faster than they can talk."[29]

This total distrust of feeling, of intuition, of nuance which can be conveyed only in personal contact was costly for McNamara. On his frequent early trips to South Vietnam, it led him to ignore the unquantifiable but real signs that the war was not going well, signs that, behind the body count and barrage of statistics about villages secured, the political structure of South Vietnam was falling apart. It led him to disregard the repeated warnings from the CIA that things were not what the numbers made them seem, that the bombing would not, in the phrase of the day, "break Hanoi's will to resist."

Most important, McNamara kept his professional life separate from the "unmasculine" values and impulses that would have led him to question the assumption that the United States had to win in Vietnam: compassion for our soldiers and the people of Vietnam; doubt about his mandate and ability to impose his view of the world on others; and the willingness to feel, through an act of empathy, what the other side is feeling and so understand that their "logic" might be different from his own. This schism made it impossible for him to challenge the objective of victory. Basic policy objectives, the starting point for strategic and tactical analysis, always grow out of underlying personal values. And values are closely linked to—in fact are the organized expression of—the emotions we consider legitimate and allow ourselves to express.

McNamara was not alone in his attempt to cut the "soft," "subjective" element out of his professional life. Secretary of State Dean Rusk cabled his ambassadors to stop using the word "feel" in their dispatches.[30] He and Rostow were not torn by the war. They were true believers. Rusk's career had been built on the cold-war dogmas of the late forties and fifties and he thought them eternal verities. They felt no conflict and, later, no remorse over the war.

McNamara's role, on the other hand, was tragic. He had great drive, an incredibly organized intelligence, and a strong commitment to public service. And he had deeply humane and liberal impulses—and what goes with them, a strongly held ethical framework. But this side of his personality was compartmentalized, walled off from his professional life. In this tension, he exemplified the *best* in American public men and, in the end, the war tore him apart. He could not bring the humane side of himself to bear in thinking about the war. Instead, the cult of toughness went unchallenged as the unarticulated major premise of all the systems analysis, war gaming, and policymaking. For all his other sensitivities, he was as much a victim of it as the others. His spontaneous response in a hostile confrontation with a group of students after a speech at Harvard in November 1966 was to shout at them that he was tougher than they were— although that had nothing to do with the issue in dispute.

In Lyndon Johnson there was no foil, no wellspring of opposing values and perspectives that would have allowed him to understand the limitations of these men. He was more openly insecure about his masculinity than John Kennedy and often made explicit the connection between these doubts and his decisions of state. No one has captured this better than Halberstam in his discussion of Johnson's decision to begin the bombing of North Vietnam:

He had always been haunted by the idea that he would be judged as being insufficiently manly for the job, that he would lack courage at a crucial moment. More than a little insecure himself, he wanted very much to be seen as a man; it was a conscious thing. . . . [H]e wanted the respect of men who were tough, real men, and they would turn out to be the hawks. He had unconsciously divided people around him between men and boys. Men were activists, doers, who conquered business empires, who acted instead of talked, who made it in the world of other men and had the respect of other men. Boys were the talkers and the writers and the intellectuals, who sat around thinking and criticizing and doubting instead of doing. . . .

*   *   *

As Johnson weighed the advice he was getting on Vietnam, it was the boys who were most skeptical, and the men who were most sure and confident and hawkish and who had Johnson's respect. Hearing that one member of his Administration was becoming a dove on Vietnam, Johnson said, "Hell, he has to squat to piss." The *men* had, after all, done things in their lifetimes, and they had the respect of other men. Doubt itself, he thought, was almost a feminine quality, doubts were for women; once, on another issue, when Lady Bird raised her doubts, Johnson had said of course she was doubtful, it was like a woman to be uncertain.[31]

Others played on Johnson's fear of not being manly enough. In late 1964 and 1965, Joseph Alsop, a prowar Washington columnist, wrote a series of columns which suggested that the President might be too weak to take the necessary steps, weaker than his predecessor was during the Cuban missile crisis. The columns hit Johnson's rawest nerve. He was very angry about them, but not unaffected. Bill Moyers, one of his closest aides, recalled that the President told him, after a National Security Council meeting, of his fear that, if he got out of Vietnam, McNamara and the other ex–Kennedy men would think him "less of a man" than Kennedy, would call up Alsop and tell him so, and that Alsop would write it up in his column. In dealing with a man with these anxieties, the military always had the advantage. "In decision making," Halberstam put it, "they proposed the manhood positions, their opponents the softer, or sissy, positions."[32]

Johnson was more open than the other men in his Administration about the connection between his views about the war and his preoccupation with aggressive masculinity and sexuality. The day after ordering the bombing of North Vietnam PT-boat bases and oil depots, the first act of war against North Vietnam, Johnson buoyantly told a reporter, "I didn't just screw Ho Chi Minh. I cut his pecker off."[33] Speaking of Johnson's psychological stake in the war, Moyers has said,

> It was as if there had been a transfer of personal interest and prestige to the war, and to our fortunes there. It was almost like a frontier test, as if he were saying, "By God, I'm not going to let those puny brown people push me around."

The tragedy of Vietnam for Lyndon Johnson was that he fought the war in part to protect the political capital he needed to push through his Great Society programs at home, and in the end it was the war that destroyed his credibility and brought the Great Society to a dead halt. Unlike John Kennedy and the men of the Eastern Establishment he brought into the government to run the country's foreign affairs, Johnson's real interest lay in the domestic sphere. He cared deeply about civil rights, education, and poverty; the place in history he wanted would come from progress on these fronts, not through the execution of grand designs in the international arena. But he thought he had to be tough in dealing with Vietnam or, even after his landslide victory in 1964, the Congress, sensing "weakness," would turn on him as he thought they had turned on Truman for "losing China."[34] But even his reading of domestic political history, like Kennedy's before him and Richard Nixon's later, was biased by his preoccupation with toughness.

Just as they did not examine carefully the question, "What exactly is the U.S. interest in Vietnam?", Kennedy and Johnson and their experts did not look to see if their fears about a reaction from the right were supported by the facts. If they had, the McCarthyite storm clouds would not have appeared so near and so dark. During the years that our Vietnam policy was shaped,

1954–1965, public awareness of and interest in Vietnam was low. Presidents Eisenhower, Kennedy, and, until 1965, Johnson, were not acting under pressure of aroused public opinion, even from the right.[35] Their Administrations *made* Vietnam into news, by treating events there as significant, by making predictions of victory which did not come true, and, ultimately, by sending in United States forces and their inevitable companions, the television and writing press.

Even after Vietnam was forced into the headlines, our Presidents have consistently dragged public opinion behind them. Support for United States policy has risen after dramatic military moves or initiatives which promised peace, and then trailed off as the war continued. In fact, a key concern which runs consistently through the Pentagon Papers is how to create and maintain public support for the war. Somehow it never struck Johnson, and later Nixon, as paradoxical that they should have to strain so hard to justify the war—preserving American honor; saving democracy in Southeast Asia; keeping our word; stopping the spread of communism—and at the same time fear a strong political reaction from the right if they withdrew.

In the 1940s and 1950s a powerful and vocal group of Americans naively believed that we had a special relationship with China which could be "lost." There were no comparable myths about South Vietnam. Joe McCarthy's appeals took root during the Korean war and during a period of adjustment to the fact that victory in World War II was followed by the cold war instead of the tranquility we expected. The real lessons of the era—that Eisenhower was elected in large part to end the Korean war, and that the end of that war, even on the ambiguous terms of the armistice, decreased rather than increased McCarthy's influence—seem to have been ignored. Finally, political scientists examining the results of the 1952 elections have shown that, contrary to myth, McCarthy's charges of being "soft on communism" did not translate into votes. Democrats lost the 1952 election generally, but Democrats whom McCarthy had attacked did no worse than the others. Senator William Benton of Connecticut, who was attacked by McCarthy and whose defeat was widely attributed to McCarthy's political clout, for example, lost no more support in the Eisenhower landslide than other Democratic candidates in Connecticut.

In short, Presidents Kennedy, Johnson, and Nixon and their advisers drew an analogy between the politics of the fifties and the politics of the sixties without examining the realities of either. This failure of analysis and the readiness to believe that the right, which might accuse them of being too soft and weak if they withdrew from Vietnam, had great political power, was in large part the result of their personal preoccupation with toughness and the projection of that preoccupation onto the voting public.

Another rebuttal to the suggestion that the cult of toughness directly influenced our policymakers is to suggest that individuals did not feel personally threatened by the idea of backing down in Vietnam but, rather, realistically recognized that advocating withdrawal would discredit them within the decision-making bureaucracy. As Richard Barnett has pointed out, one can be a "hawk," have one's advice rejected, and still maintain credibility in Washington, while unsuccessful advocacy of a "dovish" position is permanently discrediting. But this explanation only proves the point. What created the climate in which the "soft" position is riskier than the "hard" position? It grows out of the fears of the powerful individual members of the bureaucracy that they themselves will appear soft.

The cult of toughness has also biased the Vietnam policies of President Nixon and Henry Kissinger, his chief foreign-policy adviser, but in a subtler and, in some ways, purer form than in previous administrations. Richard Nixon turned out not to be the rigidly doctrinaire anti-Communist we believed him to be. The *détente* with China and his willingness to deal with the Soviet Union on a broad range of issues from arms control to trade made that clear. There is no question that he is aware of the depth of the split between the Soviet Union and China and that the Communist nations of the world do not now, if they ever did, constitute a monolith with a coordinated foreign policy aimed at subverting the non-Communist world. Henry Kissinger, his chief White House adviser and then Secretary of State, has an extraordinarily sophisticated view of foreign affairs.

Kissinger became convinced in 1967–1968, as the result of his analysis of the political forces at work in Vietnam, that the United States could not win there in the sense of keeping a non-Communist government in power indefinitely.[36] And despite Nixon's public pronouncements, there is strong evidence that he shared this belief. Richard Whalen, a Nixon adviser and speechwriter during the 1968 campaign, quoted Nixon as saying in March of that year, "I've come to the conclusion that there's no way to win the war. But we can't say that, of course. In fact, we have to seem to say the opposite, just to keep some degree of bargaining leverage."[37] And, at least privately, Kissinger explained that a genuine victory was not a vital United States objective. What he and Nixon did believe was critical—critical enough to justify four more years of war, ten thousand American casualties, countless Vietnamese killed, maimed, and homeless, endangerment of the Arms Limitation Agreement with the Soviet Union, and social and political upheaval at home—was that the United States avoid the *appearance* of losing. It was vital, in Kissinger's off-the-record words, that there be "a decent interval" between United States withdrawal and the collapse of the Saigon government, a period of time which would allow the Communist takeover of the South to appear to be the result of political forces within the country rather than the failure of United States assistance.[38] Again the rationale was that this was necessary to prevent a right-wing McCarthyite backlash at home as well as to preserve American "credibility"—a favorite Kissinger term—abroad. Kissinger wrote, in January 1969, that

the commitment of five hundred thousand Americans has settled the issue of the importance of Vietnam. For what is involved now is confidence in American promises. However fashionable it is to

ridicule the terms "credibility" or "prestige," they are not empty
phrases; other nations can gear their actions to ours only if they
can count on our steadiness. . . . In many parts of the world—the
Middle East, Europe, Latin America, even Japan—stability depends on confidence in American promises. Unilateral withdrawal or a settlement which, even unintentionally, amounts to it
could therefore lead to the erosion of restraints and to an even
more dangerous international situation.[39]

The principal audience for the demonstration of credibility is the
Soviet leadership and it is their restraint that is the focus of the
Nixon-Kissinger foreign policy. So far so good; it is hard to argue
with the premise that the United States has some responsibility
for restraining the Soviet Union from efforts, however unlikely,
to overrun Western Europe, from sending their own forces to
fight in a "war of national liberation," or threatening Japan with
nuclear weapons, or decisively shifting the military balance in
the Middle East. Such actions are less likely if the Soviet Union,
and this nation's friends, believe that the United States will
respond, to the point of meeting force with force if necessary. But
the other key premises of the Kissinger-Nixon foreign policy are
more leaps of faith than applications of logic. "Credibility" is
made into an absolute virtue, independent of the context in
which it is demonstrated and the situations to which, like ac-
cumulated savings, it is later to be applied. Responding to a
"challenge" where we have nothing at stake except credibility
itself is considered just as important in maintaining this elusive
virtue as responding firmly where national security is directly
and immediately threatened; maybe, in the Nixon-Kissinger
calculus it is even more important—if Americans are willing to
fight over tiny, remote South Vietnam, maybe the other side will
believe that we are ready to fight over anything. As Nixon wrote
in *Six Crises*,

we should stand ready to call international Communism's bluff on
any pot, large or small. If we let them know that we will defend
freedom when the stakes are small, the Soviets are not encouraged
to threaten freedom when the stakes are higher. That is why . . .

> all the . . . peripheral areas are so important in the poker game of world politics.[40]

This is a very high-risk strategy, since it is based on the assumption that the Soviet Union will follow a "weaker" policy of *not* turning every confrontation with the United States into a test of its own credibility. In 1961, for example, Kissinger wanted our forces to invade East Berlin and tear down the Berlin Wall to maintain United States credibility, although he recognized the essentially nonaggressive motivation of the Soviet Union.[41] The second key premise of the Nixon foreign policy is "linkage," the idea that

> all the world's trouble spots exist on a single continuum which connects the Soviet Union and the United States. In this context, the resolution of individual issues depends not so much on the merits of the specific issues as on the overall balance of power between the two sides. And the underlying assumption of linkage is that the settlement of a crisis in one area of the world can be predetermined by the strength and degree of resolution which one or both of the contending parties have shown in other areas.[42]

As applied by Kissinger to Vietnam, this meant that if the United States appeared to fail there, the enemies of our allies elsewhere would feel less constrained in resorting to force; and even where our allies were not the object of armed attack, some might feel coerced into one or another form of voluntary submission.[43] It is indisputable that many international developments are in fact linked, or at least—in the phrase of James C. Thompson, Jr.—have "ripple" effects on each other depending on the geographical and conceptual distances between them.[44] But, as David Landau—writing in 1972, before our "peace with honor" exit from the Vietnam war and before the October war in the Middle East—prophetically suggested:

> At a certain remove linkage becomes unjustified; it is silly to think that Soviet assistance to the Arab nations in the Mideast is in any way comparable to, or closer to a solution by virtue of, America's

prosecution of a full-scale Indochina war. And it is even less reasonable to suppose that America's steadfastness in Southeast Asia measurably affects Washington's credibility in the European theatre, with the Soviet Union, or even with the West European Allies; from Europe's vantage point, the war is an exercise not in credibility, but in irrational and absurd theatricality.[45]

* * *

Nixon and Kissinger cannot satisfactorily demonstrate to themselves or to anyone else that a high degree of "resolution" in one area will have the desired effect in other areas. From a detached outsider's view, it seems as plausible to say that this approach builds tension by encouraging Soviet toughness as to claim that it relaxes hostility by forcing Moscow to be more reasonable.[46]

In short, the search for "peace with honor" in Vietnam, after Kissinger's sophisticated intellectual gloss and skilled diplomatic tactics are stripped away, was shaped and governed by the same tired, dangerous, arbitrary, and "masculine" first principles: one must never back away once a line is drawn in the dust; every battle must be won; and, if one fails to observe the first two injunctions and by some fluke the rest of the world doesn't care, the domestic right—the "real men"—will get you for being too soft.

Kissinger is too subtle and private a person for these underlying personal imperatives to be seen directly in what is known of his character and work. But the same is not true of Nixon.

Nixon's particular variant of the cult of toughness is, in Garry Wills' phrase, the "cult of crisis," the ultimate embodiment of the self-made man, he is always remaking and testing himself, watching from some disembodied vantage point to make sure his machinery is working. And the test that counts, the action that separates the men from the boys, that allows him to parade his efforts and virtue, and to experience his worth in the marketplace of competition most vividly, is the crisis. This can be seen in "his eagerness, always, to be 'in the arena,' his praise of others for being cool under pressure, for being 'tested in the fires.'"[47] The title and format of Nixon's book, *Six Crises*, also reflects this preoccupation. Each chapter describes a problem he faced, his efforts to deal with it, and the lessons he learned, mainly about his own reactions to pressure. Some of these lessons are quite revealing.

The most difficult part of any crisis, he wrote, "is the period of indecision—*whether to fight or run away*."[48] But the choice, as he poses it, is not a real choice at all. What self-respecting man, let alone a President of the United States, can choose to "run away"? Even within the limited range of options he posits, he could have used other words—"walk away," "avoid the issue," for example—which encompass the possibility that retreat can be rational and dignified. "Run away" permits none of these overtones; it sounds just plain cowardly. More important, the *substance* of the issue, what is actually at stake (apart from honor and "credibility"), has dropped from sight. The emphasis is not on the problem at hand, not on trying to determine what objective is worth pursuing at what cost, but on *himself*—on his courage or lack thereof. In his October 26, 1973, press conference, for example, he said of himself in answer to a question about Watergate, "the tougher it gets the cooler I get"; he responded to another question about the Middle East conflict with "when I have to face an international crisis I have what it takes."[49]

During Nixon's 1958 tour through South America, he was told that violent anti-American demonstrations were likely at a planned visit to San Marcos University in Lima. There was real danger of physical injury. The decision: should he cancel the visit or go through with it? Here's how he saw it in *Six Crises:*

> The purpose of my tour was to present a symbol of the United States as a free, democratic, and powerful friend of our South American neighbors. In this context, my decision became clear. If I chose not to go to San Marcos, I would have failed at least in Peru. But if I did go, I would have a chance to demonstrate that the United States does not shrink from its responsibilities or flee in the face of threats. . . .
>
> * * *
>
> But the case for not going was also compelling. I would be risking injury, not only to myself but to others. If someone was hurt, I would be blamed. And if I took the easier and safer course of

canceling the visit to San Marcos and going to Catholic University
I might well be able to put the blame on both the Peruvian officials
and the Communists.

* * *

But my intuition, backed by considerable experience, was that I
should go. . . . [If I did not go, it] would not be simply a case of
Nixon being bluffed out by a group of students, but of the United
States itself putting its tail between its legs and running away
from a bunch of Communist thugs.[50]

Two things stand out: first his view of the challenge to
him—which was, after all, only a small, transitory, and propa-
gandistic piece of the mosaic of relations with Latin America
—as affecting the long-term realities of this country's for-
tunes; and, second, his tendency, like Kennedy and Johnson, to
sweep away all complexities in a conflict and reduce the issue
to the question of whether to stand up to the schoolyard bully.
(In Caracas, another stop, Nixon's car was stoned by demonstrators and he was also physically threatened. Every year
Nixon celebrates the anniversary of that brush with danger
with a small party.)

In his meeting with Khrushchev while Vice-President, also
described in *Six Crises*, he took the same approach, even in
private sessions where propaganda was not involved. Khrushchev blustered away, boasting about the strength of the
Soviet military. In that forum, Nixon said, "I could answer him
and counterattack, point by point, and I proceeded to do so. It
was cold steel between us all afternoon." His account of the
meeting and his tactics read like a debating manual, Nixon
describing how he countered this point with that, got the Pre-
mier off balance or was momentarily thrown off balance himself.
Again, what is striking is the extent to which Nixon, like Kennedy in Vienna, identified the fate of the United States with his
"showing" in the meeting and his ready assumption that the
most important aspect in the meeting was to demonstrate, while
not seeming belligerent, that he could not be pushed around.

Outstanding among Nixon's unacknowledged feelings, Bruce

Mazlish pointed out in his psychohistorical study, *In Search of Nixon*, is his fear of passivity:

> He is afraid of being acted upon, of being inactive, of being soft, of being thought impotent, and of being dependent on anyone else. . . . He is constantly talking about an enemy [the Soviet Union used to be the chief villain; these days it is "those who would use the smokescreen of Watergate. . . "] probing for soft spots in him (and thus America). To defend us or himself, Nixon must deny he is "soft" on communism, or Castro, or anything else.[51]

He compensates with an inordinate preoccupation with strength and fighting. The apparent ability to "hang tough" or "tough it out" appears to be the main conscious criterion on his choice of key advisers. A President needs, Mazlish recorded him as saying, "people who aren't panicking . . . somebody who brings serenity, calmness or strength into the room."[52]

In 1969, long after it became clear that "international communism" as a working entity did not exist and that the North Vietnamese could not create or control revolutionary movements in other countries, Nixon's rhetoric focused even more explicitly on credibility and face. Speaking to the nation after the invasion of Cambodia by American troops he declared, "It is not our power but our will and character that are being tested tonight." (Sounds like Kennedy's description of West Berlin as "the great testing place of Western courage and will.") And deeply moved by the vision of the United States acting like "a pitiful, helpless giant," he vowed that he would not see the country become a "second-rate power" and "accept the first defeat in its proud 190-year history." Mazlish noted,

> In the first two short paragraphs of that speech, . . . the pronoun "I" is used six times. The speech as a whole is filled with "I have concluded," "I shall describe," "this is my decision," and other similar phrases. We also have "we will not be humiliated," "we will not be defeated," and the repetitive threat that if the enemy's attacks continue to "humiliate and defeat us," we shall react accordingly.[53]

Vice-President Agnew, doing Nixon's gut work during the 1968–1972 Administration, compared then-Senator Charles Goodell to Christine Jorgensen, a man surgically changed into a woman, literally an emasculated man, in describing Goodell's shift from hawk to dove.

Foreign affairs is an ideal area into which to project the need to be tough and aggressive. There are fewer constraints in that sphere than in domestic affairs. Domestic affairs are characterized by wide dissemination of information and fast political response which tends to check the transformation of psychological needs into policy. Basic objectives in foreign affairs are necessarily stated in highly abstract terms—"a world safe for diversity"—and are achievable, if at all, only in the long term, making strategy and programs difficult to evaluate. How, for example, could it be proven that progress toward the objective of an economically strong, politically liberal Latin America did or did not result from United States intervention in the Dominican Republic in 1965? In foreign affairs, one can more easily get away with labeling the other side in a confrontation as thoroughly evil, a description which justifies complete victory and makes a defeat less acceptable. There is less pressure to deal with the enemy up close, as human beings rather than abstractions. And only in foreign affairs can the President's advisers gather in the White House communications center at three in the morning to read freshly decoded cables describing battles in progress and use their analytical skills to map out "scenarios" involving aircraft carriers, generals and troops and real guns to "break the will of the enemy." For the foreign-policy intellectuals of the Kennedy and Johnson Administrations the Vietnam conflict was an opportunity to exercise overt, direct power usually denied to scholars and foundation executives. It was their chance to play in the big leagues.

The arms race is another area in which judgments have been

distorted by male values. Two mistakes have characterized United States policy. First, our government has assumed that the Soviet Union would build as many and as advanced planes or missiles as was economically and technically possible—known among defense planners as "worst-case analysis." The illusory missile gap of 1959–1961 is an example. If American men are brought up to believe that they should be constantly aggressive and dominant, it is only natural that they assume their opponents will act the same way, regardless of the objective evidence. Second, despite strong indications that additional missiles are not necessary or particularly helpful as a deterrent, we have frequently made arms policy as though the key objective were to maintain a force larger in numbers or megatons of deliverable bombs than the Russians'. The United States rushed into equipping its missiles with multiple independently targeted warheads (MIRVs) while arms limitation talks were in progress. The rationale was that MIRVs were needed to establish a strong bargaining position. Since the United States was in fact in a position of strength before the MIRV program started, this suggests a commitment to competition for the sake of competition, the influence of the psychological need to feel bigger and more powerful than opponents regardless of actual national security needs. The result, predictably, was to make it inevitable that the Russians push ahead with their own MIRV program.

Not every male policymaker is driven by the masculine ideal, but most are significantly moved by it. Even among men who are subject to its pressures, however, decisions are the result of a complex set of influences, some of which, for particular individuals in particular areas, tip the balance away from the masculinist imperatives. Former Undersecretary of State George Ball, for example, who advised President Johnson against escalation, had a long history of diplomatic involvement with Europe and the idea of an American-European political and economic union. This helps explain why, of all President Johnson's senior advisers, he was most predisposed to play down the importance of conflict in Southeast Asia in favor of an emphasis on Europe. I do not mean to denigrate in any way the value of Ball's courageous and clear-headed opposition to the Vietnam war, I am simply suggesting that a confrontation between the United States and the Soviet Union in Europe would have posed a greater test of objectivity for someone with his professional history.

It is fair to ask whether the need to dominate and win in every confrontation situation isn't likely to be characteristic of anyone, male or female, who climbs to the highest ranks of government in our competitive society. The answer is a complicated no. Most women are not as personally threatened as most men by the suggestion that they are not tough enough. As Daniel Ellsberg pointed out, "In almost every case the wives of [the] major officials [directing the United States' participation in the Vietnam war] *did* manage to see both the impossibility of what their husbands were trying to achieve and the brutality of it and immorality of it."[54] The comprehensive Harris poll of American women's opinion conducted in 1970 supports Ellsberg's observation. Seven out of ten women and eight out of ten men are willing to go to war to defend the continental United States. But women are much less willing than men to go to war over actions that do not threaten the United States directly: invasion of Canada (78% of women willing compared to 84% of men willing); Communist invasion of Western Europe (42% to 60%); Russian takeover of West Berlin (37% to 50%); Communist invasion of Australia (37% to 54%); Communist takeover of South Vietnam (33% to 43%); takeover of South American country by Castro (31% to 43%); imminent Israeli loss in a war with the Arabs (17% to 28%). Significantly more women than men felt that the pace of Nixon's withdrawal of American forces from Vietnam was "too slow." Two out of three women but only 49% of men say they would become upset upon hearing "that a young draftee has been killed in Vietnam."[55]

Women have also been brought up to shy away from rigorous intellectual pursuits and vigorous initiative and leadership, so it *is* more difficult for a woman in this culture to maintain the self-confidence and drive needed to achieve a position of responsibility in government or elsewhere.

In the past women who did make it were able to do so only by adopting male values; it seems unlikely that these women would have done a better job on Vietnam, or the arms race. But, in the last five years under the influence of feminism, substantial numbers of women have broken away from the traditional female self-images and roles without adopting the compulsive toughness of the male stereotype. These women, and the smaller number of men who have begun to question the validity of the traditional male sex-stereotype, have the self-confidence to achieve positions of responsibility and power without feeling a personal need to respond to every challenge. Female or male, this kind of human being might well have kept us out of Vietnam.

The reasoning of this chapter will sound strange and illegitimate to many readers. American foreign policy is almost never analyzed in terms of the psychology of its makers. By unwritten consensus, this influence on public policy has been regarded as too personal and too subjective to be reliable. In fact, the taboo exists because the men who make the policy and analyze it are often uncomfortable with and ill-equipped to understand the role that their personal feelings and values play in decisions of state. As a result, men tend to be not only unwilling to focus on the role that their own psychology plays in their decisions but also only dimly aware that they have distinct psychological biases. Feeling that way about themselves, government officials and their male critics are more comfortable dealing exclusively with the "objective" elements of public policy, despite a growing awareness that analyses of military strength, political support, and cost-benefit ratios often involve leaps of subjective intuition.

Armchair psychoanalysis of public figures is unreliable. Conclusions are usually drawn about personality characteristics and problems unique to the individual on the basis of inadequate evidence and, for that reason, are useful neither to the individual involved nor to society at large. But analyses of the influence of

widely shared psychological biases which are created by common conditioning steers clear of these pitfalls. As psychohis-
torian Mazlish wrote,

> [The] "style" of politics may be vastly different among political
> leaders—for example, John F. Kennedy and Richard Nixon
> —while the substance of personality may be greatly alike. From
> different backgrounds and different life experiences, political
> figures may arrive at the same character traits of competitive-
> ness, fear of softness, and so forth. The reason must be sought in
> the fact that they all emerge from the same mold of American
> values; in short, from the constant corresponding processes and
> the basic "character" of the American people as it has been up to
> now. [56]

Analyses of this kind will not alone fully explain complex gov-
ernmental decisionmaking. Along with the failures of judgment
examined here, our nation's long involvement in Vietnam was
grounded on our World War II role as defender of the Free World;
our attempt in the early fifties to barter aid to the French in
Indochina for France's membership in a projected European
Defense Community; Cardinal Spellman's lobbying, during
the Eisenhower Administration, for United States support of
Diem, a devout Catholic; and the bureaucratic inertia created
once officials staked their careers on recommendations that we
intervene. But these other causes, like the "objective" arguments for and against United States involvement, have been
exhaustively and repeatedly analyzed over the last decade.
And all those articles, war games, area studies, and systems
analyses—the accepted tools for exploring public issues—have
not dented the basic attitudes of men like Richard Nixon who,
as late as 1968, could describe the Vietnam war as "one of
America's finest hours." Nixon got our troops out of Vietnam,
but only because their withdrawal was required for his political
survival and because he was able to avoid, at least in his eyes,
the appearance of losing.

We may even avoid exact, carbon-copy Vietnams of the future.
But the lesson of enduring value—the lesson that our policy is in

danger of being pushed in stupid, costly, and dangerous directions by the cult of toughness—has not and will not be learned from public debate which does not focus critically on the existence and influence of the biases created by the masculine ideal. A decade of traditional dialogue and interpretation of the Vietnam experience did not stop Nixon from continuing to support the prosecution of the war—at a cost of two billion dollars a year and a million new refugees; it didn't stop him from bombing Cambodia; it didn't stop him from believing that our prestige required an SST which was a disaster from every other point of view;* and it didn't stop him from adding MIRVs to the nation's existing nuclear overkill capacity.

To learn the real lessons of Vietnam for our foreign policy, we need desperately to broaden the scope of public debate. Let us make mistakes at the outset if we must, but let us begin to talk about what is really going on in the minds of the men who spend our blood and our treasure to save their sacred honor.

---

* Vice-President Ford, Nixon's choice, said, arguing in Congress for the SST, that the vote would determine whether each Congressman was "a man or a mouse". [57]

13. Speculations on Watergate

> . . . . the Watergate matter was an inevitable outgrowth of a climate of excessive concern over the political impact of demonstrators, excessive concern over leaks, an insatiable appetite for political intelligence, all coupled with a do-it-yourself White House staff, regardless of the law.
>
> —John W. Dean, III (testifying before the Senate Select Committee on Presidential Campaign Activities, June 25, 1973)

The tangle of events known as Watergate cannot be fully explained by reference to masculine values or any other single cause. The question of causation is too slippery for that, the incidents too varied and complex. Yet it seems to me that some of the necessary propensities for the most disturbing Watergate crimes do bear the stamp of the Nixon Administration's extreme and defensive masculinism. Specifically, without the paranoia and absence of moral restraint described by John Dean and the unquestioning loyalty and deference the Administration required of its servants, it seems to me, they would not have occurred.

Let's look first at the paranoia. From July 1970 on, according to Dean, the White House continually sought intelligence information about demonstration leaders and their supporters to indicate that the demonstrations were sponsored by a foreign enemy or Senate Democrats opposed to Nixon's war policies.[1] When intelligence agencies repeatedly reported that such connections did not exist, the White House staff, according to Dean "disbelieving and complaining," decided that "the entire system for gathering such intelligence was worthless."[2] This led directly to the Huston plan, approved by Nixon but later withdrawn because J. Edgar Hoover refused to go along. The plan, involving the CIA in clear violation of its legal mandate, authorized burglary, spying on students and other Americans abroad, intensification of electronic surveillance of Americans here at home "who pose a major threat to the internal security" as well as foreign embassies; listening in on Americans making overseas telephone calls, and the surreptitious and illegal opening and copying of mail.[3]

Nixon's personal hatred and fear of those who openly opposed him was so great that Dwight Chapin, his appointments secretary felt compelled to order up some "thugs" to remove a lone demonstrator Nixon had seen in a park across the street from the White House. H. R. Haldeman, Nixon's chief of staff, authorized the use of "any means—legal or illegal" to deal with demonstrators confronting the President on his travels.[4]

When the Pentagon Papers were published in 1971, Nixon was more than annoyed. He labeled the release of this four-year-old study "a security leak of unprecedented proportions" creating, as he still insisted two years later—with the Republic still intact—"a threat so grave as to require extraordinary actions."[5] The White House apparently found it impossible to believe that Daniel Ellsberg had acted out of a sense of duty to the country and not in collaboration with the Soviet Union, a charge so unsupported by evidence that it was never even raised at Ellsberg's trial. Mistrusting the FBI, Nixon created the plumbers unit, and charged Egil Krogh, the head plumber, with the task, "vitally important to national security," of finding out all he could about Ellsberg's associates and motives.[6] The result was the burglary of Ellsberg's psychiatrist's office.

The famous "enemies" lists of 1971, collections of individuals slated to be "screwed" through harassment by the Federal machinery,[7] as R. W. Apple, Jr., wrote: "showed the siege mentality at work":

> On them were not just "radic-libs" such as Paul Newman, the McGovernite actor; not just liberal establishment newspapers such as The New York Times, The Washington Post and The St. Louis Post-Dispatch, with their fierce opposition to the Vietnam war; not just the 12 black Representatives in Congress at the time . . .; not just the Presidents of Harvard, Yale and the Masschusetts Institute of Technology; but also executives at the companies that make Otis elevators, IBM computers, Van Heusen shirts and Volkswagen advertisements; and Joe Namath . . .; Arnold Picker, a relatively conservative Democrat who raised money for Lyndon Johnson and Edmund Muskie; and Samuel M. Lambert, formerly head of the National Education Association, who had voted for Nixon."[8]

And in 1972, when, in the eyes of the White House if not the poll takers, the "enemies" were gathering menacingly under George McGovern's banner, the Administration applied the dirty tricks developed by the CIA to domestic politics. Operatives like James McCord were still being fed the stories about connections between the Democrats and "such violence-oriented groups as the Vietnam Veterans Against the War."[9] But for Nixon and his aides the distinction was unimportant; anyone working against the President's re-election became the enemy, just as menacing and "out to get him" as the Communist-inspired demonstrators of the year before and entitled to no better treatment. It took only a small further step for aides operating in that climate to forge Senator Edmund S. Muskie's name to the "Canuck letter," and wiretap and burglarize the Democratic National Committee.

The paranoia shaping this vision of the world grew, it seems to me, out of Nixon's need for total control.[10] As he has never tired of telling us, Nixon sees the part of life that really counts as a series of crises, a not uncommon version of the heroic stance fostered by the masculine ideal. His constant fear is of losing control, of going "soft" or flailing wildly under the pressure of these confrontations. To avoid this, "he lives," as Garry Wills wrote, "in a cleared circle, an emotional DMZ, space razed and defoliated, so he cannot be 'got to' unexpectedly."[11] His familiar efforts to withdraw to higher and higher ground, to avoid direct contact with individuals actively espousing particular views (a former White House aide describes him as "abhorring confrontations, particularly those based on philosophical convictions"[12]), to govern with a cabinet of yes-men, to have all his information filtered, boiled down, and drained of emotional content all reflect this preoccupation. The result has been that those who oppose him, because they stir up the feelings he fears as unmanly, become threats to his personal equilibrium, not just his policies and programs. Since Nixon has not been able to admit that the struggle, which he has professed to love, is exactly what he cannot tolerate, the exaggerated menace he has felt from those who oppose him had to be found outside himself, by disregarding evidence turned up by his own agencies if necessary. His opponents take on for Nixon a menace far out of proportion to reality. Thus although the White House "never found a scintilla of viable evidence indicating that [anti-Nixon] demonstrators [in 1972] were part of a master plan, nor that they had any direct connection with the McGovern campaign," the President, John Dean testified, "believed that the opposite was, in fact, true."[13] "Nobody is a friend of ours. Let's face it!" he said a year later to Dean in one of the conversations set out in the Presidential transcripts.[14]

The same alchemy made it possible for Nixon to believe that security leaks which might stimulate domestic political opposition—like those regarding the 1969 B-52 raids on Cambodia, which were by their very nature already known to the other side—were hideous threats to national security. With his personal demons externalized and inflated to these proportions, the stage was set for extreme measures.

The absence of moral restraint in the original Watergate crimes and, as revealed by the transcripts, in the coverup is nonetheless startling, the more so because it was not based on conventional greed. Much of it grew instead out of something deeper—the market mentality ingrained in the American male character. If every aspect of a man's self-esteem, including his moral worth, turns on competitive success, then everything else—fair play, representative government, constitutional guarantees of basic freedoms, respect for the law—will be subordinated to the pursuit of victory. The veneer of self-righteousness created by regular exercise, eating cottage cheese for lunch, church attendance, or abstinence from drink only makes men with this market ethic more dangerous. Other presidents have been subject to it, but Nixon and the men he chose to keep around him have given themselves to it without reservation. Kennedy at least had the Eastern Establishment's sense that there are some things one just does not do. Johnson had a respect for the potential power of Congress bred of long years there and a deeply felt commitment to help the disadvantaged, a legacy of his days in the Roosevelt Administration. Nixon, a total captive of our emulative individualism, has wanted only to win.

Not all of the men who participated in the initial Watergate crimes and the cover-up did so because they personally shared Nixon's paranoid view of the world. A fair number seem simply to have accepted or done what they were told. Hugh Sloan, the treasurer of the Committee to Re-elect the President and one of the few Nixon men who refused to go along with the cover-up, told an interviewer, "There was no independent sense of morality [at the White House]. I mean if you worked for someone, he was God and whatever the orders were, you did it—and there were damned few who were able to make or willing to make independent judgments."[15] The awe of authority in the White House was so great, for example, that when Haldeman called one of his key aides on his red-light-flashing private line, the aide, not a military man by training, would leap to his feet, stand at attention, and declaim, "Yes sir," into the phone. A summons to meet with Haldeman sent him into a panic: "Don't talk to me, *Bob* wants me!" He would comb his hair, pull a bottle of Binaca out of his desk, squirt himself with it, and rush out of his office.[16]

Some of this kind of servility is the inevitable result of raising young men without independent stature to positions of responsibility and power. By contrast, whatever their other faults, Kennedy Administration men like McGeorge Bundy had attractive options other than service in the White House to protect. But it also seems fair to ask how much of this awe of authority and willingness to remain on the Watergate "team" was due to blind male idolatry of the winner, the man who had climbed farther up the greasy pole. One of the White House secretaries—a woman—would say to the Haldeman aide when he panicked at Haldeman's calls, "He's just a human being, just a man. And one of these days he's not going to be here in the White House, and neither will you. He's going back to J. Walter Thompson, and you're going back to your law firm." Exasperated, the aide would tell her, "You just don't understand how things work around here."[17]

Finally, one wonders how it came to be that the dull, gray, buttoned-down Nixonians hired a maniac like G. Gordon Liddy, known for carrying a pistol and threatening to kill Jeb Magruder, and kept him around long enough to plan the break-in at the Democratic National Committee headquarters. Or why they signed up an ineffectual romantic like E. Howard Hunt, who, after leaving the CIA, could not talk for ten minutes without dropping the fact that he had been a spy? Could it be that the James Bond poses of these individuals struck an irrational chord of masculine fantasy in John Mitchell, Charles Colson, H. R. Haldeman, and their junior alter egos—men fervently dedicated to the cult of toughness?

14. Androgyny

Identify with that which haunts you, not in order to fight it off, but to take it into yourself; for it must represent some rejected element in you.

—Rollo May, *Love and Will*

Perhaps in the future, our lives will be shaped by a view of personality which will not assign fixed ways of behaving to individuals on the basis of sex. Instead, it would acknowledge that each person has the potential to be—depending on the circumstances—both assertive *and* yielding, independent *and* dependent, job- *and* people-oriented, strong *and* gentle, in short, both "masculine" *and* "feminine"; that the most effective and happy individuals are likely to be those who have accepted and developed both these "sides" of themselves; and that to deny either is to mutilate and deform; that human beings, in other words, are naturally androgynous.

This integration of the "masculine" and "feminine" aspects of the self is possible because opposition between them, sometimes characterized as "doing versus being" or "instrumental versus expressive," is false. Consider, for example, the central positive "masculine" trait: the ability to organize oneself and one's actions rationally and concentratedly in pursuit of large objectives. And the central positive "feminine" trait: the ability to discern, accept, value, express, and be guided by one's feeling responses to people and situations. Our sexual stereotypes tell us that these are "opposing" abilities. But exactly the reverse is true. Each is essential to the other.[1]

Feeling gives imagination, richness—in short, content—to the ability to act. The ability to act, on the other hand, gives focus, maturity, and the necessary connection with reality to one's feeling responses. The male sex role, which teaches men to ignore or suppress their emotional responses, makes it difficult for them to know what it is they want. Instead, they tend to run single-mindedly down the track in pursuit of standardized success, and, when that fails to satisfy, lose impetus altogether. We have seen this phenomenon in men's sexual as well as professional lives. Conversely, the female sex stereotype exerts pressure on women to believe "I can't" rather than "I can" except in certain carefully delimited spheres. To the extent that this message is accepted, their freedom to feel loses meaning. Without the possibility and discipline of action, feeling degenerates into sentimentality and is ultimately extinguished. "Feelings are not just a chance state of the moment," May says, "but . . . a way I *want* something to be,"[2] a wish for the future, and one cannot wish totally without hope. Women are too often left with a sense of apathy underneath a surface welter of unfocused emotion —the housewife's syndrome identified by feminists.

This same relationship holds for other supposedly opposing personality characteristics. Independence without a selective admixture of dependence ("interdependence") leads to blind, solipsistic isolation. On the other hand, total dependence on other individuals in important aspects of life is infantilizing and inevitably destructive of self-esteem.

Toughness—the ability to persevere in the face of physical or emotional pressures to desist—has value only as protection for concerns with deep claims on our bodies or emotions. Otherwise, as an independent value, it is just a disconnection, a disregard of feedback from the environment and one's own organic responses. But tenderness and care, extended indiscriminately, become ineffective. They have meaning only as "a delicate vein in a strong constitution."[3]

The growth of either side of any one of these paired capacities requires a concentration of emotional energy. For this reason, the initial development of one tends to be at the expense of the other. Furthermore, the relationship between them is dynamic and dialectical, never fully or permanently resolved, a continuous give-and-take always involving some degree of tension and anxiety. So it may be, as Dr. Daniel Levinson suggests, that the growth of the complementary "masculine" and "feminine" qualities in a particular individual is inevitably uneven, with one side lagging behind the other and the ability to integrate them developing last.[4]

This argues against attempts to force a lockstep, symmetrically androgynous pattern of maturation on our children. But it in no way negates the importance of an environment which permits and ultimately encourages the growth of a full androgynous flexibility. (Psychologists have found, it is worth noting, that boys and girls who conform less closely to sex stereotypes exhibit higher over-all intelligence, higher spatial ability, and more creativity.[5])

In such a society girls will be allowed to play baseball, and boys will be allowed to play with dolls; girls will call boys for dates, and boys won't always pay for the movie; girls will learn to fix cars, and boys will learn to sew buttons on their shirts; girls will like math and science, and boys will learn modern dance—as well as vice versa.

As adults, women will take their kids camping and fishing, and men will leave work early to take them to the doctor; women will fix flat tires, and men will change diapers; women will be architects, Secretary of Defense or State, labor lawyers, surgeons, and engineers, and men will be secretaries and heads of departments of consumer affairs.

The family, of course, is the most critical factor in the development of the individual. And within the family today, there is a strong impetus for a shift toward androgyny in the increase in the number of mothers working outside the home.

As women participate more in the larger, goal-oriented world outside the domestic sphere, men, of necessity in many cases, will take on a greater share of responsibility for homemaking and child care. As a result, both will broaden their repertories of sensibilities and capacities by adding those previously ruled out by the traditional sex roles, and children will have more androgynous parents as models.

Equally important, the *relationship* of such parents will not be the conventional one of the father being catered to and serviced by the mother, all in the name of his role as economic provider. As women move into positions of status equal to that of their men, a shift takes place in the balance of power—the hierarchical structure of the relationship breaks down. The model from which children draw their earliest and most powerful expectations that men will and should dominate women is replaced by a more balanced, egalitarian structure.

As Philip Slater has observed, mothers (especially upper-middle-income women confined to the home) have conveyed conflicting messages to their children. The son becomes both the vicarious vehicle for the mother's frustrated aspirations and unexpended energies and the scapegoat for her resentment of masculine domination. This combination not infrequently results in a "bizarre and fanatical obsession" with the child's well-being and achievements, alternating with rejection of his masculine pretensions—a combination that perpetuates masculine narcissism and defensiveness toward women.[6] The daughter, on the other hand, is encouraged to follow the traditional pattern of subordination to and dependence on men. But at the same time, she is made aware of her mother's unhappiness with exactly that role and of her contempt for the man to whom she must cater—a combination that encourages in the daughter a low self-esteem and a desperate, often unconsciously hostile search for a man who will make her into someone. Women with substantial career involvements do not overload their relationships with their sons,[7] nor are they likely to disparage a daughter's capacity to become a person in her own right.

One of the processes by which boys in traditional families learn and come to accept the male sex role is described by contemporary psychoanalytic theory. Based on a reinterpretation, by feminist writers[8] among others, of the Oedipus complex first proposed by Freud*, the essential dynamic is as follows: Young children first identify with and are attached to their mother because of her greater role in caring for them. This attachment, including a sensual component, is a response to the broad range of emotional and physical satisfaction they derive from her. Beginning at about age five or six, the time children start school or nursery school, boys (the female version diverges at this point) are often subjected, as we have seen, to insistent and forceful demands to renounce "feminine," "baby" ways for tougher more manly behavior. This demand, often initiated within the family by the father, provokes a great deal of anxiety. The boy is asked in effect to switch his identification from his mother to his father, to trade her unconditional love for a world in which he must prove, by conforming to a murky and difficult standard, that he has any value at all. Feelings of fear and antagonism directed toward the father develop as a result. In addition to direct pressure, what induces the boy to repress this hostility and make the painful transition is the substance of the choice put before him. Does he want to be like his mother: warm, loving, but leading a dull, subordinate life? Or is his father's harsher but more adventurous, powerful masculine world more attractive? With his own demands for his mother's attention being progres-

---

* The original explanation for the Oedipal conflict, and one that classical Freudians still adhere to, rested heavily on biological impulses—the young boy's thwarted heterosexual drive toward his mother. But this literal interpretation of the Oedipal myth is now generally discredited: at ages five and six the boy is too young to imagine intercourse with his mother and has no need yet for orgasmic release.

sively rebuffed, he may also covet his father's apparent ability to command her affections.

Although this theory does not offer a totally adequate account of the boy's emerging personality, fifty years of clinical practice have shown that the conflicts it describes have been real and painful experiences for many men and one of the principal mechanisms for transmission of the traditional masculine ideal, including men's fear and repression of the "feminine" in themselves. An androgynous division of labor within the family would defuse these conflicts.*

If work and child care are fully shared by the father and mother, the boy will be more or less equally attached to them. Each parental relationship will have its unconditional nurturing and its conditional, performance-oriented sides. Rivalry with one parent for the other parent's affection and attention will be diminished since the child's dependence will be more evenly divided. And each parent will provide a model of both aspects of human behavior from which the boy, because of the insignificance of sex roles, will be free to choose what best suits his individual temperament and needs. Any general tendency to identify with and imitate the father as opposed to the mother will be slight, limited to those few areas—having to do primarily with sexual orientation—in which gender is still a differentiating factor, and will be the result of the boy's gradual elaboration of these differences rather than pressure from parents suddenly anxious that he be "a man." Most important, growing up will not pose a sudden, painful choice: because the models presented by both parents will be more balanced, the development of adult autonomy and competence will not be perceived as requiring either the near-total repression of the boy's needs for physical and emotional warmth and comfort or the equally problematic de-

---

* The parallel dynamic for girls,[9] because it does not involve a shift in identification away from the mother, the first object of attachment, but rather envy of masculine prerogatives reluctantly abandoned, does not establish an equivalent fear of the "masculine" in girls and is thus less important in the establishment of the female sex role. However, it, too, would be subject to dissolution in an androgynous household.

velopment of what appears to be an all-encompassing invulnerability and superiority to women.

This analysis is supported by Margaret Mead's observations in
her classic anthropological study of Samoan society, where both
men and women develop an adult personality remarkable for its
stability, smooth sexual adjustment, warmth, and flexibility.
There, the sex roles, although differing in some particulars, are
not distinguished as aggressive-passive, tough-tender, inde-
pendent-dependent, superior-subordinate. [10] Boys are made to
feel that becoming men is largely a matter of gradual inevitable
growth. Children are encouraged to model themselves on
slightly older playmates of the same sex rather than adults; and
there are no rites of passage involving difficult personal effort of
initiatory ordeal. [11] As a result, Oedipal conflicts and problems
simply do not appear. "Samoan culture," Mead writes, "demonstrates how much the tragic or the easy solution of the Oedipus
situation depends upon the interrelationship between parents
and children, and is not created out of whole cloth by the young
child's biological impulses." [12]

What impact will androgyny have on our sexuality? Physically, of course, men and women will still be different and the
sexual appeal of this difference will undoubtedly persist. Nor
will the abandonment of sharply differentiated male and female emotional and social styles destroy the attraction between
the sexes. The mismatched expectations of the transitional
period, as we have seen, can highlight and in some cases ag-
gravate sexual problems—mostly for men. But, once accepted,
freedom from stereotyped constraints will make sex more
rather than less interesting.

Androgyny would end men's preoccupation with dominance
and control and the discomfort they tend to feel with sexual
excitement and tension. For women, the shift—already un-
derway—would create the all-important freedom to express and
act on their own desires, to take as well as to give. Both would be
able in their sexual encounters, as in other areas of life, to ask for

and receive responses to a wider range of feelings and desires, rather than following a more or less standardized script, where each approaches the other with the same degree of aggression and submission, lust and tenderness, and so on, every time. A relationship satisfying to both partners does require the development of a rough balance in matters like this (something couples bound by stereotypes find difficult to achieve), but it must be a dynamic, shifting balance attuned to the actual moods of the moment. So androgyny would encourage more rather than less variety and spontaneity in sex. It is true, however, that to be manageable, spontaneity and variety require a higher level of consciousness. One must be able to perceive both the other person's feelings and one's own and find a way of meshing them without violating either—more difficult, as well as a lot more rewarding, than a set pattern of love-making.

Will the depolarization of sex roles lead to an increase in bisexuality or homosexuality? This question, like others involving the causes and meaning of homosexual activity, is fraught with uncertainty and bias. But let me attempt a tentative answer, at least with respect to men.

It does seem likely that lowering the inhibitions to personal communication and displays of affection between men will lead in time to more bisexuality. There appears to be no logical stopping point in the progression from social intimacy to physical affection to sex. On the other hand, it would be a mistake to underestimate the ability and inclination of human societies to create barriers at essentially arbitrary points. It is possible to be less phobic about homosexuality and freer emotionally and physically with friends of the same sex without engaging in overtly sexual acts—this is probably as far as most exclusively heterosexual men now past puberty will move. That is what I project for myself at this point, not only because of my own general negative conditioning about homosexuality but also because my specific formative sexual experience has been with women—that is what I know. For generations reared in an androgynous society, a lack of fear of homosexuality seems likely to result in more early homosexual experience—it is not that uncommon even now*—and not require its repression as an aspect of mature sexuality.

Something like this is taking place among certain women influenced by the feminist movement. Women have never been as strongly conditioned against homosexuality as men. Drawn to other women by new-found bonds of personal friendship, ideology, and the celebration of their female bodies and identities, women with full heterosexual experience and capacity are experimenting with lesbian sex. They do not play the old butch-femme roles or act "masculine." Nor do they lose their heterosexual capacity—although, repelled by the sexist attitudes, in bed and out, of the men they know, they are exercising it with considerable discrimination. If we remove the negative element introduced into this situation by sexism, and the temporary impetus given these relationships by the surge of sisterly feeling created by the feminist movement, it may be close to where men raised in an androgynous society will be in the future. In short, homosexual activity may become for larger numbers of men than at present an accepted, if occasional and subsidiary part of life, unassociated with effeminacy, heterosexual incapacity, or any other maladjustment. There have been, and still are, many human societies with patterns of sexual behavior like this. [14]

On the other hand, it also seems likely that the incidence of exclusive homosexuality will decrease. In a society in which homosexuality is accepted, homosexual activity will not label an individual as a member of a separate caste. He will not be cut off by his own internalization of that identity and by social pressure from sexual relationships with women and involvement with heterosexual society in general. For example, "One surprising result of the gay activist movement," a psychiatrist wrote, "is

---

* According to a recent study, seventeen percent of boys between the ages of sixteen and nineteen have had one or more homosexual experiences. [13]

that some of its members have gone from exclusive homosexuality to a predominantly heterosexual or bisexual orientation."[15]

Moreover, some homosexual behavior, like some heterosexual behavior, is prompted by fear. The image of masculinity as requiring constant toughness, competitiveness, and dominance, especially over women, leads some men, in attempts to prove their masculinity, to hyper-aggressive, exploitative, and humiliating behavior in their sexual relationships with women. Another reaction to the same extreme version of the male stereotype is to shun entirely the role it implies, giving up full masculine status and taking refuge in the alternative of homosexuality.[16] An androgynous society, which would not teach the association of maleness, constant dominance, and aggressive sex, would make both compulsions less likely.

From Daniel Boone to our mobile corporation executives to our most dedicated scientists, American men have tended to travel light, to steer away from human entanglements the better to pursue larger, more abstract goals. Our success myths, as we have seen, are about an individual (virtually always a man) who by his lonely, independent efforts raises himself above and away from his fellow men and accomplishes great things, preferably of the kind that can serve as a monument to himself. That fulfillment of all his human needs flows automatically from such success is also part of the myth.

Androgyny would discredit this masculine idealization of emotional and professional autarchy. It would declare its personal costs unacceptable and would lead, in ways suggested in earlier chapters, to the placing of a higher value on emotional responsiveness and human connection. It would recognize, along with the uniqueness of human beings, their need for and dependence on others.

Instead of recognizing this side of life—the first step toward harnessing its energies and controlling its dangers—Americans have been urged by the theorists of individualism to deny their social instincts, to be totally "inner-directed," with results exactly opposite to those intended:

> By raising the spectre of immersion in group life—of losing one's narcissistic consciousness—they frightened and shamed people into an ever more frantic pursuit of autonomy and self-sufficiency. . . . Ripped out of their social fabric, their social responses are constantly seeking a missing stimulus to which they can attach themselves. . . . Humans deprived of community become, in a sense, "imprinted" on rules, machines, ideologies, and bureaucratic structures. The anti-conformity critics, therefore, helped create precisely what they were attacking. By heaping scorn on social responses fundamental to humankind, they helped further the process of disconnection in the society, thus making the population ever more vulnerable to authoritarian and impersonal manipulation. For the forms in which conformity and authoritarianism appear in modern society are a *product* of ideology of freedom and individualism—desperate and shame-faced efforts to fill the hole left by the every - man - should - strive - to - be - a - lonely - genius - head - and - shoulders - above - the - worthless - gregarious - dependent - masses guilt trip.[17]

The achievements of traditional individualism *are* important. Individualism has fostered respect for civil liberties and the recognition of at least the potential dignity and worth of every person. And it has given us an ingenious, if less than wholly successful, collection of regulatory mechanisms aimed at keeping our intellectual, economic, and political markets open to newcomers. But one need not discard these legacies in order to question the value of this ideology as a psychodynamic engine of progress today. This social philosophy, closely tied to the male stereotype, encourages men to set their sights on an impersonal competitive goal and to push single-mindedly toward it—regulated, ideally, only by competition itself. The system thus created encourages and rewards what Philip Slater has called "linear" behavior: efforts directed at making more of something (money or widgets), building a bigger enterprise as an end in itself, being the best person at task X or the first person to do Y (almost any X or Y will do). The search for a piece of turf each can stake out as distinctively his own pushes scientists and academicians into greater and greater specialization. This system can and does produce more cars, higher-fidelity record players, and better surgical techniques. But it has conspicuously failed to serve our needs as whole human beings—because many of these needs are not reflected in the competitive market place.

The most difficult and pressing problems today have to do not with the individual parts of our society but with the relationships between them. Straight-line growth—in industry, in scientific exploration, in the treatment of human beings as ever more mobile economic machines—is no longer possible. The inherent connections are forcing themselves to our attention: environmental constraints on economic growth can no longer be ignored; advances in science and technology do not automatically result in human progress; a patient is more than a collection of organs—in fact, researchers are discovering that the quality of a person's relationships are often as important as medical procedures in curing disease. The fragmentation and dehumanization of work in the name of efficiency has begun to backfire, producing inefficiency and illness.[18] The injunction that we be totally free, independent of everything but the drive to achieve, has created a nation of lonely men who are prey to impersonal substitutes for personal connection, ranging from overinvestment in gadgets to xenophobic conformity (country-club or "ethnic" style, it is the same phenomenon) to grandiose attempts to leave a permanent mark on the world.

It is time for a more organic and less cosmic vision of the human enterprise, one which honors the relatedness of human beings, which values feeling as well as tangible or measurable achievements. What a modern society built on such a vision would look like is hard to predict. Efforts to return to the simple communities of an earlier time—seen today in communes and other separatist experiments—are more an attempt to avoid the problem than to deal with it. Socialism is no panacea; without fundamental changes in personal values the priorities in socialist states have not been and will not be noticeably different.[19] Nor is the conservative vision of a fixed, hierarchical social order —everyone with his or her place, be it ever so lowly, with a few safety valves of individual mobility—acceptable.

Perhaps the place to begin is not with grand new designs, but with a new sensitivity to our networks of interdependence, both the tangible, material connections and those created by our social, relational needs. Our institutions and living patterns have to be adjusted to reflect these complex networks. To do this, we need people shaped by an interest in the here and now, prepared to listen carefully and critically to the full range of their own and others' feelings, since feelings—properly sorted out—are the most sensitive indicators that an essential human need, some link in the chain, is being slighted. We need temperaments able to work patiently and creatively with what now exists, taking advantage of opportunities more, trying to force them less —personalities not too proud for maintenance and rehabilitation functions, for as the social engineering efforts and psychotherapeutic fads of the 1960s demonstrated, quick fixes slapped onto complex systems do not work, and solutions are never permanent. And most of all, we require a conception of human purpose which accepts both the limitations and opportunities of our emotional and physical interdependence, which values the uniqueness of each individual but understands that it is given shape and meaning only through "our participation in a larger entity."[20]

Men who have given themselves over to the masculine ethic of competitive individualism cannot strike this balance, for they lack its internal counterpart. To resolve, however temporarily, the opposing forces in society, to release the energy bound in opposing positions and make it fruitful, one must be able to accept and integrate the corresponding opposites in oneself.

Notes*

2. Friendships Among Men

1. Owen Wister, *The Virginia* ([Macmillan: 1902] Grosset & Dunlap ed.: 1929), pp. 397–98.

2. *Ibid.*, p. 343.

3. *Ibid.*, p. 373.

4. Lionel Tiger, *Men in Groups* (Random House: 1969), p. 185.

5. Don Clark, "Homosexual Encounter in All-Male Groups," in L. Solomon and B. Berzon (eds.), *New Perspectives on Encounter Groups* (Jossey-Bass: 1972), pp. 376–77. See also Alan Booth, "Sex and Social Participation," *American Sociological Review*, Vol. 37 (April 1972), p. 183, an empirical study showing that, contrary to Lionel Tiger's much publicized assertion *(Men in Groups)*, women form stronger and closer friendship bonds with each other than men do.

6. Fernando Bartolomé, "Executives as Human Beings," *Harvard Business Review*, Vol. 50 (November-December 1972), p. 64.

*In notes where the page reference is to paperback or later editions of a work, the publisher and year of publication of the original hardcover edition are set out in brackets.

7. The contrast with women on this point is striking. Casual observation will confirm that women's conversations move more quickly, with fewer long speeches and more frequent changes of speaker.

8. *Boston Globe*, March 12, 1972, p. B-1.

9. Bartolomé, *op. cit.*, p. 65.

10. *Ibid.*, p. 64.

11. *Ibid.*, p. 66.

12. *Ibid.*, p. 64.

13. *Ibid.*, p. 65.

14. Claude Brown, *Manchild in the Promised Land* ([Macmillan: 1965] Signet ed.: 1965), p. 171.

15. Clark, *op. cit.*, p. 378.

16. Margaret Mead, *Male and Female* ([William Morrow: 1949] Mentor ed.: 1949), p. 214.

3. The Conquest of Sex

1. Rollo May, *Love and Will* (W. W. Norton: 1969), pp. 311–12.

2. Dave Meggyesy, *Out of Their League* ([Ramparts Press: 1971] Paperback Library ed.: 1971), p. 158.

3. Kate Millett, *Sexual Politics* (Doubleday: 1970), pp. 324–25 (footnotes omitted).

4. Mary Ellman, *Thinking About Women* (Harcourt, Brace & World: 1968), p. 52.

5. Mickey Spillane, *I, the Jury* (E. P. Dutton: 1947), p. 62.

6. *Transaction* (February 1970), p. 10.

7. Julius Fast, *The Incompatibility of Men and Women* (M. Evans: 1971), p. 91.

8. Fernando Bartolomé-Pardo, "Intimate Feelings and the Executive" (unpublished doctoral dissertation, Harvard Business School, 1972), p. 173.

9. May, *op. cit.*, p. 73.

10. *Ibid.*, p. 74.

11. *Ibid.*, p. 315.

12. Ingrid Bengis, *Combat in the Erogenous Zone* (Alfred A. Knopf: 1972), pp. 163–64.

13. Ellmann, *op. cit.*, p. 123.

14. Henry Miller, *Tropic of Capricorn* (Grove Press ed.: 1969), pp. 182–83.

15. May, *op. cit.*, pp. 54–55 (italics in the original).

16. Philip Nobile, "What is the New Impotence, and Who's Got It?" *Esquire* (October 1972), p. 95.

17. *Ibid.*, p. 96.

18. George L. Ginsberg, *et al.*, "The New Impotence," *Archives of General Psychiatry*, Vol. 26 (1972), pp. 218–19.

19. William Masters and Virginia Johnson, *Human Sexual Inadequacy* (Little, Brown: 1970), p. 160.

20. May, *op. cit.*, p. 75.

21. Ellmann, *op. cit.*, p. 106.

22. Bengis, *op. cit.*, pp. 161–62.

23. Grace Helen McCabe, "The Nurturant Father" (undergraduate thesis, Goddard College, 1973).

4. The Roots of Misogyny

1. *Ms.* (July 1973), p. 8.

2. CBS Evening News, August 17, 1973.

3. Ruth Hartley, "Sex Role Pressure in the Socialization of the Male Child," *Psychological Reports*, Vol. 5 (1959), p. 458.

4. *Ibid.*, pp. 461–62.

5. Virginia Kidd, "Now You See" (unpublished paper, Sacramento State College).

6. Marjorie B. U'Ren, "The Image of Women in Textbooks," in Vivian Gornick and Barbara K. Moran (eds.), *Women in Sexist Society* ([Basic Books: 1971] Signet ed.: 1971), pp. 318–28.

7. Hartley, *op. cit.*, pp. 460–61.

8. *Ibid.*, p. 461.

9. *Ibid.*, p. 458.

10. Inge Broverman, *et al.*, "Sex-Role Stereotypes: A Current Appraisal," *Journal of Social Issues*, Vol. 28 No. 2 (1972), pp. 59, 65. Between five to twelve times as many women as men recall having wished they were of the opposite sex. Moreover, investigators have found that both boys and girls between six and ten years express greater preference for "masculine" things, and activities than for "feminine" things and activities.

11. Hartley, *op. cit.*, p. 462.

12. *Ibid.*, p. 461.

13. Friedrich Nietzsche, "Women De-Feminized," reprinted in Betty Roszak and Theodore Roszak (eds.), *Masculine/Feminine* (Harper Colophon: 1969), p. 7.

14. Mary Ellmann, *Thinking About Women* (Harcourt, Brace & World: 1968), p. 60.

15. See, for example, Robert Graves, *Mammon and the Black Goddess* (Doubleday: 1965), pp. 101–14, reprinted in Roszak and Roszak, *op. cit.*, pp. 31–38.

16. Broverman, *et. al.*, *op. cit.*, p. 59. Dr. Broverman and her co-workers surveyed more than 600 men and 380 women, married and single, ranging in age from seventeen to sixty, and in education from elementary school to advanced graduate degrees, and including members of all major religions. The data were tabulated separately for groups based on each of these characteristics with statistically identical results. Regardless of age, sex, religion, education, and martial status, Americans agree that, in comparison to each other, men and women typically displayed the following differences in behavior:

Men	Women
Very aggressive	Not at all aggressive
Very independent	Not at all independent
Not at all emotional	Very emotional
Almost always hide emotions	Do not hide emotions at all
Very objective	Very subjective
Not at all easily influenced	Very easily influenced
Very dominant	Very submissive
Like math and science very much	Dislike math and science very much
Not at all excitable in a minor crisis	Very excitable in a minor crisis
Very active	Very passive
Very competitive	Not at all competitive
Very logical	Very illogical
Very worldly	Very home oriented
Very skilled in business	Not at all skilled in business
Very direct	Very sneaky
Know the way of the world	Do not know the way of the world
Feelings not easily hurt	Feelings easily hurt
Very adventurous	Not at all adventurous
Can make decisions easily	Have difficulty making decisions
Never cry	Cry very easily
Almost always act as a leader	Almost never act as a leader
Very self-confident	Not at all self-confident
Not at all uncomfortable about being aggressive	Very uncomfortable about being aggressive
Very ambitious	Not at all ambitious
Easily able to separate feelings from ideas	Unable to separate feelings from ideas

Not at all dependent	Very dependent
Never conceited about appearance	Very conceited about appearance
Think men are always superior to women	Think women are always superior to men
Talk freely about sex with men	Do not talk freely about sex with men
Not at all talkative	Very talkative
Very blunt	Very tactful
Very rough	Very gentle
Not at all aware of feelings of others	Very aware of feelings of others
Not at all religious	Very religious
Not at all interested in their own appearance	Very interested in own appearance
Very sloppy in habits	Very neat in habits
Very loud	Very quiet
Very little need for security	Very strong need for security
Do not enjoy art and literature at all	Enjoy art and literature
Do not express tender feelings at all easily	Easily express tender feelings
Use very harsh language	Don't use harsh language at all

Asked to list traits desirable for each sex, all groups, including a sample of male college graduates, reproduced the profiles set forth above, indicating that the stereotypes are viewed as the ideal.

The Broverman study also confirmed that "masculine" characteristics are believed by both sexes to be more desirable than "feminine" characteristics.

Psychologists and psychiatrists were also surveyed, revealing a belief in the stereotypes and higher valuation of "masculine" traits no different from the supposedly more culture-bound lay public.

17. Carol Tavris, "Woman and Man," *Psychology Today*, Vol. 5 No. 10 (March 1972), pp. 83–84.

18. E.g., Konrad Lorenz, *On Aggression* (Harcourt, Brace & World: 1966); Anthony Storr, *Human Aggression* (Atheneum: 1968).

19. Lionel Tiger, *Men in Groups* (Random House: 1969); Steven Goldberg, *The Inevitability of Patriarchy* (William Morrow: 1973).

20. George Gilder, *Sexual Suicide* (Quadrangle: 1973).

21. G. D. Mitchell, "Paternalistic Behavior Among Primates," *Psychological Bulletin*, Vol. 71 No. 6 (1969), p. 399.

22. G. D. Mitchell, W. Redican, and J. Gomby, "Lesson from a Primate: Males Can Raise Babies," *Psychology Today* (April 1974), p. 63.

23. L. Harrison Mathews, "Overt Fighting in Mammals," in J. O. McCarthy and E. J. Ebling (eds.), *The Natural History of Aggression* (Academic Press: 1964).

24. For a thorough analysis of the differences which make analysis between animal and human behavior treacherous, see Gregory Rochlin, *Man's Aggression* (Gambit: 1973), Chapter III.

25. Michael Lewis, "Parents and Children: Sex Role Development," *School Review*, Vol. 80 (February 1972), p. 229.

26. John Money and Anke Ehrhardt, *Man &Woman, Boy & Girl* (Johns Hopkins Press: 1972).

27. *Ibid.*, pp. 151–66.

28. *Ibid.*, pp. 95–116.

29. Estelle Ramey, "Sex Hormones and Executive Ability," *Annals of the New York Academy of Sciences*, Vol. 28 (1973), p. 237:

> An examination of the data reveals that of the 15 girls studied, 7 were thought at birth to be . . . males with undescended testicles. Presumably the proud parents were told they had a son. The sex assignment was changed within the first 7 months in this group but it is a matter of some importance that in these, as in all the other cases, the sex ambiguity was a problem for the parents from the time of birth. The effect of parental concern about the true sex identity of these children despite medical corrective procedures must inevitably have conditioned their behavior towards the child and the child's response. For example, the data reveal that in at least half of the matched control groups of normal children, sex education was derived in large part from communication in the home while the adrenogenital children reported as the chief source of information the hospital input. These children were examined frequently as regards their genitalia and could not have escaped the knowledge that they were not entirely the little girls that their parents might have wished for.
>
> How is one to interpret the finding of a greater career interest in these young girls as compared to normal adolescent girls in this society? For Freudians it is tempting to postulate that fetal masculinization of the brain induces the development of a special neuronal pathway for "career orientation." It is more likely, however, that a girl who sees herself as less desirable as a woman then her peer group may seek other avenues of ego development.
>
> Lower interest in motherhood and personal adornment—the latter clearly a cultural variable, since in many human societies it is men who wear the feathers—are also explainable on the basis of uncertainties and fears of inadequacy.

30. J. L. Hampson and G. H. Hampson, "The Ontogenesis of Sexual Behavior in Man," in W. C. Young (ed.), *Sex and Internal Secretions* (Williams & Wilkins: 1961).

31. Money and Ehrhardt, *op. cit.*, p. 13.

32. Norman Mailer, "The Prisoner of Sex," *Harper's Magazine* (March 1971), p. 50.

33. Ian Fleming, *Casino Royale* (Macmillan: 1953), p. 149.

34. Ellmann, *op. cit.*, pp. 86–87.

5. Women as Colleagues

1. G. W. Bowman, N. B. Worthy, and S. A. Greyser, "Are Women Executives People?" *Harvard Business Review*, Vol. 43 (July–August 1965), p. 14.

2. Caroline Bird, "Demasculinizing the Professions," in Ronald Gross and Paul Osterman (eds.), *The New Professionals* (Simon and Schuster: 1972), pp. 293–94.

3. Michael Korda, *Male Chauvinism: How It Works!* (Random House: 1973), p. 124.

4. Women's Bureau, U.S. Department of Labor, "Women Workers Today" (U.S. Gov't. Printing Office: revised ed. 1973), p. 6.

5. Mary Kathleen Benet, *The Secretarial Ghetto* (McGraw-Hill: 1972), p. 74.

6. Albert E. Schwabacher, Jr., "The Repository of Wealth," in Seymour M. Farber and Roger H. L. Wilson (eds.), *The Potential of Women* (McGraw-Hill Paperbacks: 1963), pp. 251–52 (emphasis added).

6. In the Social Arena

1. Gary Shaw, *Meat on the Hoof* (St. Martin's Press: 1972), p. 153.

2. *Ibid.*, p. 176.

3. Norman Mailer, "The Prisoner of Sex," *Harper's Magazine* (March 1971), p. 92.

4. H. R. Hays, *The Dangerous Sex: The Myth of Feminine Evil* ([G. P. Putnam's Sons: 1964] Pocket Books: 1966), pp. 53–68, 124–31.

5. Lionel Tiger, *Men in Groups* (Random House: 1969), pp. 146–48.

6. Mirra Komarovsky, "Cultural Contradictions and Sex Roles: The Masculine Case," *American Journal of Sociology*, Vol. 78 (1973), p. 874. The other forty percent of the sample either felt intellecually superior to the women they dated or had little interest in intellectual concerns.

7. Lynda Lytle Holmstrom, *The Two-Career Family* (Schenkman: 1972), p. 15:

   The marriage rate among certain groups of career women is often quite low. . . . In a recent study of women with successful careers in business, half married and half did not. . . . This rate of marriage is low, both in comparison to males with similar education and occupation and in comparison to women in the general population.

   While it is possible that these findings are due in part to career women's own aversion to marrying men who demand subservience, that is just a different variation of the theme of men wanting women they can control. See also Komarovsky, *op. cit.*, pp. 879–80; Marvin R. McMillin, "Attitudes of College Men Toward Career Involvement of Married Women," *Vocational Guidance Quarterly*, Vol. 21 (September 1972), p. 8.

7. Marriage and Other Intimate Arrangements

1. Mary Ellmann, *Thinking About Women*, (Harcourt, Brace & World: 1968), pp. 103–104.

2. Alfred Lord Tennyson, "Locksley Hall," in G. B. Harrison, *et. al.* (eds.), *Major British Writers*, Vol. II (Harcourt, Brace & World: 1959), p. 403.

3. *Blackstone's Commentaries on the Law of England*, (Strahan and Woodfall: 12th edition 1768), p. 441.

4. Leo Kanowitz, *Women and the Law: The Unfinished Revolution* (University of New Mexico Press: 1969), pp. 5–6.

5. Gunnar Myrdal, *An American Dilemma* (Harper & Row: rev. ed. 1962), p. 1073.

6. Kanowitz, *op. cit.*, pp. 40–41.

7. *The New York Times*, June 4, 1972, reprinted in Michael Korda, *Male Chauvinism: How It Works!* (Random House: 1973), p. 168.

8. *Ibid.*, pp. 169–70.

9. Susan Jacoby, "Feminism in the $12,000-a-year Family," *The New York Times Magazine* (June 17, 1973), p. 11.

10. *The New York Times, op. cit.*,

11. Jesse Bernard, *The Future of Marriage* (World: 1972), pp. 29–30.

12. *Ibid.*, p. 30.

13. Myron Brenton, *The American Male* ([Fawcett: 1970] George Allen & Unwin: 1967), p. 61.

14. Bernard, *op. cit.*, p. 17 and Afterword, Tables 1–9.

15. *Ibid.*, p. 19.

16. *Ibid.*

17. Leslie Farber, "He Said, She Said," *Commentary* (March 1972), p. 53.

18. Rollo May, *Love and Will* (W. W. Norton: 1969), p. 148.

8. Family and Fatherhood

1. Women's Bureau, U.S. Department of Labor, "Highlights of Women's Employment and Education" (U.S. Gov't. Printing Office: 1973).

2. Lynda Lytle Holmstrom, *The Two-Career Family* (Schenkman: 1972), p. 141.

3. Mirra Komarovsky, *Blue-Collar Marriage* ([Random House: 1962] Vintage ed.: 1967), p. 72.

4. *Ibid.*, pp. 70–73.

5. Holmstrom, *op. cit.*, p. 141.

6. *Ibid.*

7. *Ibid.*, p. 147.

8. *Ibid.*, p. 108.

9. *Ibid.*, p. 110.

10. *Ibid.*

11. Diana Lurie, "Living With Liberation," *New York* (August 31, 1970), p. 29.

12. L. J. Axelson "The Working Wife: Differences in Perception Among Negro and White Males," *Journal of Marriage and the Family*, Vol. 32 (1970), pp. 457–64.

13. Pat Mainardi, "The Politics of Housework," in Robin Morgan (ed.), *Sisterhood is Powerful* ([Random House: 1970] Vintage ed.: 1970), pp. 448–49.

14. Holmstrom, *op. cit.*, p. 155; Komarovsky, *op. cit.*, pp. 70–73.

15. Mary Ellmann, *Thinking About Women* (Harcourt, Brace & World: 1968), pp. 135–36.

16. Holmstrom, *op. cit.*, pp. 72–77, 92–93.

17. Robert A. Fein, "Men and Young Children" (unpublished paper, July 1973).

18. *Ibid.*

19. *Ibid.*

20. John Nash, "The Father in Contemporary Culture and Current Psychological Literature," *Child Development*, Vol. 36 (1965), pp. 262–66.

21. E.g., Milton Kotelchuck, "The Nature of the Child's Tie to His Father" (unpublished doctoral dissertation, Harvard University, 1972), p. 28; Mary C. Howell, M.D., Ph.D., "Effects of Maternal Employment on the Child," *Pediatrics*, Vol. 52 (1973), p. 327; study by University of Kentucky psychologists showing that children who attend child-care centers do not differ mentally or socially from children who stay home with their mothers, *The New York Times*, December 9, 1973, p. 100.

22. R. J. Podell, H. F. Peck and C. First, "Custody to Which Parent?" *Marquette Law Review*, Vol. 56 (Winter 1973), p. 51.

23. *Jenkins* v. *Jenkins*, 181 N.W. 826 (Wisc. 1921).

24. See cases collected in footnote 23 of Podell, Peck and First, *op. cit.*

25. Case YNY-3, CCH Employment Practices Guide ¶95137 (December 29, 1972).

26. By-Law 107, Board of Education of the City of New York.

27. Fein, *op. cit.*

28. Interview, December 27, 1973.

29. *Ibid.*

30. *Ibid.*

31. *Ibid.*

9. Sports: The Training Ground

1. Nancy Gager Clinch, *The Kennedy Neurosis* (Grosset & Dunlap: 1973), p. 266.

2. Clayton Riley, "Did O. J. Dance?", *Ms.* (March 1974), p. 96.

3. Judith Krantz, "Jean-Claude Killy and the Winter Woman," *Ladies' Home Journal* (November 1969), p. 87.

4. *The New York Times*, August 20, 1970, p. 45.

5. See Brenda Feigen Fasteau, "Giving Women a Sporting Chance," *Ms.* (July 1973), p. 56, for a discussion of court challenges to the exclusion of women from participation in sports.

6. *New York Post*, March 14, 1974, p. 38.

7. Bil Gilbert and Nancy Williamson, "Programmed to be Losers," *Sports Illustrated* (June 11, 1973), p. 60.

8. David F. Aberle and Kaspar D. Naegele, "Middle-Class Fathers' Occupational Role and Attitudes Toward Children," *American Journal of Orthopsychiatry*, Vol. 22 (1952), p. 366.

9. *The New York Times*, June 2, 1973, p. 33.

10. Gary Shaw, *Meat on the Hoof* (St. Martin's Press: 1972), p. 38.

11. Aberle and Naegele, *op. cit.*, p. 374.

12. Bruce C. Ogilvie and Thomas Tutko, "Sport: If You Want to Build Character, Try Something Else," *Psychology Today* (October 1971), p. 61.

13. *Ibid.*

14. *Ibid.*, p. 63.

15. Telephone interview with Bruce C. Ogilvie, September 21, 1973.

16. Dave Meggyesy, *Out of Their League*, ([Ramparts Press: 1971] Paperback Library ed.: 1971), p. 87.

17. Norman Mailer, *Advertisements for Myself*, "The T Formation" (G. P. Putnam's Sons: 1959), pp. 394–95.

18. Philip Roth, "My Baseball Years," *The New York Times*, April 2, 1973, p. 35 (emphasis added).

19. Ogilvie and Tutko, *op. cit.*

20. *The New York Times*, January 15, 1973, p. 37.

21. Clinch, *op. cit.*, p. 31.

22. See, for example, Robert Lipsyte, "When You Lose, You Die a Little," *The New York Times Magazine* (September 16, 1973), p. 13.

23. *Ibid.*

24. *Ibid.*

25. *Ibid.*

26. *The New York Times*, May 16, 1973, p. 47.

10. Work

1. "Work in America," Report of a Special Task Force to the Secretary of Health, Education and Welfare, (United States Department of Health, Education, and Welfare: December 1972), p. 2.

2. Elliot Jaques, *Equitable Payment* (John Wiley & Sons: 1961), p. 25.

3. Garry Wills, *Nixon Agonistes* (Houghton Mifflin: 1970), pp. 237–38.

4. *Ibid.*, pp. 162–63.

5. See Philip Slater, *Earthwalk* (Anchor/Doubleday: 1974), pp. 94–97, for a detailed and devastating analysis of Jonathan.

6. *Ibid.*, p. 96.

7. W. Lloyd Warner and James Abegglen, *Big Business Leaders in America* (Atheneum: 1963), p. 83.

8. David F. Aberle and Kaspar D. Naegele, "Middle-Class Fathers' Occupational Role and Attitudes Towards Children," *American Journal of Orthopsychiatry*, Vol. 22 (1952), p. 371.

9. Wills, *op. cit.*, pp. 573–74.

10. Judith Bardwick, "Men and Work" (unpublished paper, University of Michigan, 1973), p. 12.

11. *Ibid.*, p. 10.

12. *Ibid.*

13. Gary Shaw, *Meat on the Hoof* (St. Martin's Press: 1972), p. 17.

14. Nancy Gager Clinch, *The Kennedy Neurosis* (Grossett & Dunlap: 1973), p. 256.

15. *Ibid.* pp. 228–38.

16. Caroline Bird, "Demasculinizing the Professions," in Ronald Gross and Paul Osterman (eds.), *The New Professionals* (Simon and Schuster: 1972), p. 298.

17. "Work in America," *op. cit.*, p. 18.

18. Philip Haberman, "Hiring a New Associate?" *Case and Comment*, Vol. 78 No. 5 (September–October 1973), p. 42.

19. Chris Argyris, "Interpersonal Barriers to Decisionmaking," *Harvard Business Review*, Vol. 44 (March–April 1966), p. 84; and *Organization and Innovation* (Irwin-Dorsey Press: 1965), *passim*.

20. Enid Nemy, "Intuition? It's Not a Woman's Monopoly," *The New York Times*, July 5, 1971, p. 15.

21. Argyris, *Organization and Innovation*, *op. cit.*, pp. 97–98.

22. Irving L. Janis, *Victims of Groupthink* (Houghton Mifflin: 1972), p. 174.

23. *Ibid.*, p. 175.

24. *Ibid.*, pp. 178–79.

25. Bardwick, *op. cit.*, p. 1.

26. Argyris, "Interpersonal Barriers to Decisionmaking," *op. cit.*, p. 92.

27. John Cuber and Peggy Harroff, *Sex and the Significant Americans* (Pelican: 1965), pp. 172–75, 180.

28. Slater, *op. cit.*, p. 119.

29. Bardwick, *op. cit.*, p. 20.

30. *Ibid.*, p. 30.

31. Daniel J. Levinson, "A Psychological Study of the Male Mid-Life Decade" (unpublished paper, Yale University, 1972), p. 11.

32. *Ibid.*, p. 12.

33. Bardwick, *op. cit.*, *passim*.

34. Abraham Maslow, *Motivation and Personality* (Harper & Row): [1934] 1970).

35. "Work in America," *op. cit.*, Chapters I–II.

36. *Ibid.*, p. 76.

37. *Ibid.*, pp. 78–80. (See pp. 80–83 and the Appendix to the report for other examples of work reorganization.)

38. *Ibid.*, pp. 86–90.

11. Violence: The Primal Test

1. Kate Millett, *Sexual Politics* (Doubleday: 1970), p. 331, quoting Norman Mailer, "A Wandering in Prose for Hemingway, November 1960," in *Deaths for the Ladies* (G. P. Putnam's Sons: 1962), no pagination.

2. Owen Wister, *The Virginian* ([Macmillan: 1902] Grosset & Dunlap: 1929), p. 399.

3. *Ibid.*, pp. 409–10.

4. Mickey Spillane, *I, the Jury* (E. P. Dutton: 1947), p. 29.

5. Peter Schjeldahl, "Can Blood Baths Make Men of Us?", *The New York Times*, Arts and Leisure, p. 11, February 20, 1972.

6. Carolyn Heilbrun, "The Masculine Wilderness of the American Novel," *Saturday Review* (January 29, 1972), p. 41.

7. James Dickey, *Deliverance* ([Houghton Mifflin: 1970] Dell ed.: 1971), p. 104.

8. Ernest Hemingway, *For Whom the Bell Tolls* (Charles Scribner's Sons: 1940), p. 236.

9. Millett, *op. cit.*, pp. 319–20.

10. Gary Shaw, *Meat on the Hoof* (St. Martin's Press: 1972), p. 27.

11. Dave Meggyesy, *Out of Their League* ([Ramparts Press: 1971] Paperback Library ed.: 1971), p. 146.

12. *Ibid.*, p. 156.

13. Charles J. Levy, "ARVN as Faggots: Inverted Warfare in Vietnam," *Transaction* (October 1971), p. 18.

14. Samuel A. Stouffer, *American Soldier*, Vol. 2 (Princeton University Press: 1949–50), p. 132.

15. Claude Brown, *Manchild in the Promised Land* ([Macmillan: 1965] Signet ed.: 1965), pp. 267–68.

16. Lionel Tiger, *Men in Groups* (Random House: 1969), p. 177.

17. Brown, *op. cit.*, p. 265.

18. See, for example, Norman Mailer's account of the notorious·Paret-Griffith prize fight in *The Presidential Papers* (G. P. Putnam's Sons: 1963), p. 243.

19. Julius Fast, *The Incompatibility of Men and Women* (M. Evans: 1971), p. 89.

20. Song by Carol Hall in *Free To Be . . . You and Me* (Bell Records: 1972; McGraw-Hill: 1974). The words are: It's all right to cry/Crying gets the sad out of you./It's all right to cry/It might make /you feel better. /Raindrops from your eyes/Washing all the mad out of you./Raindrops from your eyes/It might make you feel better./ It's all right to feel things/Though the feelings may be strange./Feelings are such real things/And they change and change/And change . . ./ Sad and grumpy, /Down in the dumpy/Snuggly huggly,/ Mean and ugly,/ Sloppy slappy,/ Hoppy happy, Change and change and change . . ./ It's all right to know/Feelings come and feelings go./ And it's all right to cry/ It might make you feel better.

21. Garry Wills, *Nixon Agonistes* (Houghton Mifflin: 1970), p. 134.

22. Brown, *op. cit.*, p. 153.

23. Rollo May, *Power and Innocence: A Search for the Sources of Violence* (W. W. Norton: 1972), Chapter 8.

24. *Ibid.*, p. 173.

12. Vietnam and the Cult of Toughness in Foreign Policy

1. The New York Times (ed.), *The Pentagon Papers* ([Quadrangle: 1971] Bantam ed.: 1971), p. 278.

2. CIA Memorandum, June 9, 1967, reprinted in *The Pentagon Papers, op. cit.*, p. 254.

3. *The Pentagon Papers, op. cit.*, pp. 449–54.

4. See the author's article, "Munich and Vietnam: A Valid Analogy?" *Bulletin of the Atomic Scientists* (September 1966), p. 22, for a full statement and critical discussion of this analogy.

5. *The Pentagon Papers, op. cit.*, p. 432.

6. *Ibid.*, p. 89.

7. Nancy Gager Clinch, *The Kennedy Neurosis* (Grosset & Dunlap: 1973), p. 100.

8. *Ibid.*, p. 114.

9. David Halberstam, *The Best and the Brightest* (Random House: 1972), p. 273.

10. *Ibid.*, p. 124.

11. Clinch, *op. cit.*, p. 98 (emphasis added).

12. Joe McCarthy, *The Remarkable Kennedys* (Dial: 1960), p. 30, quoted in Clinch, *op. cit.*, p. 131.

13. Halberstam, *op. cit.*, p. 122.

14. *Ibid.*, p. 151.

15. See also Halberstam, *op. cit.*, p. 72.

16. Arthur M. Schlesinger, Jr., *A Thousand Days* (Houghton Mifflin: 1965), pp. 380–81.

17. Louise FitzSimons, *The Kennedy Doctrine* (Random House: 1972), pp. 97–98, quoted in Clinch, *op. cit.*, p. 192.

18. Halberstam, *op. cit.*, p. 75.

19. *Ibid.*, p. 76.

20. Clinch, *op. cit.*, p. 194.

21. *Ibid.*, p. 195.

22. Halberstam, *op. cit.*, pp. 156–62.

23. *The Pentagon Papers, op. cit.*, p. 98.

24. Richard J. Walton, *Cold War and Counterrevolution* (Viking: 1972); Louis Heren, *No Hail, No Farewell* (Harper & Row: 1970); FitzSimons, *op. cit.*; Sidney Lens, *The Military Industrial Complex* (Pilgrim Press: 1970).

25. Halberstam, *op. cit.*, p. 274.

26. Clinch, *op. cit.*, pp. 219–21.

27. Halberstam, *op. cit.*, p. 56.

28. *Ibid*, p. 63.

29. *Ibid.*, p. 215.

30. *Ibid.*, p. 312.

31. *Ibid.*, pp. 531–32.

32. *Ibid.*, p. 178.

33. *Ibid.*, p. 414.

34. *Ibid.*, p. 425.

35. Charles Yost, *The Conduct and Misconduct of Foreign Affairs* (Random House: 1972), pp. 39–40.

36. David Landau, *Kissinger: The Uses of Power* (Houghton Mifflin: 1972), pp. 155–58.

37. Richard Whalen, *Catch the Falling Flag: A Republican's Challenge to His Party* (Houghton Mifflin: 1972), p. 137.

38. Landau, *op. cit.*, pp. 158, 180–82.

39. Kissinger, *American Foreign Policy* (W. W. Norton: 1969), p. 112, quoted in Landau, *op. cit.*, pp. 186–87.

40. Richard M. Nixon, *Six Crises*, (Doubleday: 1962), p. 273.

41. Landau, *op. cit.*, p. 71.

42. *Ibid.*, pp. 118–19.

43. *Ibid.*, p. 158.

44. *Ibid.*, p. 120.

45. *Ibid.*, pp. 119–20.

46. *Ibid.*, p. 125.

47. Garry Wills, *Nixon Agonistes* (Houghton Mifflin: 1970), p. 166

48. Nixon, *op. cit.*, p. xv (emphasis added).

49. *The New York Times*, October 27, 1973, p. 14.

50. Nixon, *op. cit.*, p. 199.

51. Bruce Mazlish, *In Search of Nixon* (Basic Books: 1972), p. 116.

52. *Ibid.*

53. *Ibid.*, p. 117.

54. *New York Post*, June 22, 1971, p. 67.

55. Virginia Slims American Women's Opinion Poll, Louis Harris and Associates (1970), pp. 74–77.

56. Mazlish, *op. cit.*, p. 170.

57. *Boston Globe*, March 19, 1972, p. 2.

13. Speculations on Watergate

1. The New York Times (ed.), *The Watergate Hearings* ([Viking: 1973] Bantam ed.: 1973), pp. 266–67.

2. *Ibid.*, p. 267.

3. *Ibid.*, pp. 756–57.

4. *Ibid.*, p. 268.

5. *Ibid.*, p. 697.

6. *Ibid.*, p. 698.

7. *Ibid.*, p. 768.

8. *Ibid.*, pp. 34–35.

9. *Ibid.*, p. 166.

10. "What moves and excites [Nixon] is not principle or policy or result, but an endless struggle for control. First to control himself. . . . Then to control others. . . . But above all to control doubt . . . doubts of his manliness." James David Barber (author of *Presidential Character*), *The New York Times*, November 8, 1973., p. 47.

11. Garry Wills, *Nixon Agonistes* (Houghton Mifflin: 1970), p. 409.

12. Arthur M. Schlesinger, Jr., *The Imperial Presidency* (Houghton Mifflin: 1973), p. 218.

13. *The Watergate Hearings, op. cit.*, p. 268.

14. Washington Post (ed.), *The Presidential Transcripts* (Dell: 1974), p. 77.

15. *The Watergate Hearings, op. cit.*, p. 866.

16. Interview with former member of the White House staff (name withheld by request), December 11, 1973.

17. *Ibid.*

14. Androgyny

1. I have drawn heavily in the discussion that follows on Rollo May's analysis of the inseparability of "wish" and "will." *Love and Will* (W. W. Norton: 1969), p. 218.

2. *Ibid.*, p. 91.

3. Ingrid Bengis, *Combat in the Erogenous Zone* (Alfred A. Knopf: 1972), p. 162.

4. Telephone interview with Dr. Daniel Levinson, Yale University, October 16, 1973.

5. Sandra L. Bem, "Psychology Looks at Sex Roles: Where Have All the Androgynous People Gone?" (paper presented at the UCLA Symposium on Women, May 1972), and studies cited therein.

6. Philip Slater, *The Glory of Hera* (Beacon Press: 1968), pp. 45, 450–51.

7. Lynda Lytle Holmstrom, *The Two-Career Family* (Schenkman: 1972), pp. 158–60.

8. Shulamith Firestone, *The Dialectic of Sex: The Case for Feminist Revolution* (William Morrow: 1970), Chapter 3.

9. *Ibid.*, pp. 58–62.

10. Margaret Mead, *Male and Female* ([William Morrow: 1949] Dell ed.: 1967), pp. 107–108, 181.

11. *Ibid.*, pp. 129–32.

12. *Ibid.*, p. 133.

13. Robert C. Sorensen, *Adolescent Sexuality in Contemporary America* (World: 1973), pp. 285–86.

14. See, for example, the discussion in John Money and Anke Ehrhardt, *Man & Woman, Boy & Girl* (Johns Hopkins Press: 1972), pp. 130–45.

15. Robert E. Gould, "What We Don't Know About Homosexuality," *The New York Times Magazine* (February 24, 1974), p. 62.

16. Lionel Ovesey has explored this association of masculinity, dominance, and sex, and its effects, in both heterosexual and homosexual men in *Homosexuality and Pseudohomosexuality* (Science House: 1969). The value of his work, however, is marred by the implicit assumption that men who react to this association by becoming homosexuals are sick while those who remain heterosexual, although hostile and aggressive in their sexual relationships, are not.

17. Philip Slater, *Earthwalk* (Doubleday/Anchor: 1974), p. 55.

18. "Work in America," Report of a Special Task Force to the Secretary of Health, Education, and Welfare (U.S. Department of Health, Education and Welfare: December 1972), pp. 62–70.

19. See Susan Sontag, "The Third World of Women," *Partisan Review*, Vol. 40 No. 2 (1973), pp. 191–92.

20. Slater, *op. cit.*, p. 209.